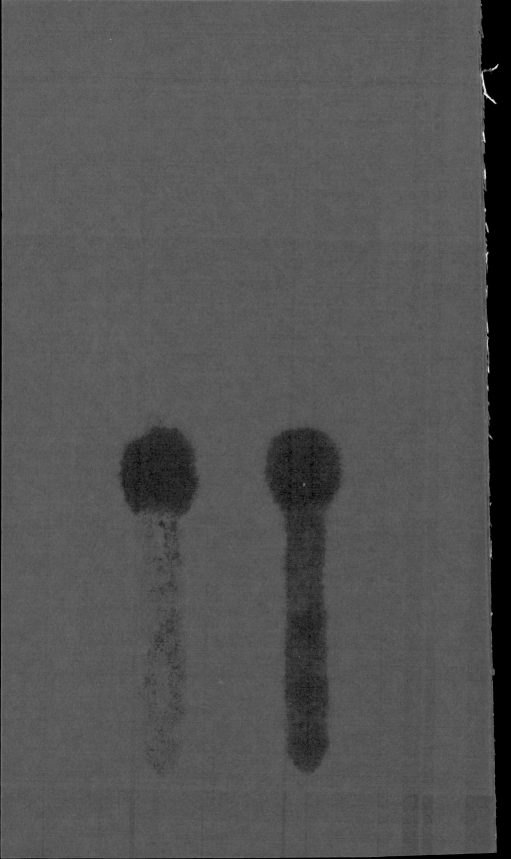

THE SECRET CAUSE

THE SECRET CAUSE

A
Discussion of Tragedy

————◄◆►————

NORMAND BERLIN

UNIVERSITY OF MASSACHUSETTS PRESS

AMHERST 1981

Copyright © 1981 by
The University of Massachusetts Press
All rights reserved
Printed in the United States of America
Library of Congress Cataloging in Publication Data
Berlin, Normand.
The secret cause.
Includes bibliographical references and index.
1. Tragedy.   I. Title.
PN1892.B43   809.2'512   81–4089
ISBN 0–87023–336–x   AACR2

For Barbara
and Adam
and David

CONTENTS

PREFACE

This book on tragedy is an "essay" in an older sense of the word—an "attempt" to discuss what I believe to be the essence of tragedy. From the moment I decided to put my thoughts on paper I realized the precarious and tentative nature of such an enterprise, because tragedy is the most difficult genre to discuss with assurance and clarity. It is impossible to get too close to mystery, to penetrate completely the dark seed of a shriek, to stare too long into the abyss. I have made no attempt to offer a definition of tragedy, nor is it my aim to refute definitions offered by others. Perhaps the most sobering thought that pressed against me throughout the writing of this book was that after 2,500 years of discussing tragedy no one definition or description has emerged as *the* way to approach this complex genre. Some of the greatest and most subtle minds have confronted tragedy, coming from different directions and from different ages, each deepening our insight but each falling short of an unqualifiedly satisfying definition or analysis. This is as it should be. The value of a work of art cannot be exhausted by analysis and is always limited by definition. The nature of tragedy and its unique appeal is a subject for argument and discussion, and the discussion will continue as long as men and women question the forces, within themselves and outside of themselves, that make life a terrible puzzlement. It goes without saying, although I here say it, that my discussion depends on the insights of those who have come before. What I offer in this book is not original, in the way we usually use the word (for how can a subject touching human nature and discussed over a period of 2,500 years still produce "original" thoughts?), but I do believe that my concentration on the secret cause makes explicit what was felt before. Ultimately, of course, the book is subjective, the product of my own understanding of a subject I have been thinking about for years.

Throughout I have avoided the Greek catchwords found in most discussions of tragedy—hamartia, hubris, ethos, etc.—because they have lost whatever original clarity they possessed. I have not avoided more modern phrases, like Jaspers's "boundary situation" and Arrowsmith's "turbulence," which are clearly useful. Throughout I have cut through chronological and geographical lines, for an obvious reason: if the concept of tragedy is a viable one, if there *is* a tragic tradition, then what is said about tragedy must apply to all tragedies, no matter where written or when. I believe, despite the forceful arguments of Joseph Wood Krutch and George Steiner, that tragedy is not dead, that the term points to a clear, although flexible, tradition that was begun by the Greeks when they put on their larger-than-life masks to play against a background of mountain and sky, and which is still with us when equal-to-life hippies ride their motorcycles in a film that captures mountain and sky on celluloid. Throughout I am interested less in tragedy's changing form than in its enduring substance. That substance touches "the secret cause," the focus of my attention. The phrase comes from James Joyce's *A Portrait of the Artist as a Young Man*. Presenting his theory of tragedy to Lynch, Stephen Dedalus haughtily indicates that Aristotle did not define pity and terror, but that *he* has: "Pity is the feeling which arrests the mind in the presence of whatsoever is grave and constant in human sufferings and unites it with the human sufferer. Terror is the feeling which arrests the mind in the presence of whatsoever is grave and constant in human sufferings and unites it with the secret cause." Pity and terror have been the objects of much critical examination. The secret cause, however, although touched by almost every critic in one way or another, in one guise or another (the phrase itself being rarely used, with the notable exceptions of Richard Sewall and Louis Martz), has not received the concentrated attention it demands. The secret cause is the prey I hunt throughout this book, always with the realization that any highly focused critical discussion tends to distort the uniqueness of a particular work of art. I like to think that what is here presented emerges gracefully and genuinely from the specific plays under discussion. That tragedy as a concept can be discussed outside of drama has been demonstrated by some of our finest critics. What I have to say about the essence of tragedy could apply to works other than plays, but my discussion deals exclusively with drama because in drama the tragic spirit is most *immediately* felt (given the nature of drama), in drama it had its first push, and in drama it continues to find its most effective manifestations. (I must add that drama is what I know best.)

A critic, resting on a small point in space and occupying but a moment in time, situates himself where all previous critical roads seem to meet. The list of those to whom I am in debt reads like an index to a history of dramatic criticism: Lionel Abel, Aristotle, William Arrowsmith, W. H. Auden, Eric Bentley, A. C. Bradley, Geoffrey Brereton, Cleanth Brooks, Robert Brustein, Kenneth Burke, Robert Corrigan, Una Ellis-Fermor, Gerald Else, Francis Fergusson, Leslie Fiedler, Northrop Frye, John Gassner, Charles Glicksberg, Thomas Gould, Richmond Hathorn, Hegel, Robert Heilman, T. R. Henn, Karl Jaspers, Walter Kaufmann, Walter Kerr, H. D. F. Kitto, Bernard Knox, Jan Kott, Murray Krieger, Joseph Wood Krutch, Susanne Langer, Clifford Leech, Harry Levin, F. L. Lucas, Maynard Mack, Oscar Mandel, Louis Martz, Laurence Michel, Arthur Miller, Roy Morrell, Herbert Muller, Henry Myers, Nietzsche, William Van O'Connor, Elder Olson, D. D. Raphael, I. A. Richards, George Santayana, Nathan Scott, Richard Sewall, George Steiner, J. L. Styan, Miguel Unamuno, Maurice Valency, Herbert Weisinger, Raymond Williams. As in an index, I list them alphabetically because each writer, in his or her own way, has probed the dark corners of this difficult subject. Some have been acknowledged in the footnotes; the ideas of the rest have been so absorbed that no specific footnote is possible. I also have a debt to those students at the University of Massachusetts—in my courses on Shakespeare, Elizabethan-Jacobean Drama, Modern Drama, O'Neill, and Tragic Drama—who were prodded by themselves or by me to state exactly how they *felt*, rather than how they were supposed to feel, while reading and after reading *Oedipus Rex* or *Hamlet* or *Waiting for Godot* or *Desire Under the Elms*. I am grateful to the Research Council of the University of Massachusetts for a Faculty Research Grant.

As always, my deepest debt is to my wife Barbara. She and our sons, Adam and David, were always there when I returned from the darkness.

Amherst, 1981

1 THE INVISIBLE PIPER

Einstein and Oedipus

Approximately sixty years ago the new physics began to call all in doubt. The strict causality of Newton's teaching gave way to principles of relativity and uncertainty. The comfortable coherence of Newton's world was shattered by the remarkable intuitions and findings of Albert Einstein. Parallels meet; space is curved; a ray of light bends. Einstein discovered a restless universe. Nothing is stationary, everything must be described as moving relative to something else. The notion of time is purely arbitrary, as are the notions of size and shape. Even mass is merely contained energy. Relativity was the concept that exploded modern man's sense of a self-contained system of physical causality. The exact progression from cause to effect became uncertain; the cause of "cause and effect" became more mysterious. But relativity was only a temporary resting place in the questionings of skeptical scientists. Inevitably, the next step in the progression from certainty to relativity is uncertainty. It became impossible to describe events accurately; one could only deal with probabilities. *How* one observes affects *what* one observes, and, as Heisenberg's uncertainty principle indicates, the closer a scientist comes to measuring accurately the position of a particle, the further he gets from measuring accurately the momentum of that particle. It was this principle of uncertainty, the focal point in the controversy over indeterminacy, that caused Einstein to part company from Werner Heisenberg and Niels Bohr and other giants of his time. Not that he did not understand or appreciate their imposing findings. "An inner voice" told him that their theories were not the whole story, that they did not "really bring us any closer to the secret of the Old One."[1] He realized that it would never be possible to decide whether the world was causal or not, but he believed instinctively that everything was determined.

> Everything is determined, the beginning as well as the end, by forces over which we have no control. It is determined for the insect as well as for the star. Human beings, vegetables, or cosmic dust, we all dance to a mysterious tune, intoned in the distance by an invisible piper.[2]

Shedding the cloak of skeptical science, assuming the stance of religious faith without giving up the notion that the source is unreachable, the most remarkable scientist of our time offers us a potent image for a discussion of tragedy. Human beings dance to a mysterious tune played by an invisible piper. The writers of tragedy dramatize the dance. Sometimes they concentrate on the piper; sometimes they emphasize the quality of dancing; sometimes they focus on the dancer. But always—for this is essential to tragedy—they are haunted by the mysteriousness of the tune.

Einstein, the clearest of thinkers, believed that "the most beautiful experience we can have is the mysterious. It is the fundamental emotion which stands at the cradle of true art and true science."[3] A serious examination of the tragic tradition confirms the validity of this view. It *is* a fundamental emotion and contains the very seed of tragedy and religion and science. However, whereas religion offers answers to the mystery, whereas science strives to comprehend portions of the mystery, tragedy enhances the mystery by dramatizing the question. Religion leads to a period, science leads to a comma, tragedy raises a question mark.

The fundamental emotion of the mysterious that for Einstein is at the heart of true art and science is given its first important dramatic life in Sophocles' *Oedipus Rex*. This, I believe, is the reason for the play's abiding potency as tragedy and for its important place in the history of the tragic tradition. *Oedipus Rex* has been the touchstone of tragedy from the time that it provided Aristotle with his generalizations on tragic art.[4] It deservedly is the focus of any discussion of tragedy, not merely because Aristotle's precepts seem to derive from his having witnessed and been moved by this play, not merely because *Oedipus Rex* seems to contain many of the popular, and often misleading, notions about tragedy (the hero is high, he has a flaw, he suffers, he achieves wisdom, the society is sick), but because for the first time in the Western dramatic tradition, a dramatist, brilliantly using all the resources of his art, puts a question mark at the heart of his play. For the first time, a character in a play pursues the crucial questions that tragedy pursues, and he embodies both the strengths and the limits of reason in trying to answer the questions. In terms closer to the main thrust of my thesis, for the first time a character's ordeal causes him to face the fact of mystery, the darkness of self and the darkness of gods. In search of a period, Oedipus finds a question mark. The core of mystery in *Oedipus Rex* is the core of tragedy, and the pervading interrogative mood of the play is the essential mood of tragedy.

A riddle is at the center of Oedipus' story and a Sphinx haunts that story. A young man, having met and with justified anger killed some belligerent strangers on a spot where three roads meet, comes to a Thebes devastated by a creature, half lion with wings and half woman with beautiful face and breasts, that destroys men who fail to solve the riddle she asks. Oedipus—fleeing from Corinth because the Apollonian oracle stated that he would kill his father and have sexual intercourse with his mother—confronts the Sphinx's riddle and solves it, thereby freeing Thebes, becoming king (since the Theban King Laius had recently been killed on the spot where three roads meet), and marrying Laius' wife, Jocasta. The riddle itself is not presented in *Oedipus Rex* but would have been familiar to Sophocles' audience: What thing on land has a single voice but changes shape, going on four feet in the morning, on two feet in the afternoon, and on three feet in the evening? The answer, known by Oedipus but by no one else, including the blind seer Teiresias, is "Man," who moves on four feet as an infant, walks erect as an adult, and needs the aid of a stick in old age. A seemingly frivolous riddle, almost childish, yet his solution of it is enough to give Oedipus the reputation of being the most intelligent of Theban men and enough to make Oedipus confident and proud of his own intelligence and ability to reason. We must, of course, accept the difficulty of the riddle and the brilliance of the answer at face value, although the superficiality of the enigma forces itself on us when the larger questions of the play seem to reduce the riddle to a childish endeavor. Who *is* that man, the answer of the riddle? Crawling, walking erect, or stumbling, what road does he travel, and who controls his journey? Clearly, the riddle points to man's outside, his physical nature. The play's riddle, as opposed to the Sphinx's riddle, points to darker shadows, shadows both microcosmic and macrocosmic. In fact, "riddle" becomes too frivolous a word for the mystery.

As saviour of his city, as good King for many years, Oedipus, in the play's beginning, is understandably implored by the priests to come to the aid of Thebes, which is suffering once more, this time from a mysterious plague. He has deep concern for his people and has already begun to act in their behalf, having sent Creon to Delphi to learn from the oracle what he, as the king, can do to save the city. He will not, he reveals, "scant whatever duty God reveals."[5] Dutifully listening to Apollo's oracle which orders him to punish or kill Laius' murderers, Oedipus curses them and vows to the chorus of honored elders that he will obey the god, he will "bring what is dark to light . . . with the help of God"; in fact, he will "associate" himself with the oracle. Oedipus' search for the murderers, his search for the cause of the city's plague and blight, constitutes the play's action.

That Oedipus believes in the gods, that he is a pious man, is indisputable. It was precisely *because* he believed in the truth of Apollo's assertion that he would be a parricide and commit incest, that he left Corinth. It is precisely *because* he believes in the oracle's assertion that Laius' murderers must be caught if Thebes is to be cleansed, that he actively and relentlessly pursues the investigation. Those critics who claim that Oedipus is guilty of not believing in the gods because he tries to avoid the fate they give him are paying attention neither to Oedipus' piety as presented in the play nor to the very human impulse to take precautions against parricide and incest, especially when these horrendous dangers are couched in the dark words of an oracle. This last point needs emphasis, I believe. The oracles are accurate, as the play clearly and forcefully demonstrates. But the terms of their messages are often enigmatic, bathed in ambiguity, leading to deeper questions. The oracles seem to force the listener *not* to interpret them in a literal way. Certainly Oedipus, who is a fundamentally good man, who does not wish to commit sins so grievous, who is morally innocent of the sins that he does commit, certainly Oedipus—pious man that he is, with a firm belief in the justice of the gods—would be forced by his very nature *not* to interpret the oracles so literally. In his case, to face the literal accuracy of the gods is to face the essential injustice of things, at the very least to face a question mark about the gods' actions when a satisfying period was always operative.

As we witness Oedipus' actions throughout the play; as we listen to his justifiably angry denunciation of Teiresias, who appears not to wish to heal the country, and who, like the gods, expresses his truths both enigmatically and clearly (and again, as with the gods, his clear statements are not taken literally); as we listen to Oedipus' accusations against Creon (mistaken accusations, but surely based on intelligent assumptions); as we see Oedipus accumulate evidence which ultimately will devastate him but which he reasons or explains away, again in intelligent fashion; and as we experience the agony of his discovery of the truth about himself, we must *feel* the mysterious workings of the gods and the injustice of the fate they have given Oedipus. Oedipus vigorously and admirably narrows the gap between appearance and reality, while Sophocles offers the audience the double vision associated with irony. The horrible *truth* that sits in the middle of the play's action, the tip of the spinning top, is ever present in the audience's consciousness and informs the play's unique atmosphere. Oedipus strips away veil after veil of illusion, only to find his real self, naked, exposed, polluted. And the play, which dramatizes the riddle, reveals the more full answer, "the man Oedipus." This riddle is posed not by a Sphinx who throws herself off a cliff when the correct answer is given, but by Apollo, who remains alive—god that he is—to destroy or heal, whatever he wishes, for whatever reason he may or may not have. "What has God done to me?" is Oedipus' momentous and agonizing question when he returns to the stage as a blind man leaning upon a stick. It is a question that cannot be lightly dismissed, because it is asked by the answerer of questions and because it indicates that the intelligent Oedipus has not lifted and cannot lift the last veil. "What has God done to me?" allows us to realize we have moved from a Sphinx's riddle to more important riddles and questions. "What had two of its four feet bruised in the morning, went on two seemingly steady feet in the afternoon, and hobbled on three feet when that afternoon suddenly turned into evening?" The answer: Oedipus. But "Who leads man on a horrible path to parricide and incest, and who does not permit a basically good man, both pious and intelligent, to escape his horrible destiny?" The answer: the gods. And this riddle forces the largest question of all. "Why?" The answer is silence. The cause remains secret.

The gods. A troublesome element for modern audiences, and, I suspect, for the Greeks watching *Oedipus Rex* in the bright light of an Athens day. The human drama that unfolds before us seems to be played not only against the *background* provided by the gods—the "system of co-ordinates against which we are to read the significance of what the human actors do and suffer," as Kitto suggests[6]—but also with the gods taking an active role *in* the drama and touching the most potent source of mystery in the play. The gods are without and within, not only presenting oracles that seem designed to trick the hearer, but also operating within the human protagonist, that is, becoming inherent in the character to such an extent that we can with assurance describe Oedipus as an "Apollonian" man. Apollonian in that he believes in Apollo's oracle and associates himself with that oracle, and Apollonian because he conducts himself *like* Apollo when he attempts to shed light on a mystery, to change chaos and plague to order and health. Apollo, like most Olympian deities, is both healer and polluter, both saviour and destroyer, epithets which clearly describe Oedipus.[7] The doubleness of the god and the doubleness of the man reflect one another to such an extent that they seem at times to be one. That a man should contain a god within him, that man and god should be bound in one body, that the God should destroy part of himself by destroying the man—these are all mysteries. (Need one point to the Christian parallel, the destruction of God-in-man by the God who "forsakes" the man?) In *Oedipus Rex* the mystery is compounded because the Apollonian man, working with Apollonian reason and intelligence against a background of Apollonian oracles, discovers that another god has possessed him, has been *in* him all along, and this discovery is filled with terror. This god, of course, is the Nietzschean Dionysus, the instinctual reality, the chaos seething within all men, the sensuality and cruelty and irrationality at the base of man's existence. In the third choric ode, immediately before the slow entrance of the shepherd who will reveal the truth of Oedipus' wretched fate, the chorus mentions Dionysus, asking "was it he who found you there (on Mt. Cithaeron), / And caught you up in his own proud / Arms . . . ?" (p. 57). Dionysus has indeed caught him up. By uncovering the truth about himself, Oedipus discovers his Dionysian self, and this knowledge causes suffering and pain. Although an Apollonian man, Oedipus discovers that he is closer to Dionysus because of his *actions* before the Sophocles play began: he killed his father; he had, and continues to have, sexual intercourse with his mother. He *sees* the full horror of these deeds. That a mortal man is closer to Dionysus than to Apollo should come as no surprise to modern readers, for we have behind us the momentous discoveries of Sigmund Freud who, like Oedipus, ventured into territory unknown, seemingly inaccessible, dark and awesome. Sophocles anticipated Freud, as Freud himself acknowledged, in presenting the terror of natural inheritance. For the Greeks the affinity of Oedipus and Dionysus would have been recognized simply by the knowledge that Dionysus was the *only* Greek god born of a mortal woman, and by the knowledge that both Oedipus and Dionysus stem from the same Cadmus, founder of Thebes, and that both Oedipus and Dionysus were born in Thebes.

We can say, therefore, that when Oedipus looks into his own Dionysian abyss he is discovering both kin and kind. But that is as far as mortal man can go. He can recognize Dionysus and his own guilt *in action;* he can blame the gods, especially Apollo, for forcing him to travel a path leading to parricide and incest. [We must not forget that his simple question to the oracle of whether he was indeed the son of Polybus and Merope was *never* answered; we cannot forget that Oedipus does blame the gods for his plight—"Ah, what net has God been weaving for me?" (p. 38). "Ah, / If I was created so, born to this fate, / Who could deny the savagery of God?" (p. 42).] But as mortal man he cannot look too long into that dark reality of self, so, in despair, he blinds himself physically. And he cannot lift the last veil hiding the secret cause of the gods' actions, a cause not accessible or approachable by any efforts of mortal man's reason. Man by reason can destroy a Sphinx, but he cannot know the mysterious workings of an Apollo or Dionysus. And what little he does learn causes pain and suffering, and produces ever-darker questions about the forces within himself and outside himself.

That Oedipus was born to his fate, that his "abomination" was "destined him," is an indisputable fact of the play, but, strange to say, a fact that many critics and teachers and students wish to avoid. Free will as a *necessary* condition of tragedy has taken such firm hold on students of tragic drama that it seems impossible to dislodge it. Admittedly, free will does operate in many tragedies, and certainly it is easier to discuss "tragic flaw" in the light of free will. But a clear —I would almost say pure or innocent—investigation of *Oedipus Rex* reveals a man who has not been treated justly. How often do we find that students, who have been "taught" *Oedipus Rex,* blame Oedipus for his pride, his anger, his desire to escape his fate, and therefore, his impiety; how often they posit a system of poetic justice where a man pays for the sins he committed. The didacticism of their ideas belies the turbulence and mystery found in the play and, I suspect, belies their genuine responses to Oedipus' condition. Ask students who have *not* been conditioned to tragic flaws and Aristotelian theory what they think, and they will say, "Oedipus was screwed!" The rawness of the expression, not to mention its appropriate sexual overtone, more closely indicates Oedipus' condition as we genuinely feel it than do the usual academic responses. For here at least we get the sense of injustice, here at least we are pointing at the inscrutability of the gods and the frailty of man. The security of Oedipus' illusions is shattered. Stripped of security, precariously balancing on the edge of the abyss, Oedipus gets to see more of himself and more of the condition of the world. He recognizes his dreadful conduct, the sheer horror of his violent murder of father and incestuous marriage to mother, and this allows him to recognize the irrational, dark, demonic forces within him and the mystery, the appalling mystery, of the behavior of the gods. He, like all men, is bewildered by the indiscriminate workings of the gods. The illusion of God's justice is broken and man's plight becomes desperate—for how much darkness can a man contemplate? Oedipus' problem is a basic human problem; his groping toward the truth of his life is a basic human groping; and his realization that the last veil—the secret cause, the "why" of the gods' actions—cannot be lifted is a discovery that most men can understand and appreciate. And when we look back at Oedipus' story—so remarkably told by Sophocles, with the strong and steady progression of the play re-enforcing Oedipus' strong search for the truth—do we remember his pride, his anger, his "flaws," or do we remember the horror of his situation and the dark shadows in which the gods function?

That Oedipus is born to his condition does not erase his individual characteristics. He is proud, he is angry, he has an inner turbulence, he is *active* (as opposed to the chorus of elders declaring their disease and bemoaning their plight), he does run toward his destruction, he does travel on a journey into night, Karl Jaspers's dark night of the soul. His determination is a measure of his greatness. When the shepherd asserts, "Ah, I am on the brink of dreadful speech!", Oedipus' answer indicates the nature of the man: "And I of dreadful hearing. Yet I must hear." He may suspect the worst, but he "must" hear, the "must" of a stubborn, intense man who, despite every kind of obstacle (the dark silence of Teiresias, the pleadings of

Jocasta, the prayers of the shepherd), rushes toward the brink of painful knowledge. That he must play a part written by the gods does not mean he will not play it well and that we, as audience, will not be interested in *him* as a man, and, in fact, proud of him as our man. (Those who feel superior to Oedipus because we have knowledge he does not have should beware. He also thought he knew.) Using Einstein's metaphor, we can say that when Oedipus dances to that mysterious tune, he dances brilliantly and he dances for us. He looks into the abyss for us, he asks the questions we ask, and he acknowledges the darkness, as we must. The catharsis the audience feels at the end of the play stems, I believe, from this basic idea: we are forced to openly acknowledge terrible aspects of life, buried deeply and darkly in our minds. The tragic dramatist makes us face the fact of darkness, and this facing the mystery, facing the reality of the abyss, acknowledging the secrecy of the secret cause, gives us relief. Looking into an abyss can afford pleasure as well as pain.

Oedipus killed his father where three roads meet. On that spot, that dark spot where Oedipus does his devastating deed, three men, traveling their separate roads, meet. Einstein, Freud, and Sophocles all believed in causal determinism, all affirmed the sense that there *is* a cause that explains the workings of the physical universe and the workings of man's psyche. Einstein and Freud were determined to search for the cause. Sophocles—here the representative of all tragic dramatists?—affirms the secrecy of the cause. Life's uncertainty and mystery is the center of the tragic vision, and the *recognition* that life is indeed based on mystery, on the question mark —that *we will never know* what shape our lives will take or how our lives are directed, if at all—is itself a catharsis. "What has God done to me?" is a question that touches the mystery, and just asking the question puts the tragic focus within the realm of our sensibility and experience. We witness what we know—a knowledge connected with pain and suffering—and we know that we do not know, forever feeling the pressure of uncertainty and mystery. That is a paradox that life forces us to share with every other thinking and feeling person—today and in the past and in time to come.

2 LOVE

Sophocles' *Antigone* & Anouilh's *Antigone*

Sophocles' *Antigone* has been the focus of much critical attention. It is a play that can be approached from different angles and it raises wide-ranging issues and questions. A popular play in university courses, it allows the teacher to demonstrate the relevance of ancient drama to our contemporary situation. *Antigone* dramatizes problems that always seem modern: the conflict between the state and individual conscience; the clash between written and unwritten laws; the claims of family affection vs. the claims of political stability. In addition, students of drama have posed and attempted to answer more academic questions: Is Antigone an ideal tragic heroine? Whose tragedy is it—Antigone's or Creon's? How "romantic" is the play? Does the play conform to Aristotelian principles? Or, on the other hand, is it an excellent example of Hegelian tragedy?

One of the results of such heavy attention is that Antigone's tragedy has been sentimentalized. This is understandable, because her youth, her sex, her betrothal to Haemon (Creon's son and therefore the son of her executioner), her fate-crossed birth—we can never forget she is Oedipus' daughter—her family affections, her defiant personality, all of these have helped make her a popular tragic heroine and have prompted modern dramatists, like Jean Anouilh, to retell her story. But these same considerations, based on her charismatic character, combined with the relevant issues that the play raises, have diverted attention from the exact nature of the tragedy. William Arrowsmith is surely correct in asserting that we are not "stirred" by the usual interpretations of the play, and that these interpretations have neglected the play's "turbulence," its emotional experience.[1] I would like to help correct this situation by concentrating on what I see as the essential core of Sophocles' play, what makes it a tragedy, what gave it a potency before we moderns pounced upon its "relevance," and what is the deeper reason for the play's hold on the imagination: its presentation of the radical contradictions of man's experience, Sophocles' handling of the vital and shifting relationship of love and death and the gods; in short, the play's confrontation with the secret cause.

The first appearance of the titular figure in a Greek tragedy presents his character note. We are dealing with masks, of course, and the mask, necessarily immobile, freezes the character into a stance, at least when the character first enters. As the play progresses, we may see a different mask, or we may discern more clearly what is *behind* the mask, but the mask, in its first appearance, is not meant to deceive us. (I see it as a truth-teller, comparable to the Shakespearean soliloquy.) When we first see Oedipus in *Oedipus Rex* he is a concerned, pious king. When we first see Antigone in her play, she is a defiant, fiery young woman, filled with love for brother, loyalty to family, anger against Creon, and piety toward the gods. Between her entrance, with Ismene, from the central door of the palace to her departure alone as she takes her long walk across the large pit of the Greek amphitheater, Sophocles offers us her entire present being and a sense of her past.

Her first words to Ismene, her "dear sister," bring up the "curse of Oedipus," which has informed her past life and which she will confront directly just before going to her death. She tells Ismene of Creon's decree that Polyneices, their dead brother, cannot be buried on penalty of death, and she expresses her horror that his body is food for carrion birds. There is no hesitation in her voice when she asserts "there is something we must do" and in her straight-forward challenge to Ismene: by helping with the burial, "you can prove what you are: / A true sister, or a traitor to your family."[2] Ismene thinks Antigone is "mad," a word that pinpoints Antigone's irrational, instinctive defiance of Creon's decree. It is difficult to interpret Antigone's attitude toward the decree as incorrect because Sophocles seems relentless in presenting her act of burial in the most praiseworthy terms. She is obeying divine laws; the "crime" of burying the body is "holy"; if the act means death, "it will not be the worst of deaths—death without honor." What she says to Ismene now, we, as audience, know to be right because we, like Antigone, instinctively recoil from the idea of an unburied dead body; we, like Antigone, realize the outrage to humanity when the body of a man is left for carrion. We are willing, therefore, to take Antigone's comments on "the laws of the gods" to be true as well. But if we have any doubts that the *human* thing to do coincides with the wishes of the gods, the sentry's report to Creon dispels them. The sentry, naturally troubled because what he has to say may reflect on him, fearfully presents the details of the symbolic burial of Polyneices: "someone" has put "new dust on the slimy flesh," just enough dust "for the ghost's peace"; there was "not a sign of digging, no, / Not a wheeltrack in the dust, no trace of anyone"; and "no sign / Of dogs or any wild animal." The sentry does not know "how to put it," and for good reason—the burial is inexplicable if we think in terms of a mortal's having buried the body. The question, Who buried Polyneices? is answered immediately by the question of the leader of the chorus: "Can it be that the gods have done this?" Sophocles is calculatingly placing this burial in the context of mystery, and raising a question that he answers with a question, the interrogative mood of tragedy always with us. The chorus leader's question must be taken seriously, very seriously, especially because Creon the tyrant rejects it so vehemently. The gods are operating in this burial, just as they are operating in Antigone's entire life. It seems that Antigone and the gods are working together in burying a body, and that they are working together in challenging Creon's inhuman and ungodly decree.

The rightness and essential piety of Antigone's attitude toward the burial, as she utters it to Ismene, seem irrefutable. But the *way* she voices her attitude toward Ismene must give us pause. Her family affections, her great love for a dear brother, make her defiant and fearless, heroic qualities indeed. However, this defiance and fearlessness seem so heightened in the face of a death to come that Antigone appears inhuman. Ismene stresses the point: "You are mad"; "think of the danger"; "we are only women"; "I am so afraid for you!"; "you should be cold with fear." And inhuman too, or at least cold and forbidding, are Antigone's words, which are first of sarcasm and then of hatred, to a sister who rejects her offer of complicity: "Go away, Ismene: / I shall be hating you soon, and the dead will too, / For your words are hateful." Ismene leaves the stage praising Antigone as "a loyal friend indeed to those who love you." No words come from Antigone as she takes her long walk to the dead body of Polyneices. Her righteous cause of burying a beloved brother has produced a coldness of heart for a dear sister.

Later, Antigone will not allow Ismene, who now realizes her duty to the dead, to die with her. "You shall not lessen my death by sharing it." Ismene rightly feels that she is being mocked. Family affection stifles family affection. Here is the first of many paradoxes in the play: love has led to a negation of love; a cause based on love has made "a stone of the heart," to use Yeats's phrase when he was describing another cause. This is what causes do. Which of us does not hear the words, "It is the cause, it is the cause," as Othello for the sake of justice is ready to murder Desdemona. Sophocles forces us very early in the play, in this first exchange between sisters, to think of the terrible paradox of love leading to a denial of love.

The coldness and fiery defiance that we associate with Antigone return to the stage in the person of Creon. They are, after all, related to each other, and they are both related, we can never forget, to the fiery Oedipus. But Antigone's coldness still clings to a cause that is right; Creon's always clings to a cause that is wrong. Perhaps one should not be too dogmatic about right and wrong in so complex a play, but, many critics notwithstanding, Creon is the unequivocal tyrant of the play, relentlessly narrow in his views and destructive in his behavior. He stands firmly against every idea of compassion and love; he goes against every principle of democracy in government; he epitomizes the principle of calculation.[3] In short, he represents hatred in a play about love. It is difficult, therefore, to accept the Hegelian interpretation of *Antigone* as a clash between two rights, what Hegel calls "the equal validity of both powers engaged in conflict."[4] The neatness of Hegel's tragic formula does not fit the tragedy that he seems to have based it on. Creon's cause has no validity, as it is presented in the play. The issue of the validity of the claims of the state vs. the claims of family and individual is always a debatable one, and helps explain the popularity of the play, but it is not an issue in *this* play. Creon is clearly a tyrant, and his denial of the gods and of love will cause his eventual suffering in terms of the coldest kind of poetic justice. To think of Creon as the possible tragic hero, as many have, seems a gross misreading of the play. And to see a resemblance between Creon and his brother-in-law and nephew Oedipus in anything more than their anger is forgetting the important issue of piety to the gods. Creon works against the gods and is punished—as if a logical equation is being worked out. Oedipus works with the gods and for the gods but is their victim—thereby producing the large inexplicable questions about man's relationship to the gods. And this brings us back to the tragic heroine, Antigone, who in burying Polyneices is doing the work of the gods.

When the sentry appears a second time, he brings Antigone with him, whom he has caught placing dust on the stinking corpse and sprinkling wine three times "for her brother's ghost." Even in this second burial the gods seem to have been at work. These are the sentry's words:

> But nothing happened until the white round sun
> Whirled in the center of the round sky over us:
> Then, suddenly,
> A storm of dust roared up from the earth, and the sky
> Went out, the plain vanished with all its trees
> In the stinging dark. We closed our eyes and endured it.
> The whirlwind lasted a long time, but it passed;
> And then we looked, and there was Antigone!
> (p. 201)

Antigone's act is given a macrocosmic dimension. This is no ordinary burial; the gods who helped to accomplish the first burial seem to be watching this second burial.

In her agon with Creon, Antigone denies nothing, reaffirms the "unrecorded laws of God," asserts that "there is no guilt in reverence for the dead," and is sure that she will have "praise and honor" for what she has done. Here too she seems to welcome death. She knows she must die eventually—"I am only mortal"—so sees no hardship in dying now, before her time, for the pious act of burying her brother. In fact, in a world of evil, she sees death as a "friend." Her last phrase in this scene is ". . . I belong to Death." Headstrong, bitter in her condemnation of Creon, cold to Ismene, weary of words, and intellectually accepting the death that she knows is the price of her action, Antigone displays an "inflexible heart," to use Creon's phrase. But she is attached to a pious cause, and, cold though she is in her behavior, she is acting in behalf of love. Surely her most important line in this entire encounter with Creon is: "It is my nature to join in love, not hate."

Love is the power that informs the play.[5] It is the essential instinctive motive of Antigone when she buries Polyneices; the reason Ismene asks to share her sister's fate; the bond between Antigone and Haemon; the force that prompts Haemon to rebel against his father and then to kill himself; the idea that even Creon asserts when he suggests that love can only exist within an orderly society.[6] (Obviously, Creon has his private notion of what love is, for he emerges as the apostle of hate. Throughout, he denies love or cheapens it; he has no understanding of its hidden power or mystery.) Love is what connects Antigone's human act of burying Polyneices with her pious obedience to the gods. In the third choric ode, the chorus sings about love's power, informing us of "a girl's glance working the will of heaven." This ode concludes with an important idea, usually neglected in discussions of the play. Love is "pleasure to her alone who mocks us, / Merciless Aphrodite." Love, we know, causes pain and suffering, it causes hardness of heart, it brings about the death of Antigone, the deaths of Haemon and Eurydice, and the living death of Creon. It has awesome power over men and gods. But it is a "pleasure" to the goddess Aphrodite who "mocks" us. Here is a note of cruelty, the kind of mocking cruelty that is often associated with the gods, and in this play is associated with mortals as well. Ismene felt she was being mocked by Antigone; Creon mocked his son's love, the chorus, and the gods; Antigone, when going to her death, will feel she is mocked by the chorus and the gods. A tragic heroine, a tyrant, and a goddess all mock, all look at those around them from a heightened position, but only the goddess prevails, for the tyrant and heroine are themselves mocked—Creon when he is justly punished by the gods for his impiety, Antigone when she for the first time in the play (and the last time that we see her) displays confusion and anxiety and doubt. Only the immortals can *remain* mockers; the heightened mortals, because they are human, must fall *down* to their humanity and must eventually become the victims of the gods' mockery. But in the fall to humanity, the wounded and mocked mortals rise in our estimation, achieving dignity. Creon does not rise much because of his narrow tyranny and lovelessness, although he does learn, too late, that he was a "fool," that he is guilty of the deaths around him, but that some of the guilt rests on the gods who crushed him, driving him headlong to barbarism. Antigone rises enormously, for in her confusion at being mocked and in her horror at facing death alone, she appears to take upon herself "the mystery of things," and she is never more human and, paradoxically, more heightened than in her last moments.

Sophocles carefully prepares for Antigone's last appearance on stage. She enters just as the chorus completes its ode on love with the words on the mocking, merciless Aphrodite. Indeed, love has brought her to this final scene and she will feel mocked. Antigone's words:

> Look upon me, friends, and pity me
> Turning back at the night's edge to say
> Good-by to the sun that shines for me no longer;
> Now sleepy Death
> Summons me down to Acheron, that cold shore:
> There is no bridesong there, nor any music.
> (p. 219)

Here is the first time that Antigone displays fear in the face of death; her words betray the softer emotions of a young girl going to her end. She realizes that she is on the edge of night, having come to her boundary situation, and she knows that the night she is entering contains neither light nor song. Her loneliness seems to overwhelm her as she goes on to mention the story of Niobe, "how the stone / Clung fast about her." When the chorus mentions her "glory" because she is dying with "a kind of honor," Antigone thinks herself mocked. "You laugh at me. Ah, friends, friends, / Can you not wait until I am dead?" When the chorus, pursuing the idea of justice, mentions her father's guilt, Antigone, in moving terms, recalls, for us and for herself, her dark beginnings, mentioned in her first speech and surely always lurking in her mind.

> You have touched it at last: that bridal bed
> Unspeakable, horror of son and mother mingling:
> Their crime, infection of all our family!
> O Oedipus, father and brother!
> Your marriage strikes from the grave to murder mine.
> I have been a stranger here in my own land: '
> All my life
> The blasphemy of my birth has followed me.
> (p. 220)

It is unjust that an innocent girl is suffering for her father's sin, and this injustice reminds us that her father too was an innocent sufferer, and that the gods continue to play their demonic and inexplicable role. However, the chorus, forever upholding established law, denies her innocence: "You have made your choice, / Your death is

the doing of your conscious hand." The coldness of the sentiment
—precisely echoing the coldness that Antigone herself displayed
to Ismene: ("You have made your choice")—leads Antigone to
despair.

> Then let me go, since all your words are bitter,
> And the very light of the sun is cold to me.
> Lead me to my vigil, where I must have
> Neither love nor lamentation; no song, but silence.
> (p. 221).

She laments her isolation, the condition of most tragic heroes, and
she sees herself not only alone but neither pitied nor loved. Her act
of love in burying Polyneices, a pious act in her eyes, is branded as
impious and wrong. Small wonder that she refuses to address the
chorus any longer, finding some consolation in speaking directly to
her tomb of death, believing she will soon be "with her own again,"
especially with Polyneices for whom she is dying. She reasserts her
innocence: "And yet, as men's hearts know, I have done no wrong./
I have not sinned before God." Her tone, in the Fitts-Fitzgerald
translation, must betray her deep disappointment with the gods.
Knox's translation makes her sense of being deserted by the gods
more explicit: "Why should I in my misery look to the gods any
more? Which of them can I call my ally?"[7] Revealing human disappointment, terrible loneliness in the face of death, Antigone is
mocked not only by the people around her, but by the gods, including the merciless Aphrodite. Once again, the gods in Sophoclean
tragedy are wearing masks impossible to penetrate, performing
actions that seem unjust. It is natural for a confused young woman
on the brink of death to question their enigmatic ways. She is not
shouting against the gods as her father—a larger tragic hero—had,
but rather, in her quiet shudder and lonely desperation, she is reminding us and herself of their injustice.

But the scene does not end on this note of disappointment.
Antigone prays that if Creon is guilty in his actions, his punishment
should equal hers, and she leaves the stage still defiantly expressing
the piety of her act, this time to her native Thebes:

> Thebes, and you my fathers' gods,
> And rulers of Thebes, you see me now, the last
> Unhappy daughter of a line of kings,

Your kings, led away to death. You will remember
What things I suffer, and at what men's hands,
Because I would not transgress the laws of heaven.
(p. 222)

She walks to her death in the tomb, and as she departs we surely feel
the rightness in her questioning of the gods, the power of her instinctive love, and the heroism of her unshakable defiance. The
chorus immediately sings an ode about others who have journeyed
to darkness—Danae, Lycurgus, and the sons of Cleopatra. The
choice of these particular figures from the past and the search for the
ode's unity and relevance to Antigone have produced some interesting critical commentary,[8] but no critic, to my knowledge, has noticed the thread of mockery connecting each of the allusions. The
innocent Danae was hidden by her father in a gravelike chamber
"where the sunlight could not come" so that she could not bear a
son who, according to an oracle, would kill his grandfather. But
Zeus visited her in a shower of gold, pouring "love" upon her,
thereby mocking the merely human precautions of Danae's father.
The guilty Lycurgus was entombed in a dungeon by Dionysus because "his tongue had mocked" the power of that powerful god.
And, most appropriate to Antigone's story, the two sons of imprisoned Cleopatra had their eyes "ripped out" by a vicious woman
filled with hatred "while grinning Ares watched." Cleopatra was
"of heavenly birth" but "in her marriage deathless Fate found
means / To build a tomb like yours for all her joy." These three
stories extend the idea of entombment, as Antigone goes to her
tomb. They remind us that gods and men have mocked Antigone.
And, in the ode's climactic story, we are forced to remember the
curse on Oedipus' house, his blinding and journey from light to
dark, and—specifically touching Antigone's story at *this* moment—
the children who were victims of fate and human cruelty. The
chorus, never directly showing pity for Antigone or expressing horror at her situation, sings an ode that manages to evoke both tragic
emotions. The ode is bathed in darkness—in the situations it presents and in the language it uses. Therefore—here Sophocles seems
most brilliant in his grasp of tragic movement—as Antigone walks to
her death, we the audience also lean toward night and mystery.
From the questions on the behavior of the gods, from the darkness
of their mocking, from the mystery of a potent love, the play moves

toward the darkness of cruelty, the mystery of Oedipus' story, and finally, the darkness and mystery of death.

Before we learn the specific nature of Antigone's death, however, an unexpected god, mentioned in the ode just discussed, takes on some significance. After Teiresias reveals the anger of the gods at Creon's refusal to bury Polyneices, whose rotting corpse is polluting Thebes, the chorus, who supported Creon throughout the play, either out of fear or because of respect for law, now insists that Creon listen to Teiresias, that he immediately free Antigone and bury Polyneices. Creon readily agrees, uttering that "the laws of the gods are mighty," and leaves the stage. The chorus then sings a hymn—not to Apollo, whose priest they just heard, who is traditionally concerned with the pollution of a state, and who seems the logical recipient of their prayers—but to Dionysus. Dionysus, true to his nature, seems intrusive here. Of course, we can explain his presence by saying that he is the bringer of good gifts; the chorus, after all, is praying for deliverance from the pestilence. And we can add to this that Dionysus is a Theban god, a god of local patriotism. But the power of the chorus's hymn, as I read it, rests on its strongly *emotional* appeal to a mysterious force, a god born of Thunder to a mortal woman, the god who punished Lycurgus, the god of wine and dance and rapture, the "purest among the voices of the night!" (p. 231). This is the figure who occupies the mid-region between man and god; he connects the two, just as Antigone's act of burial connects the human impulse to the godly wish. He reminds us of the connection between Antigone and Oedipus, both of whom descended from Dionysus. But most important, at this high point in the drama, he makes us acknowledge the emotional life, the irrational and instinctive love that informs Antigone's entire being. He allows us to understand the limitations of narrow reason and cold calculation, associated with Creon. Dionysus is the god whom Oedipus discovered within himself and who must intrude into the story of Oedipus' daughter—a heroine who acted madly and instinctively out of love, and who, at the very moment the chorus is singing its song to the potent voice of the night, is herself rushing to the night of the dead.

The rest of the play seems to belong to Creon, and for this reason many have seen him as the tragic hero. I have already indicated why this is a misguided view. Antigone's play ends with Creon's punishment in order to demonstrate that Antigone was right in her action, that she indeed worked for the gods, who now punish her adversary. The result of Antigone's action is the defeat of a tyrant, and we must understand this clearly. As the miseries of Creon pile up, as he goes on his very speedy journey to suffering and wisdom, the image of Antigone, who helped bring him to his living death, haunts the stage. Haemon kills himself for love of Antigone and he does so in her tomb. Antigone, still independent, listening to her own deathly drummer, has hanged herself in the tomb. Creon's punishment is speedily dramatized in an atmosphere of the strict justice of the gods, a dramatically disappointing but absolutely necessary acting out of poetic justice. The echoes of Antigone's end in the tomb, and her life before that, fill the last part of the play up to Creon's very last line: "Fate has brought all my pride to a thought of dust." The dust that first the gods and then Antigone spread on Polyneices' body is recalled here and we are back to the play's beginning. Between that dust and this "thought of dust" a young woman has traveled her fated journey to death.

Antigone's act of burying her brother is prompted by the deep sources of her personal motivation, based on love, but in this act we also see the workings of the gods. It is the cause, it is the cause, that gives Antigone stature; and it is the cause that makes her godlike in her sureness of self, in her cold rejection of Ismene, in her relentless defiance of the tyrant Creon. When Antigone is mocked, when she realizes the gods have left her, when she clearly confronts the curse on her family, when she feels most abandoned and most alone, then she becomes most human, and in her descent rises in our estimation. She regains her humanity, retains her dignity, and reminds us once again that love was the source of her action, but this time a love that seems more precious and powerful because it forces her to face the mystery of death. In Sophocles' treatment of the Antigone story, when the mystery of love touches the mystery of death, tragedy is born. And in this tragedy, Sophocles prods us into asking the important existential questions: Why does a pious act based on love lead to death? Why do the gods mock those who are pious? Why does love lead to a denial of love? Why are the promptings of love and the workings of the gods darker than the dark earth of Antigone's tomb? What is behind such radical contradictions in man's existence?

Uncertainty, a radical uncertainty, lodges at the deepest roots of our human experience. The deeper we get, the darker the terrain;

the darker the terrain, the more uncertain our vision and our footing. That is why Oedipus needs a stick, and that is why Antigone— abandoned and mocked, facing her own death for the first time —shudders in horror, revealing her humanity and revealing the enormous power of love that can propel a fearful woman on a journey to night. The dark seed of Antigone's shudder, like the dark root of Oedipus' scream of anguish, touches mystery, the secret cause.

Antigone, like *Oedipus Rex*, is an important touchstone in any discussion of tragedy. Its appeal goes far deeper than the political, social, and religious issues that it raises, and it is more than a study of personalities or a neat example of either Aristotelian or Hegelian tragedy. It dramatizes the basic mysteries of love and death and the gods. Therefore, when a modern dramatist wishes to use the Antigone story, with Sophocles' penetrating treatment behind him, he is confronting a difficult task. This Jean Anouilh does, with verve and some brilliance and considerable insight into the tragic mode. But his play is not a tragedy, and the exact nature of its failure as tragedy helps us to understand the necessity for mystery in tragedy.

There is no doubt that Anouilh went to Sophocles' version of the Antigone myth for the situation and the plot of his *Antigone*. He clearly follows Sophocles' development of the story, and he too presents an Antigone who is young, proud, and seemingly fearless. Two new characters, Antigone's nurse and Creon's page, are added, and Anouilh offers important verbal exchanges between Antigone and her nurse and between Antigone and Haemon that have no basis in Sophocles. Also, his chorus acts as a stage manager who tells us about the characters and action, and who presents Anouilh's ideas on tragedy. All actors wear modern dress, and the language is usually colloquial. One must always keep in mind that the play was written and performed in a France occupied by Germany.

The conflict here, as in almost all of the prolific Anouilh's diversified work, is between the individual and society, or, more specifically, between the innocent, pure heroine and a corrupt, compromising, bourgeois society. Sophocles' plot was the perfect source for this kind of conflict. Anouilh reinterprets the story in the light of his abiding interest. And that is precisely why the tragic qualities of Sophocles' formulation of the myth seem lost in Anouilh. His play, although brilliantly sensitive to the problems of the modern world and valiantly shouting out against compromise and conformity, reduces the mystery, stifles the interrogative mood, and changes tragedy to something else, call it drama, call it tragicomedy.

The slowly rising curtain reveals all the characters sitting or standing on steps, Antigone on the top step sitting with hands clasped around her knees. The chorus moves downstage to introduce the play and the characters. His first words are important.

> Well, here we are.
>
> These people are about to act out for you the story of Antigone. That thin little creature sitting by herself, staring straight ahead, seeing nothing, is Antigone. She is thinking. She is thinking that the instant I finish telling you who's who and what's what in this play, she will burst forth as the tense, sallow, willful girl whose family would never take her seriously and who is about to rise up alone against Creon, her uncle, the king.
>
> Another thing that she is thinking is this: she is going to die. Antigone is young. She would much rather live than die. But there is no help for it. When your name is Antigone, there is only one part you can play; and she will have to play hers through to the end.
>
> From the moment the curtain went up, she began to feel that inhuman forces were whirling her out of this world, snatching her away from her sister Ismene, . . . from all of us who sit or stand here, looking at her, not in the least upset ourselves—for we are not doomed to die tonight.[9]

These words, and a later speech by the chorus, testify to Anouilh's clear insights into Sophocles' treatment of the Antigone story and into the tragic mode. His Antigone, like Sophocles', is willful and tense; she too is young and is going to die. She too—because her name is Antigone—has a part to play that she must play, and her doom will have some relationship to "inhuman forces." But as the play unfolds we must test its action against these words. *Is* Antigone thinking about death? *Does* she feel the inhuman forces? Do *we* feel her thinking, or think ourselves about the inhuman forces? Of one matter, however, there is no doubt. The sense of tragic inevitability is expressed here and will be functioning throughout. In Sophocles, Antigone's life is played out against the backdrop of a curse on the

Oedipus family with the gods in the wings. In Anouilh, Antigone must play her part against what seems like a "literary" backdrop of a known story. In both dramatists, Antigone's death in inevitable, and in both the action that precipitates the specific tragic movement is Antigone's burial of Polyneices against the decree of Creon.

Because Anouilh is a modern dramatist wishing to invest his character with a psychological depth never attempted by the Greek playwrights, he gives us a close look at Antigone's personality even before we learn of her defiance of Creon's statute. She has two dialogues with her nurse, two with Ismene, and one with Haemon before she reveals that she has *already* buried Polyneices. These exchanges re-enforce the chorus's statement that Antigone "would much rather live than die," and they also reveal the softer side of her nature. At times, the softer side is too soft, to the point of mushiness. Take, for example, her concern for her dog who will be without a mistress. A human sentiment, to be sure, but this worry about her dog at a time when her heroic mission should be charging the play's atmosphere dissipates the turbulence.

> *Antigone.* Nanny . . .
> *Nurse.* Yes?
> *Antigone.* My dog, Puff . . .
> *Nurse.* . . . Well?
> *Antigone.* Promise me that you will never scold her again.
> *Nurse.* Dogs that dirty up the house with their filthy paws deserve to be scolded.
> *Antigone.* I know. Just the same, promise me.
> *Nurse.* You mean you want me to let her make a mess all over the place and not say a thing?
> *Antigone.* Yes, Nanny.
> *Nurse.* You're asking a lot. The next time she wets my living-room carpet, I'll———.
> *Antigone.* Please, Nanny, I beg of you!
> (p. 15)

The dialogue continues in this way, with Antigone begging the nurse to talk to the dog as she, Antigone, talks to the dog, not the way people usually do, and finally asking the nurse to put Puff to sleep mercifully if he gets too unhappy "waiting for me." The approaching death of Antigone that Anouilh wants us to feel now is minimized by this prosy and sticky context. In a literal sense, death has gone to the dogs, and Antigone's soft side has given her humanity, but not stature.

When she speaks with Haemon in the play's only scene of love between the two young lovers, Antigone again displays softness, seemingly needing Haemon's strength to sustain her. "And hold me tight. Tighter than you have ever held me. I want all your strength to flow into me." She mentions the little boy they were going to have after they were married, and she talks of his qualities that would have come from her strength. "He wouldn't have been afraid of anything. I swear he wouldn't. Not of the falling night, nor of the terrible noonday sun, nor of all the shadows, or all the walls in the world. Our little boy, Haemon!" (p. 17). This rings somewhat false in the light of her own weakness, her own need for assurance from Haemon that he indeed loves her, really loves her.

It is in her dialogues with Ismene that Antigone displays her more resolute self, her will to live, and her joy in living. Creon, she realizes, is "bound" to put them to death but "we are bound to go out and bury our brother. That's the way it is." She boldly states the part she must play, and she clearly sees its consequences. Her uncompromising nature is more shrilly revealed in answer to Ismene's "I sort of see what Uncle Creon means." Antigone says, "I don't want to 'sort of see' anything." She believes in a pure and full commitment to whatever she undertakes in life. She doesn't "want to be right" necessarily, nor does she want to "think too much" or have to "understand" things. Time enough for that when she gets old, "if I ever am old." She knows she must do the deed (indeed, she has done it) and she understandably becomes most passionate when Ismene asks her, "Don't you want to go on living?"

Go on living! Who was it that was always the first out of bed because she loved the touch of the cold morning air on her bare skin? Who was always the last to bed because nothing less than infinite weariness could wean her from the lingering night? Who wept when she was little because there were too many grasses in the field, for her to know and touch them all? (p. 12)

At this moment, Ismene, "in a sudden rush of tenderness," clasps Antigone's hand, saying "Darling little sister!" only to be cruelly repulsed by Antigone's "No! For heaven's sake! Don't paw me!" Here is the resolute and loveless Antigone whom we met in Sophocles.

The cold heart is unequivocally displayed, but in Anouilh it is not caused by the love of a brother, which produced in Sophocles the mysterious paradox of love leading to hatred. Here Polyneices' rotting body seems so unimportant, while Antigone's personality and spiritedness and innocence flood the stage. Her defiant self is asserted, so strongly that the love for a Haemon or a dog seems forgotten, and the love for a dead brother and tender sister seems nonexistent.

Before Anouilh presents the dramatic agon between self and society, between Antigone and Creon, the chorus offers further generalizations on tragedy. Anouilh continues to display fine tragic insights, but once again the insights do not always apply to the drama unfolding before us.

> The spring is wound up tight. It will uncoil of itself. That is what is so convenient in tragedy. The least little turn of the wrist will do the job. Anything will set it going: a glance at a girl who happens to be lifting her arms to her hair as you go by; a feeling when you wake up on a fine morning that you'd like a little respect paid to you today, as if it were as easy to order as a second cup of coffee; one question too many, idly thrown out over a friendly drink—and the tragedy is on. (p. 23)

This is the first paragraph of the chorus's long speech. Its image of the spring ready to uncoil perfectly describes two potent ideas in tragedy: tragic inevitability and the sense of a powerful force ready to be triggered, often capriciously. The first is always present in this play, as the chorus's opening speech has indicated. When you are Antigone, you must play your part to its conclusion. The second idea often is attached to the force of evil, but no evil is present in *Antigone*. Creon can represent the power of the state or the force of compromise and conformity, but evil is too charged a word for his role. Later in this speech, the chorus affirms this absence of evil by saying that in tragedy "he who kills is as innocent as he who gets killed," which is true for Anouilh's play but not true for tragedy generally. In Sophocles, Antigone was right and Creon was wrong. In Anouilh we are witnessing two rights—and here Hegel's formulation of tragedy seems to find its perfect touchstone.

That the spring is triggered capriciously or arbitrarily seems correct when we think of the action of the gods in Greek tragedy, but no gods occupy Anouilh's play. Here the personality of Antigone, and that alone, causes the spring to uncoil. Her action may have no strong, concrete motive, as we shall see, but it cannot be considered arbitrary. In short, we can use Anouilh's potent image of the spring to describe many tragedies, but it is only partially useful in describing his *Antigone*.

In the same speech, while presenting distinctions between tragedy and melodrama, the chorus uses words that seem to apply directly and exactly to this play.

> Tragedy is restful; and the reason is that hope, that foul, deceitful thing, has no part in it. There isn't any hope. You're trapped. The whole sky has fallen on you, and all you can do about it is to shout.
>
> Don't mistake me: I said "shout"; I did not say groan, whimper, complain. That, you cannot do. But you can shout aloud; you can get all those things said that you never thought you'd be able to say—or never even knew that you had it in you to say. And you don't say these things because it will do any good to say them: you know better than that. You say them for their own sake; you say them because you learn a lot from them. (p. 24)

Antigone is trapped. She knows it and we know it—a tragic inevitability that makes the plot "restful," but allows the heroine to shout against her fate. This is an unequivocally right observation, and we have seen how perfectly it applies to the shout of Oedipus and the shudder of Sophocles' Antigone, her shudder closer to Anouilh's figurative "shout" than to the groans and whimpers that he deplores. But as Anouilh goes on to describe the shout, he seems to be emphasizing not a shout against one's doom (or against the capriciousness of the gods) but a shouting of one's opinions, like the last speech of a dying man who says what he thinks about life because this is his last chance to do so. And this kind of shouting—more didactic than Anouilh suggests—is not charged with the pressure of mystery, contains no question marks, in fact, rejects the interrogative. In saying things or shouting things "for their own sake," the heroine asserts her individuality, her *self*, and makes her rebellion articulate, but she does not prod the secret cause.

It is Antigone's assertion of self that causes her to bury a brother.[10] Not love, not family, not the gods. It is this self—the self of a romantic idealist—which faces the canny, political realism of Creon in the play's most important confrontation. Creon is not the tyrant of Sophocles' play. Perhaps it would have been dangerous for Anouilh to make his ruler a tyrant while the Germans were in control of France, but this can only partially explain the character he gives Creon. Creon is playing his part in a play in which two rights conflict; therefore, he is given a case. Not a more powerful case than Antigone's, but reasonable enough to indicate that he is no villain. As a leader, he has daily problems to solve, and he does his job "like a conscientious workman." The lines on his face, his tired look, his happier past as a patron of the arts, his questioning the worth of being a leader of men—all of these testify to his humanity and frailty. He realizes that rulers have jobs to do, that they cannot "surrender themselves to their private feelings." With this statement, Creon, as selfless leader, becomes the antagonist to the intensely private self of Antigone.

Creon is as curious as we are about Antigone's motive in burying her brother. Surely she does not believe "all that flummery about religious burial." She agrees that the notion is "absurd." Then why, why? "For nobody, for myself," shouts Antigone. A significant pause follows this utterance, Creon looking intently at Antigone. His next words strike to the heart of Antigone's character: "You must want very much to die. You look like a trapped animal." We cannot help feeling that Creon is correct in pinpointing an instinctive desire for death that Antigone and he and we cannot find a reason for. This despite her oft-repeated assertions that she wants to live. A deep disappointment with life seems to be the motive for her behavior. She is a pure idealist who cannot live in a sordid world that lacks ideals. Creon's strong comments on Antigone's worthless brothers, his clear emphasis that "this whole business is nothing but politics," his insistence that he hasn't the leisure to say "no" to life, that saying "no" is too easy—all of these chip away at Antigone's heroic posture and "faith." She is ready to go to her room, defeated, but Creon continues to talk. He tells her to go to Haemon; he asserts that "life is a treasure"; and he mentions the word "happiness." The last arouses Antigone to defiance and prods her to reveal the full power of her innocence and idealism.

> I spit on your happiness! I spit on your idea of life—that life that must go on, come what may. You are all like dogs that lick everything they smell. You with your promise of a humdrum

happiness . . . provided a person doesn't ask too much of life. I want everything of life, I do; and I want it now! I want it total, complete: otherwise I reject it! I will *not* be moderate. I will *not* be satisfied with the bit of cake you offer me if I promise to be a good little girl. I want to be sure of everything this very day; sure that everything will be as beautiful as when I was a little girl. If not, I want to die!" (p. 42)

This impassioned statement against bourgeois conformity and "humdrum happiness" gives Antigone dignity and gives us a glimpse, at least, of what seems to be the cause of her behavior. It is a cause, however, that touches neither love nor the gods; it reverts to *self*, to the personal feelings of a child disappointed with the world as it is. And it reflects, we must assume, Anouilh's own attitude toward a world that deserves no respect. Antigone's death in this context is purely microcosmic, and, in fact, meaningless. It is the result of what emerges as a mistaken, or at least childishly fragile, view of life, nothing but a dream of innocence. The childish perspective continues to dominate when Antigone goes on to talk about her father, he who asked questions and he who became most "beautiful" "when all his questions had been answered," when he knew he *had* killed his father and slept with his mother. But all questions were *not* answered, cannot ever be answered, least of all the important questions. Why did the gods do this? What is there in us that *causes* us to do such horrible things? Why are we born trapped? These are the kinds of questions never recognized by the young Antigone and never acknowledged by the shouting Anouilh. Although Antigone declares that she is of the "tribe that asks questions," she reveals herself as of the tribe that makes statements. In *Antigone* the declarative mood erases the question mark.

Rejecting a life of "happiness," coldly casting aside Ismene who wants to die with her, courageously defiant as she calls Creon a "cook"—alluding to his own statement that in the wings of this drama we find the "kitchen of politics"—Antigone leaves the stage in an aura of relief because finally she is going to die. But when we see her next, in her last scene, the death that she will soon embrace has made her a child again. Here, for the only time in the play—and clearly paralleling Antigone's last fearful moments in Sophocles —Antigone truly realizes that she must die. Her words to the self-centered guard—"I'm going to die soon." "Do you think it hurts to die?" "How are they going to put me to death?"—reveal a frightened child, "a tiny figure in the middle of the stage," cold and alone, who wraps her arms around herself, the perfect stage gesture for the *self* embracing *self*, echoing her posture in the play's beginning. In her love letter to Haemon, dictated to and written down by the callous guard, she declares that "Creon was right. It is terrible to die." And then: "And I don't even know what I am dying for." The sacrifice of Antigone seems meaningless, the cause abstract, but the fear genuine. She has the guard cut everything out of the letter except "Forgive me, my darling. You would all have been so happy except for Antigone. I love you." Love seems to have entered the play, after all, but the guard's presence and words—"I love you. Is that all?" —deflate the emotion, and the word "happy" brings us back to a conforming, empty world.

The rest of the play contains reports of death and seems perfunctory. Anouilh never lets us forget that he is presenting children—the hanging cord was around Antigone's neck "like a child's collar," the face of Haemon was that "of a little boy." The two young lovers embrace, dead, in "a great pool of blood," but we never feel the blood. And Creon's statement—"They are together at last, and at peace. Two lovers on the morrow of their bridal. Their work is done"—is soft, bordering on the trite. Surprisingly, he tells his page "never grow up if you can help it." One wonders why, since the destruction of innocence is inevitable in a world of kitchen politics and coarse happiness. Creon leaves the stage to go to a cabinet meeting because his work is not done.

It is left for the chorus to end the play. All who are dead, he says, were "caught up in the web," again stressing tragic inevitability. Antigone "shall never know the name of the fever that consumed her. She has played her part." Which is a statement fine and true. If only her *not knowing* were given a dramatic intensity, if only the fever acquired the horror of mystery.

Jean Anouilh has reinterpreted the Antigone myth, re-created Sophocles' *Antigone*, for modern audiences under the pressure of his own interests, and he has done so effectively. There is no point in faulting him for not writing a tragedy (although he certainly intended to write a tragedy), and there is much reason to praise him for presenting an often powerful dramatization of the destruction of innocence by the forces of compromise and practical realism, a universal theme. However, to discern why his treatment of Antigone's story, although filled with tragic insights and capturing tragic inevitability, does not produce tragedy helps us to understand why mystery is the essential core of tragedy. Of course, the expectations of a modern audience are different from those of Sophocles' audience, and we should not expect the gods, for example, to play an important part, but Anouilh presents no substitute for the gods. The fever that consumes Antigone contains no shadow of mystery, seems too abstract a cause for her behavior. The deep and essentially mysterious power of love that triggered the action of Sophocles' Antigone is absent here, and death, although feared, never touches other springs of behavior, like love or the gods (or some substitute for the gods). Tragic inevitability is present because Antigone plays a prearranged part, the story providing the spring and the web, both useful images for tragedy. But a literary destiny must of necessity produce a paler inevitability than a destiny controlled by mysterious forces without and/or within.

Antigone's personality also reduces the potential for tragedy. We can pity her because her childlike innocence is affecting and her lonely idealism is touching. But she never acquires the kind of respect that is paid to a character who broods, who goes beyond the self of her own personality to ask the larger questions about love and death and the gods. She is too young, it seems, to touch her own Dionysian qualities. Her point of view is clear—thereby allowing her to serve as the perfect vehicle for Anouilh's attack on society— but her motive is never *felt*. A brilliant mouthpiece for purity and innocence, her cause is Anouilh's cause as he asserts the integrity of idealism in an empty and corrupt, but not evil, world. In a sense, Anouilh is too involved with the issues, and even his tragic insights seem to serve a political purpose. This could still produce tragedy if the "kitchen of politics" acquired the kind of large significance that Ibsen gives to his drawing rooms, for example. But in *Antigone* the kitchen remains a kitchen, effectively presenting Anouilh's view of the world, a view essentially pessimistic.[11] In giving dramatic life to his disillusionment, Anouilh has touched some characteristics of tragedy, but has written a play that seems, because of its tone, closer to tragicomedy.

The chorus also helps to remove the play from the tragic realm. He covers the play with an Apollonian veneer, one that is never ruffled.

He stresses literary destiny, the playing of parts—but never does Anouilh allow a character to revolt against or investigate that part. The chorus mentions the fever that consumes Antigone, but Anouilh never allows us to feel the fever or the Dionysian power that can cause it. In short, the chorus, like Anouilh, tells us much, makes fine observations on life and on tragedy, but the play does not lead us to the secret caverns of the heart, or make us feel the darkness of death, or force us to ask the deep existential questions.

3 PASSION

Hippolytus, Phaedra, Desire Under the Elms

The story of Hippolytus, like that of Antigone, has been told and retold. Euripides, Racine, and O'Neill—three dramatists separated by time and place and temperament—focus on one basic story, each dramatist attempting to write tragedy for his time, each providing a crucial instance of the tragic vision. At the heart of each treatment resides the secret cause.

The Hippolytus story has the haunting resonances of an archetypal event in Man's life. A young man spurns the passionate advances of his stepmother, Phaedra, who takes revenge by accusing him of having attempted to dishonor her. The young man's father, Theseus, curses his son, who is killed when a bull emerges from the sea to frighten the horses of his chariot. The archetypal story has its parallels in the account of Bellerophon in *The Iliad* and in the biblical story of Potiphar's wife. Of course, the Oedipal myth lurks in the background, this time in reverse, with a mother loving a son. The incest motif and the forbidden fruit idea and the attractions of sin and sexuality are built into a tale possessing high dramatic potential. The story itself finds its most basic roots in the myth of a mortal lover who spurns the advances of a goddess, and thereby dies, eventually to be reborn.[1]

Of all the treatments of the story, Euripides' has caused the liveliest critical controversy—first, because his purposes and accomplishments as a dramatist are forever debated; and second, because his particular treatment of the story does not seem to conform to the usual Greek pattern, that is, he does not treat myth the way Aeschylus and Sophocles do. Euripides has been discussed as both a realist and a fantasist, a rationalist and irrationalist, religious and atheistic, debunker of myths and serious believer of myths. His plays have been condemned for their inconsistencies and structural flaws; they have been applauded for their unity and strong direction. For some, his plays are preoccupied with contemporary problems and ideas; for other, he deals with universal themes. He has been called a satirist and reformer and the least tragic of Greek tragedians; he has been called "the most tragic of all the poets" by no less an authority than Aristotle.[2]

I do not wish to enter directly into this large controversy. My purpose is to examine *Hippolytus*, a difficult play generally acknowledged to be among Euripides' best, in order to determine what its springs of feeling and action are, and to delineate as sharply as possible the nature of Euripidean tragedy. Along the way, some aspects of the large debate will be touched, of course, and perhaps indirections will find directions out.

Whether or not Euripides is satirizing the traditional mythical conceptions—a major focus of controversy—it is clear, at least, that he is *using* myth for his dramatic purposes. He places the story of Hippolytus and Phaedra in a divine framework, a framework that cannot be discounted or ignored. *Hippolytus* begins with Aphrodite as a character on stage and ends with Artemis as a character on stage. Throughout the play these deities are on stage as statues, therefore always visible to the audience, and throughout the play their power is felt in the actions of the two antagonists, Hippolytus and Phaedra. However we may wish to interpret their significance, significant they are—both outside man's world (framing it both in time, as prologue and epilogue, and in space, as statues on either side of the stage) and inside man's world. And their presence helps to universalize man's experience. The gods are so integral to Euripidean tragedy here and in most of his other plays that it seems sheer critical folly to ignore their importance or explain them away.

Aphrodite's opening monologue clearly expresses her purpose and her power. She is "mighty among men" and she is honored by men. Those who "worship" her power, she exalts, but "those whose pride is stiff-necked against me / I lay by the heels." Immediately she tells of Hippolytus, who has "blasphemed" her by considering her the "vilest of the Gods in Heaven."

He will none of the bed of love nor marriage,
but honors Artemis, Zeus's daughter,

counting her greatest of the Gods in Heaven
he is with her continually, this Maiden Goddess,
    in the Greenwood.[3]

Although Hippolytus' continual companionship with Artemis
seems to be a major source of Aphrodite's anger, she says "I do not
grudge him such privileges: why should I?" This is puzzling, for if
he is "continually" with the Maiden Goddess he cannot be in the
bed of love. Nevertheless, Aphrodite leaves this idea as a question—
"Why should I?"—and expresses her desire for revenge: "But for his
sin against me / I shall punish Hippolytus this day." Glorying in
her power, swift in her revenge, Aphrodite will use Phaedra,
Theseus' new wife, as her instrument of revenge, for Phaedra is one
who "dedicated a temple" to Aphrodite, one who worships her continually. Phaedra's heart is already "filled with the longings of love"
—which was "my work," claims Aphrodite—and Phaedra must
suffer and die in helping to accomplish Aphrodite's revenge.

Her suffering does not weigh in the scale so much
that I should let my enemies go untouched
escaping payment of that retribution
that honor demands that I have
(ll. 47–50)

The secret of Phaedra's love will be revealed to Theseus, we hear,
and his curse will "slay" Hippolytus who, coming on stage at this
moment, is "looking at his last sun" without knowing it.

Aphrodite's prologue has given us all the facts we need as we
watch the story proceed to its inevitable conclusion: Hippolytus will
die because he denies sexual love; Phaedra, filled with sexual passion, will also die as an instrument of Aphrodite's revenge; Theseus
will play his part by cursing the son who is "hateful" to Aphrodite.
In addition to information, Aphrodite reveals a need for revenge, a
crude callousness toward her disciple Phaedra, and a clear and terrible power. So powerful is she that even here, in the play's beginning, she seems more than an anthropomorphic, Homer-like
goddess. She is a force associated with sexual passion, physical
love, a force that cannot be denied without endangering one's life.
As Aphrodite withdraws physically—perhaps going behind her
statue that is always on stage—her victim Hippolytus enters to

verify her statements, and his progress through the play will be dramatic verification of the truth of her power. Aphrodite so affects the life of Hippolytus and the lives of Phaedra and Theseus, so informs the human drama, that she emerges as both the anthropological goddess of mythology and the absolute force of sexual passion whose pressure all men feel. Whatever the philosopher Euripides may think about supernatural goddesses, the dramatist Euripides is able to make Aphrodite real and her power clear. Both Hippolytus, who opposes her, and Phaedra, who worships her, will play out in human terms the revenge play that Aphrodite has written. A powerful goddess places a burden too great for either the chaste or the passionate to bear. Equally vulnerable, our two human characters can use only a small margin of freedom to act and suffer before they fall victims to a fate clear to the audience from the beginning. Aphrodite has triggered the spring; the play will dramatize its unwinding.

The clarity of the play's movement, however, does not reduce an essential mystery: if *both* worshipper and blasphemer, the passionate and the pure, will fall victim to a powerful goddess, will go on a long day's journey to death, are not the actions of the gods based on contradictions? Must not the audience feel, from the very beginning, that the world is governed by unreasonable, self-contradictory, almost whimsical gods? Either that or the gods' reasoning is incomprehensible to men, even when clearly stated. In either case, a large question mark, the shadow of the irrational or incomprehensible, hovers over Aphrodite's seemingly clear prologue.

Hippolytus sings the praises of Artemis as he enters with his huntsmen. His exclusive attention to Artemis, his willful neglect of Aphrodite, and what seems his blatant contempt for her, substantiate Aphrodite's earlier complaint and makes her desire for vengeance more understandable. Hippolytus lays a garland at the altar of Artemis, the "most beautiful of all the Heavenly Host" and praises her "inviolate Meadow," where he plucked and wove the garland, a sacred grove as untouched and virginal as the goddess and he. Hippolytus believes that the purity of the sacred place reflects his own purity and his own superiority to other men, for "with no man else I share this privilege." This note of smugness in Hippolytus' opening prayer is accentuated when his servant tells him that "men hate the haughty of heart" and that the gods also hate the haughty, alluding to Hippolytus' neglect of Aphrodite. But

Hippolytus asserts his right to choose which goddess he prefers—
"one man honors one God, / and one another." The "God of noc-
turnal prowess is not my God," he states boldly, and it is because of
such haughty disdain that this creature of day will feel the dark revengeful power of Aphrodite, that goddess of night.

Hippolytus' belief that a man cannot honor more than one goddess must give us pause. Perhaps a well-balanced man can contain
and modulate the claims of both sexual passion and chastity, thereby making each something else, but—given the reality and potency
of the two claims, and allowing them to remain distinct as mutually
exclusive claims—Hippolytus does not seem altogether wrong in
freely declaring a choice and allegiance. Can one be chaste *and* occupy a bed of love at the same time? A choice seems necessary—and
whatever the decision, the chooser has made the wrong choice in
the eyes of one or the other goddess. Man, therefore, by the nature
of his condition, is caught in a web from which he can be released
only by death. This is not to deny that Hippolytus is overly zealous
in his cause or that he is snobbish or that his words could have been
softer or that he should have acknowledged, at least, the power of
Aphrodite. Unquestionably, he is a limited man, blind to a natural
necessary force in life. But the puzzlement about man's relationship
to gods remains, and our first look at Hippolytus—with Aphrodite's
words behind us and his fate before us—must force us to wonder
about the precarious nature of man in relation to the power of terrifying forces not only beyond his control but beyond his understanding.

The condition of the exclusive worshipper of Aphrodite is equally
precarious and seems even more devastating. Phaedra's agony,
when we first see her, strikingly contrasts the calm exposition of
Aphrodite's revenge and the cool smugness of Hippolytus' haughty
heart. It is small wonder that many critics think Phaedra emerges as
the play's center. This seems a faulty judgment, albeit an understandable one because the pull of the heart is stronger than the pull
of the mind, and the vessel of passion has more human interest and
complexity than the vessel of chastity. Nonetheless, it is Hippolytus
who is the focus of Aphrodite's attention in the beginning and of
Artemis' attention at the end, who is the object of Phaedra's desire,
and the main concern of Theseus; in addition Euripides has given
him the play's title.

Phaedra's entrance is prepared for by the chorus of women who sing of her agony and speculate on its causes. They do not touch the real reason, although their various speculations indicate the many miseries that flesh is heir to. The nurse, bringing on stage a weak and delirious Phaedra, supports the notion that "the life of man entire is misery," and that we are "luckless lovers" of death, of which we know nothing. The "fever" of Phaedra's passionate heart has made her "mad," but the ravings of her mind, her wild and whirling words, lead her to a logical place—the mountains where Hippolytus hunts. Overwhelmed by the power of passion, Phaedra is sane enough to recognize that her madness was "sent from some God / that caused my fall." She suppresses the name of Hippolytus and is willing to go to her death in silence, for her "honor," she says, "lies in silence." Her moral integrity can be measured by her inner struggle; and her struggle testifies to the awesome power of Aphrodite. Prodded by the nurse's insistence, Phaedra's secret becomes revealed, but not before she thinks about her forbidden love as an "inherited curse." Too few critics have confronted this idea, important because it comes immediately before she breaks her silence, and even more important because the potency of curses in Greek drama can never be minimized. Phaedra refers to "unhappy mother, what a love was yours!" and to her "unhappy sister, bride of Dionysus!" She sees herself as the "unlucky third" in this chain. What a dark, terrifying inheritance! A mother who had sexual intercourse with a bull, thereby giving birth to a Minotaur (finally killed by Theseus), and a sister possessed and loved by Dionysus, that vital dark god, often worshipped as a bull in orgiastic rites. How helpless woman seems when confronted by the godlike power and mystery of sexual passion. And how helpless is a man, we can add, when he abuses that power, for the bull will eventually destroy him.

Enveloped by the cloud of her dark past, pressured by a loving nurse, Phaedra reveals her love for Hippolytus. The nurse initially is shocked by the idea and reasserts the power of Aphrodite with these interesting words: "Cypris, you are no God. / You are something stronger than God if that can be. / You have ruined her and me and all this house" (ll. 359–61). Phaedra, calm and reasonable now, realizes that death is the best solution for her, for death will seal her shame and keep her reputation clean—a decision that again testifies to her moral integrity. The nurse's speech on the power of love, which is "not withstandable," does not convince Phaedra, but the nurse's claim that she has a magic potion which will rid Phaedra of her passion undermines Phaedra's strong stance. She grudgingly consents to having the nurse speak with Hippolytus in order to get some token from him for the potion to work. Even a woman of high morality and dignity cannot withstand the inevitable progress of necessity. Phaedra is fated; her individual will is impotent; Aphrodite is all-powerful, even "something stronger than God if that can be."

When Hippolytus learns of Phaedra's passion, he expresses genuine horror. Understandably so, for sexual relations between stepmother and stepson would appear outrageously sinful even to a man without Hippolytus' obsessive purity. But as he gives voice to his horror, he is brutal in his callousness and blind, as usual, to the power of passion. Because we see Phaedra as she overhears Hippolytus' tirade, Hippolytus' words seem even more brutal. Once more we witness in tragedy a heart made stone by a cause. In his *self*-righteousness, Hippolytus has no understanding of Phaedra's suffering. So vehement is his rejection of Aphrodite that he condemns all womankind—"Women! This coin which men find counterfeit! / Why, why, Lord Zeus, did you put them in the world, / in the light of the sun? . . . I'll hate you women, hate and hate and hate you, / and never have enough of hating . . ." (ll. 616–18, 663–64). He finds even the idea of passionate sexual love so disgusting that he needs purification—"I'll go to the running stream and pour its waters / into my ear to purge away the filth." Perhaps the source of his vehemence, as some critics suggest, is his bitterness at being a bastard, having come into the world as a result of what he considers to be loathsome love-making. Perhaps the logical result of an obsessive chastity is intolerance. Whatever the reason for his fury, Hippolytus must be seen as unpitying and hardhearted—but he is also a noble and pure disciple of Artemis, and an honorable young man who will not reveal Phaedra's love for him because of his promise to the nurse. Both the praiseworthy and negative qualities of Hippolytus' character help push him along the road to destruction paved by Aphrodite.

Hippolytus' tirade seals his doom, for it causes Phaedra to consider revenge, prodding her to write her own revenge play within Aphrodite's larger revenge play, with Hippolytus as victim in both plays. Frustrated in her passion, concerned with her reputation, angered by so inhumanly virtuous a young man, Phaedra realizes that she has reached the limit of her suffering, her boundary situation. As she leaves the stage, she utters words which acknowledge the power of Aphrodite and the hardness of Hippolytus' heart.

> But on this day
> when I shake off the burden of this life
> I shall delight the Goddess who destroys me,
> the Goddess Cypris.
> Bitter will have been the love that conquers me,
> but in my death I shall at least bring sorrow,
> upon another, too, that his high heart
> may know no arrogant joy at my life's shipwreck;
> he will have his share in this my mortal sickness
> and learn of chastity in moderation.
> (ll. 724–31)

With her suicide note accusing Hippolytus of having raped her, Phaedra accomplishes her revenge. The returning Theseus believes without question what Phaedra has written, because words from the dead have a special force, and, perhaps more important, because Theseus knows first-hand the power of Aphrodite. Sexual affairs with women make up his past and, in fact, Hippolytus, that smug pure son facing him, is the product of Theseus' dark passion for an Amazon. Theseus is a high man of great feeling and understanding, tragically mistaken about his son, but understandably so. The passion that characterizes Theseus makes him believe that all men have powerful sexual desires. This belief overrides Hippolytus' defense against Phaedra's lying message: that "there lives no man more chaste / than I. . . ." Theseus rightly chastises Hippolytus for "self-worship," but unjustly and hardheartedly banishes his son and will not remove the curse he already uttered—that Poseidon should kill Hippolytus "this very day." It is all according to the script that Aphrodite wrote, with each actor playing a role true to character.

A messenger rushes on stage to present a vivid description of Hippolytus' violent end. As Hippolytus was riding his chariot along the seashore, a wave—"a miraculous wave"—threw up a monstrous savage bull, which caused Hippolytus' horses to panic, "maddening the team with terror," leading to the crash of wheels and Hippolytus' "dear head pounded on the rocks." Before this moment of destruction, Hippolytus had prayed to Zeus: "Zeus, let me die now, if I have been guilty!" The nature of his "guilt" is questionable, but die he will. As the chorus had stated: ". . . for what is doomed and fated there is no quittance." No quittance and no appeal to the gods, it seems.

Hippolytus' emotion-charged last scene with his father, the play's climax, is preceded by the chorus's speech on the power of love:

Cypris, you guide men's hearts
and the inflexible
hearts of the Gods and with you
comes Love with the flashing wings,
comes Love with the swiftest of wings.
Over the earth he flies
and the loud-echoing salt-sea.
He bewitches and maddens the heart
of the victim he swoops upon.
He bewitches the race of the mountain-hunting
lions and beasts of the sea,
and all the creatures that earth feeds,
and the blazing sun sees—
and man, too—
over all you hold kingly power,
Love, you are only ruler
over all these.
(ll. 1268–82)

The messenger's speech had testified to that power, and the choric speech punctuates the "inflexible hearts of the Gods," the human heart made mad by love (we think of Phaedra), and nature itself bewitched (we think not of the "inviolate Meadow" of Artemis, but of nature gone beserk sending a bull from the sea). So powerful are Aphrodite and Eros that only a goddess, it seems, can convince Theseus of Hippolytus' innocence. The epilogue begins immediately after the choric speech on love, with Artemis calmly and clearly affirming Hippolytus' "piety" and the innocence of Phaedra, who was seized by a "frenzied love" caused by "that most hated Goddess," Aphrodite. The outcome of her long explanation is Theseus' "Mistress, I am destroyed." Overwhelmed, Theseus remains mute during Hippolytus' long speech of woe, an important speech because in it Hippolytus displays no changed perception of himself. He reaffirms his "piety"; he continues to believe he "excelled all men in chastity." His physical pain is so great that he wishes for black death to give him sleep. But Artemis' presence revives him momentarily, and his allegiance to the maiden Goddess is given lovely words: "O divine fragrance! Even in my pain / I sense it, and the suffering is lightened." Artemis sees his physical suffering but cannot cry, she says, for heavenly law forbids her tears. She places all blame on Aphrodite who claimed three "victims"—Hippolytus, Theseus, and herself. (We would add a fourth—Phaedra.) Hippolytus' genuine sorrow for his father's suffering gives him a stature he never displayed before; the hardhearted young man becomes warmly compassionate. But anger against Aphrodite follows quickly: "O, if only men might be a curse to Gods!" Having previously asked important questions about man's relationship with gods—Why the labors of piety if death comes in this brutal way? Why me, who am clear of guilt?—Hippolytus resorts to cursing the gods whose power he now recognizes. Artemis tries to appease him by declaring that she will avenge his death by destroying a mortal dear to Aphrodite, so the revenge play will continue. The memory of Hippolytus will live on, she says, in the songs young girls sing before their wedding day. (A strange gift, considering Hippolytus' avoidance of the bed of love and marriage. The gods continue to puzzle.) Artemis reasserts that men are "blinded by the Gods" and that it was Hippolytus' "fate" to die. When she leaves, Hippolytus absolves Theseus of his sin, says farewell, and asks that his mutilated face be covered. So ends a lamentable tale, to use the chorus's words, a tale told, we cannot forget, by a goddess who asserts her power by means of destruction.

Hippolytus leaves the world as the same exclusive follower of Artemis, with the same obsession for chastity and high regard for self. But in his physical agony he recognizes the destructive power of love, he asks important questions about god and man, and he displays human forgiveness. His last minutes on stage give him dignity and raise him in the audience's estimation. Phaedra too has been raised in her struggle against her own passion, really her struggle against Aphrodite, and even her treacherous last act is considerably softened by her motive, by the burden of her shame, and by Artemis' assertion of her "noble innocence." Both the worshipper of Aphrodite and the blasphemer of Aphrodite suffer and die. And the suffering of both gives them height. Still, our positive feelings about these two characters, strong though they are, seem less important than the play's atmosphere of dark, destructive necessity. We leave the play not, as some critics claim, primarily thinking about the moral superiority of forgiving humans over vindictive gods, and not contemplating the positive and negative aspects of character that helped push Hippolytus, Phaedra, and Theseus along their destructive paths. We leave wondering about the condition of the world, a tragic condition. The frail and the strong, the humble and the haughty, the chaste and the passionate, operate in a dark and dangerous atmosphere, for the claims of the rival goddesses of the play are incompatible, and man—whatever his nature—plays a role that must destroy him. Euripides brilliantly confronts the contradictory nature of things, the human predicament, and he sees this predicament as insoluble. The debate as to whether Euripides believed in the goddesses he presents is beside the point because man's condition remains the same, be those goddesses real outside forces or crystallizations of real inner forces. He is never clear about religion in his plays but he does not have to be to give dramatic life to the unknown forces. He is not a reformer or a satirist but a dramatist, a humanistic dramatist of the highest order, who clearly recognizes that something greater than man, some real but mysterious forces, unfathomably deep, cause man's agony and lead to man's death. Man can shout out against this condition, can assert his dignity, but cannot avoid destruction and cannot explain the cause. No mortal can withstand the power of terrifying forces, and no mortal can penetrate the mystery of necessity, as the question mark continues to hover over tragedy. This Euripidean emphasis on man's dark condition makes him the most obviously modern of Greek dramatists—allying him with Beckett, for example—and makes him for Aristotle "the most tragic of poets." Irrationality and contradictions are at the core of man's life, and the result is destruction and terror. Whether a man is chaste or dwells in a bed of love, a mad bull is always there to threaten his precarious existence, a larger force than he can cope with or even understand. The bull can come from the sea or can surge through the heart's blood. In either case, the bull is dark and mysterious and destructive.

Jean Racine could not avoid being drawn to the myth of Hippolytus and Phaedra. Having received an exceptional classical education, raised by an aunt who fervently believed in that particular brand of theological determinism called Jansenism, always interested in the irrational aspects of man's behavior and in man's struggle against destiny, Racine obviously recognized in the Hippolytus-Phaedra story a potentially rich focus for his particular kind of tragedy. He takes the subject from Euripides, as he himself states in the preface, makes Phaedra the unequivocally central character, gives Hippolytus a lover to warm his cold chaste character, adds a subdued political element, and thereby offers what George Steiner considers to be "the keystone in French tragic drama."[4] This is no critical exaggeration. The madness of love combines with the mystery of myth to pull Phaedra along an ever-narrowing path to death, the movement producing a tragic masterpiece brilliantly dramatizing the dark workings of destiny.

The idea of destiny is the source of most of the critical controversy surrounding *Phaedra*. Because Racine is more interested in the individual psyche than were the Greek dramatists, because his heroes and heroines seem more pathetic in their struggles against the gods than their Greek counterparts, because his dramatic action seems to take place within the character, critics have tended to minimize the force of destiny, either making *Phaedra* primarily a tragedy of character, or speculating about the force that causes Phaedra's agony and destruction. Some have recognized no macrocosmic dimension; they have reduced the play to an example of Racine's rational and didactic art.[5] A close examination of the play, however—one that pays little attention to its preface (which Racine wrote in order to appease the moral critics of his time), one that does not automatically accept the usual clichés about Racine's "elegant" art and his "neoclassic" obedience to the tenets of Aristotle and Horace— reveals Racine's deep interest in the affliction of man's soul within a context of destiny, and further, reveals that only because of this context has Racine been able to capture the Greek sense of tragedy.

When we first see Phaedra, she is already in agony because of her sinful desire for her stepson Hippolytus. She has "reached the limit" of her strength, she declares, and her eyes are "blinded by the daylight." What we have is a character at the boundary situation at the play's beginning. That Racine can place Phaedra there from the start and allow us to retain an interest in her to the end is no small accomplishment. As the play progresses, Phaedra goes deeper and deeper into the abyss of her own doom. Love, guilt, and death reside heavily in Phaedra's soul, their pressure always informing her feverish behavior. A frightening passion matches the confusion and terror associated with the polytheism of ancient myth that Racine inherits from Euripides. Racine never lets us forget the origins of

Phaedra's passion, the ancestry of his sick heroine, the deep-rooted sense of destiny that drives her life. Even before her appearance, Hippolytus—telling his tutor Theramenes that he wishes to leave Troezen to seek his missing father—refers to Phaedra as "the daughter of Minos and Pasiphae." Immediately, then, we are asked to see Phaedra as the queen from Crete—the Crete of the labyrinth, we must remember—and as the offspring of strange parents who have their own strange stories. Strange because bordering on the unnatural: Pasiphae, who slept with a bull to give birth to the Minotaur, is the daughter of the sun; Minos, who commissioned the construction of the labyrinth wherein the Minotaur dwelled, is the son of Zeus who came to Europa as a white bull when he impregnated her, and is a judge of the shades of Hades. In the veins of Phaedra, therefore, flows unnatural blood, blood already connected with monsters and gods. A reading of the play that minimizes this dark dimension of Phaedra's ancestry loses the most important aspect of her dilemma. For Phaedra's unnatural desire is natural to her because she is Phaedra. She has inherited her condition, as Oedipus inherited his. She is the product of a barbaric and majestic past. And she is at present married to a man who has his own relationship to monsters and is now returning from the dead. Phaedra knows that she is controlled by the gods, especially Venus, for in the first act she tells her devoted nurse Oenone, "Since Venus so ordains, / Last and most wretched of my tragic race, / I too shall perish."[6] Racine's troubled heroine recognizes her dilemma from the play's beginning. The tragic recognition will be different here because Phaedra is not at all ignorant about her desire or her guilt, and she is able to discuss her passion with feverish precision. Although the gods have robbed her of her wits, as she claims, she is able to verbalize her agony. Much of the play's fascination rests on Phaedra's ability to watch her own progress toward doom. To err unknowingly is bad enough; to see one's own movement toward destruction, and be unable to stop it, is excruciating agony.

When Phaedra first glanced at Hippolytus, her eyes were blinded, her body was inflamed. "I knew / the terrible fires of Venus, the tortures fated / to one whom she pursues." From that moment on, the fires of Venus have burned her soul and caused her to lose her reason. She tried to avoid Hippolytus, even assuming a stepmother's "proverbial cruelty," and forcing him into exile, but "Fate intervened," "her keen wound bled again," and Venus once more "fastened on her helpless prey." She tells all this to Oenone, the admission forced from her by her faithful servant. But her death, for which she longs and which will save her good name, will bury her secret with her, she believes. We notice that Racine's Phaedra, like Euripides', displays high moral dignity because she considers her passion for Hippolytus to be abominable. Her desire for death expresses both the hopelessness of her destined position and her admirable superiority to that position. But the report of Theseus' death gives her a temporary stay, because now, as Oenone insists, Phaedra's young son, a potential successor to the throne, must be protected. This ostensible concern for her son leads to Phaedra's confrontation with Hippolytus, the central dialogue of the play, rich in symbolic significance, remarkable for its penetration into the psyche of Phaedra. Nowhere does Racine seem more modern—or, for that matter, does any dramatist between Shakespeare and Ibsen —than when he presents Phaedra and Hippolytus meeting, each on a separate track, the movement of that scene almost Beckettian in the initial noncontact of its characters.

Facing Hippolytus makes Phaedra's blood rush, causing her to forget what she meant to say. Oenone prompts her to think of her son. To "think," however, is too difficult a task when the madness of passion seethes within. Phaedra does manage to ask Hippolytus to protect the boy, but as she goes on to discuss her former cruel treatment of Hippolytus, she begins to weaken. Hippolytus, always decent and reasonable, understands that stepmothers are often jealous of and hateful toward stepsons; he is willing to forgive her past actions. When Hippolytus suggests that Theseus may be alive, Phaedra dismisses the idea—no one has ever returned from the dead—but then she catches herself:

> What do I say?
> He is not dead since he still lives in you.
> Ever before my eyes I see my husband.
> I see him, speak with him, and my heart still . . .
> I'm wandering, my lord. My foolish feelings,
> In spite of me, declare themselves.
> (p. 196)

Phaedra is now no longer in control of her thoughts, and her "wandering" leads her to the labyrinth of the Minotaur, where father and son, Theseus and Hippolytus, become one. She relives the story in her mind, but now she is playing an active role, becoming Ariadne to Hippolytus-Theseus.

> It would have been me, Prince; by timely aid,
> I would have led you through the labyrinth.
> How many cares that charming head of yours
> Would then have cost me! I would not have trusted
> To that weak thread alone, but walked before you,
> Companion in the peril which you chose:
> And going down into the labyrinth,
> Phaedra would have returned with you, or else
> Been lost with you.
> (p. 197)

A story in her past has led her deep within herself. She is trying to work through that labyrinth now; she has entered the abyss of her shame which is wound up with the darkness of rapture. Although she sees herself as lost in the labyrinth with Hippolytus, only she is lost and always was—for Phaedra was always trapped in the dark labyrinth where her own monster-passion forever dwells. Only her death will destroy her Minotaur, and the pressure of this speech, so perceptive in its psychology, so rich in its symbolism, so nervous in its cadence, allows us to grasp how bent Phaedra is on destruction. Racine has placed passion and guilt and death in that labyrinth, and he has given us the thread to help us explore some of the darkness in Phaedra's soul.

Her vision is broken by Hippolytus' exclamation: "O Gods! What do I hear? / Do you forget that Theseus is my father, / And you his wife?" This question of the decent Hippolytus indicates the limits of his understanding, for it is precisely because Phaedra never forgets she is Theseus' wife that her agony is so overwhelming. Lost though she may be in the labyrinth of her soul, she has never lost her moral way, and she says so: "By what do you judge that I / Have done so, Prince? Would I forget my honor?" This causes Hippolytus to retreat, saying his misinterpretation of her speech makes him "ashamed." But Phaedra now reveals all, in a long passionate speech beginning with a declaration of "love" that is linked to her realization that this love is not innocent, that it makes her "abhor" herself. She sees her monstrous passion as a fire caused by the gods who have made her a victim of "celestial vengeance."

> The gods are witnesses—
> Those gods who kindled in my breast the flame
> Fatal to all my blood, whose cruel boast
> Was to seduce a weak and mortal heart.
> (p. 198)

So much does she loathe her monstrous self that she calls for death at the hands of Hippolytus:

> Avenge yourself; punish an odious love,
> Son worthy of a noble father, free
> The universe of a monster who offends you.
> Theseus' widow dares to love Hippolytus!
> Believe me, Prince,
> This dreadful monster would not seek to flee.
> There is my heart: there you should aim your blow.
> (p. 198)

When Hippolytus hesitates, she takes his sword to pierce herself —the fitting dramatic climax of an emotional scene, and psychologically accurate in its sexual implications. To die (death and orgasm) by Hippolytus' sword (phallus) would be the supreme moment for Phaedra. Just as Theseus killed the Minotaur, who represents monstrous instinct, in the labyrinth of Crete, so Phaedra, the Cretan queen, wishes to have Theseus' son kill the Minotaur in the labyrinth of her soul. But Oenone intervenes, Phaedra runs off stage with the sword in her hand, and death is postponed again.

Now, more than ever, Phaedra feels that her open admission of love puts her in disgrace. Again she wishes to hide from the world, intensifying a motif that Racine has stressed from the play's beginning, when Phaedra wished to die. Oenone asks: "Would it not be better, / Worthy the blood of Minos, in nobler cares / To seek your peace?" But by this time in the play, the third act, such words acquire a rich doubleness. Indeed, Minos is a noble and worthy judge of the underworld, but he is also the son of a god-bull and connected with labyrinths and sexuality. Being "worthy" the blood of Minos —notice the charged word "blood"—is exactly Phaedra's problem. Her despair leads to a flickering of hope, for at least she has no rival, she believes, and can perhaps tempt Hippolytus with "the charms of ruling." This slight high, however, is shattered by the news that

Theseus is not dead; he has returned to Troezen. One of the potent paradoxes of the play, marvelously bound up with its structure, is that Phaedra moves through her labyrinth of passion and instinct *toward* death while her husband, an escaper from labyrinths and a killer of monsters, returns *from* death.

Her fear of disgrace and her confusion, combined with Oenone's persistence, cause Phaedra to agree to Oenone's betrayal of Hippolytus. Theseus, learning of Hippolytus' treacherous attempt to rape his wife, utters: "How harshly, Destiny, dost thou pursue me! / I know not where I'm going, nor what I am!" Theseus seems to be entering his own labyrinth now, and destiny, he believes, has put him there. Unwilling to listen to Hippolytus, who will not reveal Phaedra's secret but who does allude to Phaedra's unnatural ancestry—"Yet Phaedra's mother . . . Phaedra springs / From a race, as you well know, my lord, more filled / With horrors than mine is"—Theseus curses his son, calling on Neptune to avenge a wretched father. His passion for justice overcomes his love for a son for whom his "heart is yearning." The secret power of destiny has forced a father to sacrifice a child, and the sacrifice is unavoidable. Phaedra's attempt to save Hippolytus is thwarted by jealousy, for Theseus reveals Hippolytus' love for Aricia. This new emotion causes Phaedra to utter thoughts of destruction. Disturbed by the image of the "innocent lovers" meeting in the woods in freedom, while she is forever hiding, forever invoking death, Phaedra says that her hands "burn to plunge in innocent blood!" But the noble Phaedra suddenly recoils from the horror of her own imagination; she wonders where her reason has fled, and she reasserts her desire for death. But her wish for death is now tied to her fear of death, as was Antigone's in Sophocles' play. Racine brilliantly exploits this heightened moment.

> Wretch! And I live!
> And I endure the sight of sacred Phoebus
> From whom I am derived. My ancestor
> Is sire and master of the gods; and heaven,
> Nay all the universe, is teeming now
> With my forbears. Where then can I hide?
> Flee to eternal night. What do I say?
> For there my father holds the fatal urn,
> Put by the Fates in his stern hands, 'tis said.

Minos in Hades judges the pale ghosts.
Ah, how this shade will tremble when his eyes
Behold his daughter there, confessing sins—
Crimes yet unknown in hell! What wilt thou say,
Father, to see this hideous spectacle?
Me thinks I now behold the dreadful urn
Fall from thy hand! Me thinks I see thee search
For some new punishment, thyself become
The torturer of thine own blood. Forgive:
A cruel god has doomed thy family.
Behold his vengeance in thy daughter's lust.
(p. 215)

Her words powerfully indicate Phaedra's trapped condition. The observed of all observers, she cannot hide from her grandfather the sun—she is literally too much in the sun—and she cannot hide in the night of death, for her father Minos is there to judge her. She can never escape her ancestry; her torment seems everlasting and the sphere of her terror has no spatial bounds. The fatality of her past and the turbulence of her mind—the dark, demonic forces of destiny and psyche—inspire horror in Phaedra and in us.

Phaedra condemns Oenone for poisoning her mind, making her forget her duty, and leaves the stage. She will return only once more, at the play's end—but then a literal poison will be coursing through her veins. Between her departure and that final entrance, Racine has Panope, a lady of the court, reveal the death of Oenone, who threw herself "into the deep sea," and he has Theramenes reveal the death of Hippolytus, who was killed because of a monster that came from the sea. Theramenes' speech is especially effective because the speaker is the eminently reasonable and balanced tutor who must report a horrible, supernatural death. His inability to comprehend the situation adds to the terror. A monster—"half-bull, half-dragon"—was vomited from the sea.

The seashore trembled with his bellowing;
The sky with horror saw that savage monster;
The earth was moved, the air infected with it;
The sea which brought it started back amazed.
(p. 222)

The heroic Hippolytus wounds the monster who in rage and pain strikes terror in the horses, causing them to run wild and drag Hippolytus to his bloody, mangled death. In the confusion a god was seen spurring on the horses. Theseus' phrase, after hearing Theramenes' account, seems to say it all: "Inexorable gods." The gods—whether they arise from the sea in the form of a lovely Venus or a mad bull-dragon, whether they bring love or death—represent a primal power that is dark, deep, cruel, and destructive. Theseus, the famous slayer of the Minotaur (who was the son of Pasiphae and therefore the half-brother of Phaedra), is now devastated by a report of the bull's revenge. The bull, with all the violence of passion and instinct he represents—in the dark labyrinth of Phaedra's soul, in the labyrinth of Minos' cave, in the uncontrollable sea—forever reminds us of man's fragile condition in the face of unnatural and supernatural power.

Phaedra's last speech—uttered as the deadly poison flows through her "burning veins"—reveals to Theseus the innocence of Hippolytus and the incestuous nature of her own desire. She again insists that "the heavens / put in my breast that fatal spark," and she puts much of the blame on Oenone as well. We derive no comfort from her confession; it is right that she confesses, but it seems unimportant. Always bound up with *her* feelings, we welcome with her the death that robs her eyes of "clearness" because those eyes have constantly gazed at her own appalling progress through guilty passion to inescapable doom. This progress is the play's movement; Phaedra's conflict with herself is the play's focus. And when we look hard and long at Phaedra's condition, as we are forced to do, we realize that Racine, like Euripides who focused on Hippolytus, is raising questions without offering solutions and without offering comfort. (Which of us really cares whether Theseus will take care of Aricia?) Phaedra's dilemma—unable to walk in the sun, afraid to walk in the dark, always appalled by an obsession she cannot control, always the helpless victim of a past and a destiny and the gods—is presented so powerfully that it becomes the human dilemma. As in Euripides, we see man as a limited creature caught in a web, but trying to assert himself within the web's snare. We feel the force of Phaedra's passion as well as the force of her guilty feelings about it; we feel and applaud her resistance at the same time that we recognize its futility. Our knowledge that this woman of high dignity and deep passion is ensnared by a dark fate gives us a strange pleasure, for pleasure can come—as we have seen in Sophocles—from looking into an abyss, from looking at the dark spot where love and guilt and death meet, from realizing that however strong man is in his stand against necessity, he is still weak and limited. That is why the usual Aristotelian notions of pity and fear—supported by Racine himself in the preface and certainly operating throughout the play —describe only part of a complex tragic effect. And that is why Racine's idea of poetic justice, also stated in the preface, cannot work at all. We do not condemn Phaedra for her passion, because it was god-sent and because she, radically alone, groping in the labyrinth of her soul, is forever condemning herself. We do not see her death as a punishment for her incestuous thoughts, but rather as a relief from her torment, assuming and hoping that she will not be confronting Minos in the underworld. We are sensitive to her weakness against the dark forces that oppose her, from without and from within, and we are admiring of her resistance and her wish for death and the feverish clarity of her expression.

Racine allows us to see so much, but his greatness as a tragic dramatist is that he makes us realize the power, but not the nature, of what lies beneath even the depth of things, the hidden shadows and mysteries of the secret cause. The tragic effect, therefore, stems from feelings associated with mythic mystery, from questions concerning the nature of passion, concerning man's relationship with the gods, concerning the bull. The constellation Taurus seems to hang over the play, with the stars themselves forming a question mark. The bull's whiteness—and whiteness can be more terrible than blackness, as Melville clearly demonstrates—is what we associate with the Zeus who rapes Europa to beget a Minos and with the creature that sleeps with Pasiphae to beget Phaedra. The bull's darkness is what we see in the Minotaur, waiting for his victims in the labyrinth, and in the Dionysian passions within Phaedra's labyrinthine soul. And the monstrous bull that emerges from the sea to destroy Hippolytus is, in Racine, not white and not black, but both and neither. Mysterious, coming from the sea like Venus and like life itself, this bull rages and destroys. With Racine, as with Euripides and Sophocles, we go beyond the human conflicts to their mysterious sources. Racine has been able to combine the amplitude of myth with the innerness of psychology to produce a tragedy that never loses its sinister power because it never allows us to forget the fearful unknown that lodges at the center of both microcosm and macrocosm.

Although no bull charges through *Desire Under the Elms,* Eugene O'Neill has successfully captured the tragic spirit in his rehandling of the Hippolytus-Phaedra story. Perhaps it is a comment on tragedy in our time, or at least on twentieth-century American tragedy, that the dark strange worlds of Crete and Troezen have become a New England farm, that the power of Aphrodite has become the power of Mother, and that the important animal in O'Neill's play is not a bull but a cow. Nevertheless, tragedy prevails. Dionysian passions are still seething, and the sources of passion and love remain mysterious. In his entire career, from the early one-act plays about the sea to the painful, autobiographical late plays, O'Neill was acutely aware of "the Force behind (Fate, God, our biological past creating our present, whatever one calls it, Mystery certainly)—and of the one eternal tragedy of Man in his glorious, self-destructive struggle to make the Force express him instead of being, as an animal is, an infinitesimal incident in its expression."[7] His statement is important because it confirms the experience of his plays and because it reaffirms for a modern audience the need in tragedy for the "Force behind," whatever it may be but surely call it "Mystery," and man's self-destructive struggle against it. For O'Neill that force in *Desire Under the Elms* was not the gods we associate with Greek drama, but the "past" that creates the present, the force of the dead mother who determines the action, the mysterious power of desire which pushes man toward his end.

O'Neill in *Desire Under the Elms,* as in his later *Mourning Becomes Electra,* is consciously presenting what Travis Bogard calls "tragedy-by-analogy,"[8] grafting Greek myth on an American historical setting—New England in 1850—in order to give his play a larger significance. O'Neill has always aimed for largeness and depth; in *Desire* the largeness is strengthened by the play's use of the Hippolytus-Phaedra story as treated by Euripides, and the depth is strengthened perhaps by O'Neill's reading of Racine's *Phaedra.*[9] He considerably changes his models, but the underlying frames of reference enrich his particular tragic vision, a modern vision that substitutes Freudian determinism for Greek gods and that, although allowing more free will than Euripides or Racine, retains the mysterious forces that control men's lives.

Following the mythic account of Hippolytus and Phaedra, O'Neill has a father (Ephraim) return to a land with a new wife (Abbie) who is attracted to her stepson (Eben). Like Phaedra, Abbie at first conceals her passion; like Phaedra, Abbie wishes to banish the son from the land; and like Phaedra, Abbie eventually confronts her young lover directly. Unlike Phaedra, however, she is successful in her advances, and the son, unlike Hippolytus, enjoys the affair and seems to enjoy sexual affairs in general, as we see in his desire for Min the prostitute. Obviously, Eben is not the chaste Hippolytus of Euripides and Racine, but more like Hippolytus' woman-loving father, Theseus. Ephraim is also like Theseus in being a possessor of many women—having had two wives, the first the mother of Peter and Simeon, the second the mother of Eben, and now possessing Abbie, and having also slept with Min—but his is not a philandering nature; quite the opposite, Ephraim is the stern apostle of a hard, demanding God, and he embodies a New England Puritan tradition that is biblical and oppressive. In *Desire,* the curse of the father on the son does not come from Theseus-Ephraim on Hippolytus-Eben; it comes from the father Eben on his child with Abbie. And the instrument of that death is not Poseidon or a bull from the sea, but Abbie herself. At the end of the play, Theseus-Ephraim remains alone, as in the traditional story, but Abbie and Eben leave the stage together, hand in hand, on the way to their deaths as murderers of the infant.[10]

O'Neill's treatment of the story seems most Greek, however, not in the specific similarities or in his changes that have the conventional story as their base, but in the atmosphere of determinism. Necessity hangs over the play, not in the person of a Euripidean Aphrodite nor in the thoughts of a Racinian Phaedra, but in the "sinister maternity" of two large elms. Here is a portion of O'Neill's famous stage direction which opens the play.

> Two enormous elms are on each side of the house. They bend their trailing branches down over the roof. They appear to protect and at the same time subdue. There is a sinister maternity in their aspect, a crushing, jealous absorption. They have developed from their intimate contact with the life of man in the house an appalling humaneness. They brood oppressively over the house. They are like exhausted women resting their sagging breasts and hands and hair on its roof, and when it rains their tears trickle down monotonously and rot on the shingles.[11]

The words are charged and so obviously important on the symbolic level that it is difficult to agree with Bogard's assertion that "the novelistic rhetoric that links the elms with Eben's dead mother and with an exhausted life force holds no meaning beyond the printed page."[12] The elms dominate the play; as described, they are as visible as the statues of Aphrodite and Artemis that frame the action of Euripides' *Hippolytus*. O'Neill is stressing their importance not only in the stage direction but in the play's title—whatever is happening in the play, stemming from many kinds of desire, is happening *under* the elms, physically under them as they hover over the house and symbolically under them as they represent clearly and forcefully the dominance of Mother: Mother as female principle, Mother as the demands of the past, Mother as avenging spirit, Mother as lover. In human form, Mother is Ephraim's second wife—soft, good-natured, worked to death by Ephraim—and Abbie—who takes Eben's mother's place in the home and in his affections—and Min—the prostitute shared by father and son; in animal form, Mother is the cows that Ephraim must visit; in the form of animated nature, Mother is the elms, darkly rooted, maternally protective and oppressive, creating shadows and hidden corners, informing the play's action.

The trigger that springs the action is *desire,* in all its manifestations. Eben's brothers, seeing the gold of the sunset in the play's beginning, think of California gold: "Gold in the sky—in the west —Golden Gate—California!—Goldest West!—fields o' gold!" Their desire for easy riches, combined with their realization that the farm will never belong to them, especially now that their father is bringing home a new bride, causes them to sell their shares of the farm to Eben as they head for California with a song on their lips. Eben's desire is the farm and the land, which he believes belonged entirely to his mother before Ephraim stole it from her. This desire is bound up with his desire for revenge against his hated father. And both desires are darkly tied to his sexual desire—for Min, for Abbie, and for his mother. Abbie's desire is both material and sexual. Greed motivates her early actions in the play; she always wanted a home and she possesses one now. That is why she married old Ephraim Cabot and that is why she wants a son to make sure the farm will remain hers. Also present from the beginning is her sexual desire for Eben; her very first glance at "his youth and good looks" awakens it.

Ephraim's desire is more static than kinetic in that his passion for the farm and land is assumed; he desires the farm, he has it, he will do anything to keep it, and he does keep it at the end. Less obvious is his desire for warmth and companionship, which he can satisfy only when he is with the cows. This hidden desire and need is what makes Ephraim the most complex and interesting character in the play. The Father against whom Eben must revolt, the Father who had abused the Mother whose spirit will seek revenge, the Father who worships a lonely God and is himself a lonely, stony god of the farm, needs the warmth of the cows. O'Neill allows the desires of his characters to control the play's movement: the kinetic desires of Eben and Abbie move the play along, and Ephraim is the stone around which Eben and Abbie must move—while the elms (Mother) and the stone Ephraim (Father) control the play, and while Eben and Abbie give the play direction. At the end, the movers are gone but the stone and elms remain, which is itself a comment on O'Neill's tragic vision: man destroys himself in the battle against a stronger "force behind" that is powerful and pervasive.

In the course of the play, Eben and Abbie move from desire to true love. Along the way O'Neill gives us all the elements that could make *Desire Under the Elms* a sensational melodrama—greed, on-stage violence, sex, incest, adultery, infanticide. Yet, because each of these elements is controlled by a larger frame of reference—the past determining the present and future—we are in the realm of tragedy. In *Desire* the dead do not die; a living son will avenge the lurking spirit of a dead mother. The claims of the past make *Desire* a revenge play, and Eben's role as his mother's avenger is not unlike Hamlet's role as his father's avenger. In both O'Neill and Shakespeare the past controls the present and creates the future. Eben's mother, like Hamlet's father, seems to be saying throughout: "Remember me!" Each character in the play remembers her; their words uttered under the sagging elms make us feel her presence. Simeon and Peter reminisce: "She was good t' Sim 'n' me. A good step-maw's scurse." "She was good t' everyone." Eben, in the very beginning, reveals his closeness to her:

> Me cookin'—doin' her work—that made me know her, suffer her sufferin'—she'd come back t' help—come back t' bile pota-
> toes—come back t' fry bacon—come back t' bake biscuits—
> come back all cramped up t' shake the fire, an' carry ashes, her

eyes weepin' an' bloody with smoke an' cinders same's they used t' be. She still comes back—stands by the stove thar in the evenin'— she can't find it nateral sleepin' an' restin' in peace. She can't git used t' bein' free—even in her grave. (part 1, sc. 2)

And throughout he asserts: "I'm Maw—every drop o' blood!" It is his mother's blood in him that drives him to avenge her wrongs. Whatever he does seems to be done under her auspices; Eben is his mother's agent of retribution against Ephraim, who also feels her presence. Matter of factly, Ephraim tells Abbie about "Eben's Maw": "Her folks was contestin' me at law over my deeds t' the farm —my farm! That's why Eben keeps a-talkin' his fool talk o' this bein' his Maw's farm. She bore Eben. She was purty—but soft. She tried t' be hard. She couldn't. She never knowed me nor nothin'. It was lonesomer 'n hell with her. After a matter o' sixteen odd years, she died" (part 2, sc. 2). But she died in body only, even for him. She is alive in her son Eben—"Soft headed. Like his Maw. Dead spit 'n' image." And she is alive in spirit, for Ephraim feels something "pokin' round the corners," "somethin' onnateral," and Ephraim tells Eben at the play's end that he'll burn the farm "an' I'll leave yer Maw t' haunt the ashes." Abbie realizes that she must compete against Eben's mother: "I'm yer new Maw." "I'm all prepared t' have ye agin me—at fust. I don't blame ye nuther. I'd feel the same at any stranger comin' t' take my Maw's place." But Abbie eventually becomes one with Eben's mother—in winning over Eben as both son and lover, and in helping Eben in his revenge against Ephraim. Mother, in short, hangs over the play and lurks within the play; she acquires a deterministic force as potent as the gods in Greek drama.

The scene which brilliantly captures her mysterious presence is the parlour scene (part 2, sc. 3), in which the passionate sexual desires of Eben and Abbie are fulfilled. O'Neill prepares for this sexually and dramatically climactic moment by giving the parlour, the mother's parlour, a supernatural significance. It is the room where Eben's mother was laid out when she died, a room never occupied since then, a "repressed room like a tomb," according to O'Neill's stage direction. Abbie wishes to possess that room, the only room that is not hers yet. Possessing it will fulfill her obsessive desire for ownership of the home, but when she enters it, it is she who is possessed. O'Neill, again in a stage direction, tells us "A change has come over the woman. She looks awed and frightened now, ready to run away." When Eben enters—for she said she would be expecting him to court her in *that* room—she fearfully tells him: "When I fust come in—in the dark—they seemed somethin' here." Eben instinctively says "Maw." Abbie can still feel "somethin' " but now that Eben is with her something seems to be "growin' soft an' kind t' me." As they continue talking about Maw, Abbie at first takes Eben's hand in hers, then more passionately holds him around, becoming his mother.

> I'll sing fur ye! I'll die fur ye! . . . Don't cry, Eben! I'll take yer Maw's place! I'll be everythin' she was t' ye! Let me kiss ye, Eben! . . . Don't be afeered! I'll kiss ye pure, Eben—Same's if I was a Maw t' ye—an' ye kin kiss me back 's if yew was my son —my boy—sayin' good-night t' me! Kiss me, Eben. *(They kiss in restrained fashion. Then suddenly wild passion overcomes her. She kisses him lustfully again and he flings his arms about her and returns her kisses. Suddenly . . . he frees himself from her violently and springs to his feet. He is trembling all over, in a strange state of terror. Abbie strains her arms toward him with fierce pleading.)* Don't ye leave me, Eben! Can't ye see it hain't enuf—lovin' ye like a Maw—can't ye see it's got t' be that an' more—much more—a hundred times more—fur me t' be happy—fur yew t' be happy? (part 2, sc. 3)

Abbie is not pretending to be mother in order to seduce Eben, as some critics maintain. Abbie, in awe because of the presence of Eben's mother in the parlour, identifies herself with the mother and loves Eben as a mother would love a son. (We should remember that Abbie lost her own child.) But she goes beyond this identification with the mother by wanting to be loved for her self. She convinces Eben that his mother is blessing their physical union, that his mother wants him to have Abbie because "she knows I love ye!" Eben finds his own reason for mother's blessing on the union—"It's her vengeance on him—so's she kin rest quiet in her grave!" Abbie, however, rejects the idea of vengeance and clings to the higher value of love. "Vengeance o' God on the hull o' us! What d' we give a durn? I love ye, Eben! God knows I love ye!" Eben's passion is released: "An' I love yew, Abbie!—now I kin say it! I been dyin' fur want o' ye—every hour since ye come! I love ye!" The curtain falls as they fiercely kiss, their sexual union taking place in an atmosphere of lust and incest and Oedipal desire *and* the natural love of man and woman for each other. Reactions to this turbulent scene must be mixed and troubled. A dark psychological moment has been given dramatic life; an unnatural union seems naturally consummated; a scene of deep sexual passion is informed by what seem like the incompatible forces of vengeance and true love. At this point in the play, Abbie seems closer to true love and Eben to vengeance. At the play's conclusion, they both will leave vengeance and Mother behind them, having discovered the purer truth of their love but having chosen death in the process.

Their lovemaking, Eben and Abbie believe, has freed the ghost of Mother. The parlour's shutters are now open, the sun will be let in, and "Maw's gone back t' her grave." But the ghost remains, for the punishment of Ephraim is not complete. Eben's child is born to Abbie, and Ephraim, who thinks it is his child, is jubilant because his heir will inherit the farm. In a remarkable scene of Dionysian celebration—drinking, singing, dancing—Ephraim Cabot revels in his accomplishment while his guests, knowing the truth of the child's parentage, utter snide remarks. Of course, the true Dionysianism belongs not to the self-denying, stony Ephraim but to Abbie and Eben, the force of whose passion is vital and natural and deep. We cannot forget Abbie's sexually charged words to Eben in the beginning of part 2 when she wishes to seduce him: "Hain't the sun strong an' hot? Ye kin feel it burnin' into the earth—Nature—makin' ye want t' grow—into somethin' else—till ye're jined with it—and it's your'n—but it owns ye, too—an' makes ye grow bigger—like a tree—like them elums— . . . Nature'll beat ye, Eben. Ye might's well own up t' it fust 's last." The festive spirit in the dancing scene is displayed by Ephraim. As he dances alone, his acrobatic capers and loud boasting contrast sharply with the anxiety of Abbie and the quietness of Eben, trying to "understand his conflicting emotions" produced by the birth of a son he cannot acknowledge. But even the seemingly happy and certainly frenzied Ephraim is confused about things, for he leaves the party to go wearily to the barn, uttering these words: "Even the music can't drive it out—somethin'. Ye kin feel it droppin' off the elums, climbin' up the roof, sneakin' down the chimney, pokin' in the corners!" The elms continue to hover, and the spirit of Mother continues to haunt the darkness.

From this scene of high revelry, the play rushes to its conclusion. Immediately, Ephraim reveals to Eben that Abbie wanted a child so that she could have the farm and cut off Eben from it. Eben believes Ephraim; they have a physical scuffle, which Ephraim wins. Eben, in great anger and confusion, rejects Abbie who is attempting to express her love for him and him alone. Eben wishes the child "never was born! I wish he'd die this minit! . . . It's him—yew havin' him—a-purpose t' steal—that's changed everythin'!" His wish—the equivalent of Theseus' curse on Hippolytus in the myth—is granted. Abbie, to prove she loves Eben only for himself and to keep him with her, murders the child. She kills what she loves to prove a greater love; the suffocation of the child of love, paradoxically and tragically, symbolizes the true quality of love. When she reveals her act to Eben, he is shocked, calls to his mother—"Maw, whar was ye, why didn't ye stop her?"—and in horror, almost mad with passion, runs to get the sheriff while Abbie screams after him, "I love ye, Eben! I love ye!" An excruciating scene, touching the dark corners of death and love, tugging at our sympathies and fears.

That Eben's love for Abbie has become genuine and unequivocal is made explicit when he returns from the sheriff to share her guilt and death, unwilling to waver from that choice. She proved her love for him by choosing death for the child; he proves his love for her by choosing death for himself with her. The lovers are guilty of murder, which is the only guilt they feel in the play. The guilt that Phaedra felt because of her sinful passion in both Euripides and Racine finds no place in O'Neill's play. The only guilt here concerns murder, for the sexual passion is presented as natural and the child as a creation of love. Eben's willingness to go to death with his lover is a high, noble act, so noble that even Ephraim grudgingly admires him —"Purty good—fur yew!" Having redeclared their love for one another, Eben and Abbie walk "hand in hand" to the gate of the house as the sun rises and the curtain falls. The last words of the play belong to the sheriff—"It's a jim-dandy farm, no denyin'. Wished I owned it!"—and we are brought back to the desires that triggered the play's action.

The togetherness of Abbie and Eben at the completion of their progress from desire to love highlights the solitariness of Ephraim's end. Having boastfully upheld a puritanical tradition that represses life, having piled up the stones around his farm and around himself, having reasserted that "God's hard, not easy! God's in the stones!" and realizing that he will be lonesomer than ever, Ephraim at the end remains true to himself and unmoving in his hardness. The self-destruction of the young lovers, capable of having children, is counterpointed to the enduring quality of the sterile old man. Like Yeats's stone, Ephraim troubles "the living stream," the stone itself acquiring mythic proportions. John H. Raleigh is correct in seeing Ephraim Cabot as the play's great character.[13] Concentrating on the kinetic Eben and Abbie, critics have somewhat neglected the more complex Ephraim. True, his dominance is usually acknowledged and his representation of the archetypal (and typically O'Neill) Father against whom a son must revolt is discussed, but his own need for warmth is rarely recognized. Yet, O'Neill gives him a powerful and poignant speech (part 2, sc. 2) in which he expresses his inmost thoughts to Abbie, who is not listening, who in fact is looking through the wall of her room to Eben's room. The wall between the bedrooms of the lovers seems paper-thin; the wall around Ephraim is stone. Also, O'Neill gives Ephraim a love for the cows, conventional symbols of maternity, here the perfect animals to indicate Ephraim's own need for the warmth of Mother and female. "It's wa'm down t' the barn—nice smellin' an' warm—with the cows." His wives gave him no peace; sleeping with the cows gives him peace. His wives never listened; he can talk to the cows who "know" the farm and him. Thinking that he'll set fire to the farm, he turns the cows loose—"By freein' 'em, I'm freein' myself!" His bond to the cows is strong, necessary, and mysterious. Stone though he may be, the old Ephraim Cabot, like the young Stephen Dedalus and like all men, must meet a "moocow" on the road of life. We seem to have come a long way from Theseus with a bull in a labyrinth to Ephraim Cabot with a cow on a New England farm but the passions and needs of man remain dark and the causes remain deep and secret.

As inevitably as sunset leads to sunrise in the play (and as inevitably as sunrise leads to sunset in man's life) Eben's and Abbie's pasts lead them to their present and future. Some free will is operating, of course—and critics are pleased to discuss the free choices of Eben and Abbie because for many critics free will seems to be a necessary requirement for tragedy—but the play is essentially deterministic. The choices made by the characters must be seen in the context of the pressures that produce these choices. No gods without, as in *Hippolytus*, and no gods within and without, as in *Phaedra*, yet forces as strong as the gods. O'Neill makes us feel the power of the land, the force that through the green fuse drives the flower, which influences Ephraim, Eben, and Abbie, and which helps shape their destinies. (The soil in *Desire* is as potent a shaper of life as that "ol' devil sea" in O'Neill's *Anna Christie*.) Abbie experiences the force of nature most intensely when she feels her passion for Eben growing within her and when she sees his passion for her growing within Eben. Ephraim feels the force of a lonely and hard God whose image controls his life. But the most obvious and sinister outside force is Mother, and the Freudian pattern is clear, a pattern that emerges naturally from the play's action and characters. O'Neill is faithful to Freud's larger truth which involves the revolt of son against father, the love for mother, the Dionysian triumph of passion over self-denial, and, most important for O'Neill in all his plays, the terrible hold that the past has on the present, the last most clearly expressed by Mary Tyrone in *Long Day's Journey Into Night*, a startlingly autobiographical play that represents O'Neill's most direct insights into the life around him. In her agony, Mary Tyrone comes to realize "that no one is responsible for what happened. The past made them what they are. . . . The past is the present and the future, too. There is no way out." The past in *Desire Under the Elms* determines and controls the tragic action. Eben and Abbie operate against the background of a larger process of retribution, with the avenging Mother writing the play that both son and lover act in. Like Hamlet, who is acting in his avenging father's play, Eben could say that he was "born to set things right." In the process he destroys himself. This power of the past, this inability to avoid what the past has created, makes human beings victims of a fate they cannot control. "There is no way out." The past hangs over the present as broodingly as the elms hang over the farmhouse, as oppressively as the gods hang over Greek tragedy. Freudian determinism—the dark forces of the past, the dark corners of the human psyche, the mystery—is for a modern audience as potent a manifestation of necessity as the Delphic oracle for the Greek audience. O'Neill in *Desire* makes it a believable determinism in terms of tragic action and a dark comment on man's plight. Man and woman can, like Eben and Abbie, reach heights of dignity by self-sacrificing love, can walk into the sunrise, but we in the audience feel the paradox of true love found only when death is chosen, of a sunrise that is a sunset. And we as witnesses stand in "puzzled awe" (as Eben does in the play's beginning when he sees the sunset) at the insoluble mysteries of human desire and love and death, at the terrible power of the past, at death that does not die but returns to haunt the living, at the "Force behind." When he discussed his early plays about the sea, O'Neill said that he wished as a dramatist to "at least faintly shadow at their work . . . the impelling, inscrutable forces behind life."[14] His subsequent plays, especially *Desire Under the Elms* and the last autobiographical plays, testify to his success in achieving this goal. Their moving power stems in no small part from his abiding vision of man fighting against an inescapable determinism and inevitably losing. His plays touch the over-riding mystery, and the cause remains secret and haunting. Primarily for this reason, Eugene O'Neill, our finest twentieth-century American dramatist, has been able—like the ancient Greek Euripides and the seventeenth-century Frenchman Racine—to capture the essence of tragedy.

4 DEATH

Hamlet & *Rosencrantz and Guildenstern Are Dead*

What has come to be called the Hamlet mystery, which we try to pluck out of prince and play, challenging the sensitivity and understanding of readers and viewers and critics, must be approached with the forbidding awareness that everything about the play seems to have been said. (Seems, madam?) Yet, this vitally complex play is so central to almost every modern discussion of tragedy that it must be approached once more, if only to place the Hamlet mystery within the mystery of *Hamlet*. Interpretations both narrow and large, misinterpretations equally wide-ranging, cling to the play, but one fact is indisputable, and it must be the focus of any discussion that ensues: *Hamlet* is about death and sex, the "charnel and the carnal" (to borrow Harry Levin's apt phrase),[1] graves and beds, skulls and cosmetics, dying literally and dying sexually. Death and sex, in knot instrinsicate, prod the mystery, touch the secret cause.

The movement of the play can be plotted as the progress from question to silence. Not the silence that comes from the answer to the question; rather the silence that comes with death and the realization that questions cannot be answered. "Who's there?" shouts Bernardo anxiously on the ramparts of a fortification on a cold night —and that is the question that remains with us throughout the play, as important to this play as the phrase "Fair is foul, and foul is fair" is to *Macbeth*, Shakespeare rarely wasting words in his opening scenes. Shouted in the dark, reverberating from the heavens, "Who's there?" becomes the large ontological question of a play that contains more questions than any other play in our tragic tradition. Maynard Mack has characterized *Hamlet* as a play in the interrogative mood;[2] with this judgment there can be no dispute. The question mark pervades tragedy, as my previous chapters have demonstrated, but in *Hamlet* it not only pervades, it overwhelms. The play presents questions of every possible kind, some small ("What hour now?"), some seemingly small but becoming very important ("Where's your father?"), some conspicuously large ("To be or not to be[?]"). Some questions can be answered to everyone's satisfaction, some—those crucial to the texture of tragedy—can never be answered except by silence. But silence in the presence of mystery, silence produced by facing the fact of mystery, is cathartic, "rest," as we shall come to see.

Francisco—cold, sick at heart, guarding the fortress Elsinore, waiting for relief—hears the challenge that should have come from his own cold lips: "Who's there?" Bernardo, coming to relieve Francisco at his watch, fearful of what the night holds for him since he has already seen the "thing" for two consecutive nights, anxiously issues the challenge. "Nay, answer me"—that's my line, says Francisco. Immediately, Shakespeare makes us feel the nervousness in the air. Bernardo's "Who's there?" applies to the Ghost as well as to anything that is dark and hidden in the night. The haunting question is appropriate to the specific theatrical context and reverberatingly important to the play's larger philosophical dimension. And immediately death stalks the play in the figure of a dead king returning from the unknown for reasons unknown. Old Hamlet is silent when confronted by Horatio in the first scene, but at the end of the play's first movement (1. 5), when the Ghost speaks to his son, his anguished speech, containing the play's two most important elements, death and sexuality, gives Hamlet the charge that will propel the play forward—"revenge." However, between the Ghost's first silent appearance and his later revelation, death and sexuality are presented and played on by Shakespeare. Horatio talks about the death of Julius Caesar, having already informed us of Old Hamlet's slaying of Old Fortinbras. Claudius and Gertrude utter words about the death of Hamlet's father and the proper duration for mourning the dead. Hamlet dwells on death and sexuality in his first soliloquy. Hamlet and Horatio mention weddings and funerals just before Horatio tells Hamlet of the appearance of the Ghost. And Laertes and Ophelia and Polonius discuss the sexual habits of young princes. Therefore, by the time the Ghost presents the powerful images of death and sex, Shakespeare has already made them part of the play's emotional and intellectual atmosphere, nowhere in the first movement more brilliantly than in Hamlet's first soliloquy. This must give us pause, for here we confront the melancholy Hamlet *before* the Ghost's shattering revelation.

Oh, that this too too solid flesh would melt,
Thaw, and resolve itself into a dew!
Or that the Everlasting had not fixed
His canon 'gainst self-slaughter! Oh, God! God!
How weary, stale, flat, and unprofitable
Seem to me all the uses of this world!
Fie on 't, ah, fie! 'Tis an unweeded garden,
That grows to seed, things rank and gross in nature
Possess it merely. That it should come to this!
But two months dead! Nay, not so much, not two.
So excellent a King, that was, to this,
Hyperion to a satyr. So loving to my mother
That he might not beteem the winds of heaven
Visit her face too roughly. Heaven and earth!
Must I remember? Why, she would hang on him
As if increase of appetite had grown
By what it fed on. And yet within a month—
Let me not think on 't. —Frailty, thy name is woman! —
A little month, or ere those shoes were old
With which she followed my poor father's body,
Like Niobe all tears. —Why she, even she—
Oh, God! A beast that wants discourse of reason
Would have mourned longer—married with my uncle,
My father's brother, but no more like my father
Than I to Hercules. Within a month,
Ere yet the salt of most unrighteous tears
Had left the flushing in her galled eyes,
She married. Oh, most wicked speed, to post
With such dexterity to incestuous sheets!
It is not, nor it cannot, come to good.
But break, my heart, for I must hold my tongue![3]

Here Hamlet expresses a despair that is natural, the normal reaction of a sensitive young man to the fact of death—his father's—and the fact of his mother's too hasty remarriage. Suddenly, it seems, Hamlet's idealism—resting firmly on the belief that his parents' love for one another was strong and unequivocal—has been shaken, producing a world he has never before confronted, where love is fragile, where death of life and love must be experienced, a world, in fact, so dark and disillusioning that it is impossible to find one's way through the despair. The only solution seems to be suicide, which will stop all questioning of values, and which will stop all thoughts of death. Hamlet's despair is increased, certainly, by what he witnessed just before the soliloquy, that everything is going on as usual —the court world is functioning, the trumpets continue to resound, the costumes remain gay, the wine flows as freely, mother has a new husband, Denmark has a new king, Laertes can return to France. Everyone has forgotten the past. He, and he alone, remembers, even before the Ghost's injunction to "Remember me." The effectiveness of Hamlet's soliloquy rests on its powerful presentation of the truth of Hamlet's inner condition: his horror at what has happened to his familiar, ideal world; his grief for things lost; his fear of his own isolation in being the only one to remember, the only one wearing an inky cloak on the outside while confronting an unanswerable question on the inside. What is there in woman's nature to cause a mother to leave a Hyperion to feed on a satyr, to rush to those incestuous sheets? Remembering what *was* and witnessing what *is* make all the ways of the world stale and flat. What once had a clear surface, what once seemed a healthy garden, now is muddied and grows weeds. Dionysus, it seems, always lurked beneath the Apollonian clarity. The young prince's vision of this aspect of nature, which is new to him, of the ulcer beneath the fair outside, causes him to shout out against the frailty of woman, the seeming cause of his mother's lust. However, the cause of that frailty, connected with passion and sexuality, remains secret. If one adds the mystery of his mother's shocking behavior to the mystery of his father's death, a father whom he seems to be forever seeking in the dust, then is it not natural for Hamlet to wish to leave the scene, to die, in order to avoid groping his way through the murky thickets of a supposedly fair clear world now seen as foul and puzzling?

However, that final exit, death, intrinsically mysterious, seems even more mysterious when it becomes an entrance back into this world for the Ghost, whose revelations about his own gruesome murder and his wife's sexuality add further to the horror of Hamlet's already morbid imagination. "Oh, horrible! Oh, horrible, most horrible!" belongs to Hamlet, whether or not he utters it. The Ghost, speechlessly entering and exiting from the play's first scene on the ramparts, overlooking the cold and dark sea, re-enters in the fourth scene to beckon Hamlet to himself but also closer to the "dreadful summit of the cliff," the place itself able to "put toys of desperation" in every brain. On that summit, the dark boundary between consciousness and unconsciousness, the Ghost causes Hamlet to look into the abyss to hear the "roar beneath," to learn of unnatural death and gross sexuality, thoughts that take one "beyond the reaches of the soul." The Ghost's powerful speech invokes the terror of his own immediate situation, his doom to roam until his murder is avenged, but forbidden "to tell the secrets of my prison house," thereby making heavier the air of mystery. He then presents the details of his murder by that serpent Claudius, and he reveals his feelings of sexual disgust when he mentions the lust of that "seeming-virtuous Queen," who is now sexually gorging herself on garbage. The Ghost orders his son to avenge his murder, to stop the "royal bed of Denmark" from being a couch for lust and incest. But he also tells him not to contrive anything against Gertrude—"Leave her to heaven." The love that Gertrude draws from all the men in her life, and here the man whom she betrayed, is one of the play's many mysteries. In the paradoxical nature of tragedy, Hamlet is asked to prove his love for a dead father by killing Claudius. To prove love, the heart must be hardened. (Witness Antigone; witness Abbie as she murders her child.) Hamlet is given a dreadful mission by his father, is assigned the lead role in a play that his father has sketched but that Hamlet will have to fill in or flesh out. The past, as we saw in Greek tragedy and Racine and O'Neill, never dies; here in *Hamlet* the prince's personal past—the unnatural murder of a father, the lustful behavior of a mother, the dark combination of death and sexuality—determines Hamlet's present and future, as powerful a determinism as one is apt to find in drama, but not the play's only form of determinism. At the end of the first movement, Hamlet utters the famous words that crisply indicate his attitude toward his assigned role:

> The time is out of joint, O, cursed spite
> That ever I was born to set it right!

He realizes he was born to set it right—born to his condition, born to his royal parents, one dead, one lustful, and newborn to a world that has so suddenly revealed its ulcerous and evil foundation. The roar beneath the sea of life echoes mysterious passions and unanswered questions, and Hamlet realizes instinctively—"Oh, cursed

spite!"—that he is incapable of understanding these passions or answering these questions. Only when he accepts this realization will
the "rest" come; until then, he must strive to set the time right.

Because Hamlet does not take action immediately, because two
months have passed when we see him next—reading a book (no
less)—because he seems not to take opportunities when offered (as
when Claudius is praying), his reason or reasons for delay have produced a vast body of critical literature. The critics valiantly search for
the key to Hamlet's behavior, even though Hamlet himself warns us
against trying to "pluck out the heart of my mystery." But challenges of this kind must be met, and Hamlet is so rich a character,
the play so interesting and various, that the search continues, although one cannot find a modern discussion of Hamlet that does
not present an initial disclaimer, indicating how much has been
written about the play and how this interpretation is only one
among many possible interpretations. The hazards in attempting to
find the key to Hamlet's delay, and thus the key to the play, are generally recognized, and the sense of hopeless resignation that the
problem cannot really be solved is often felt. This is as it should be,
for we are dealing with a play in which the question mark domi-
nates, in which puzzlement is part of the play's fabric. The search for
the reason for the delay has led within Hamlet (Elizabethan and
modern psychology) and without Hamlet (sources, archetypes, the
play's "world" and "atmosphere"). The results of the search are
well known, and need not be repeated here.[4] One need only state
the obvious—that most of the various interpretations bring us a little
closer to the play, but that we are not closer to any consensus on the
truth of Hamlet's condition or the meaning of the play. The only
positive statement we can make about the maze of *Hamlet* criticism is
that there is no one answer to any of the important problems the
play raises. However, whatever critical view is held, there can be no
doubt about the importance of death and sex to the play, and whatever focus the play has—and it could be a shifting focus—its core
rests on mortality and sexuality, both aspects of a secret cause, both
manifestations of a hidden horror. The play's first movement, the
twenty-four hours between the two appearances of the Ghost,
clearly presents both motifs. Hovering over these motifs is the
question mark; powerfully introducing death and sexuality is the
"questionable" ghost; trying to find a way through the questionable

atmosphere of his world and its newly dark values is the Ghost's questioning son.

Clear answers to his many questions do not reveal themselves to Hamlet. He must—like almost everyone else in the play—find directions out by indirections. Is the Ghost from heaven or hell? Is the Ghost telling the truth? To find *these* answers, Hamlet must put on an antic disposition—"seems, madam," I *know* seems!—and must build a mousetrap, which leads almost immediately to the death of the wrong rodent, "a rat." Is Ophelia an honest lover or is she deceitful, like all women? To find this answer, Hamlet must ask "Where's your father?" Ophelia's "At home, my lord," when Hamlet knows her father is behind a curtain, produces Hamlet's vehement "Get thee to a nunnery" which now is the brothel-nunnery where women, all women, paint and jig and amble and act like whores. To find out the mission of Rosencrantz and Guildenstern, Hamlet must play the prince who wants to be king. To fool Polonius, Hamlet plays the unrequited lover. And so on. Throughout the play—mentioning all the moments would give a plot summary, so often does this happen—Hamlet is indirect or playing a role in order to find his direction, some way to approach his task as avenger and some way to know the unknowable. As if it is not enough to have a play filled with questions, the hero himself not only meets questions and puzzlements at every turn, but calculatingly decides to mystify. Only when he is alone, only when he contemplates the fact of death (thinking about father) and the fact of sexuality (thinking about mother) does he seem to be clearly himself, but because death and sexuality are themselves steeped in mystery and are, in fact, intricately bound up one with the other—to die, to sleep (in death); to die, to sleep (in orgasm)—the clarity is tainted.

Camus in his *Notebooks* says, "There is only one liberty, to come to terms with death. After which, everything is possible." This liberty comes to Hamlet only at the end of the play, when he realizes "the readiness is all"; before that he is *trying* to come to terms with death, and it is not a simplification of this complex play to suggest that Hamlet's progress in the play is a painful but increasing understanding of the nature of death. From his early thoughts on the death of his father—and his mother's reaction to it—to his later thoughts on the death of beggars and Alexander and Yorick, we have an interim in which Hamlet deals with death: its most haunting manifestation, the return of a dead father as a ghost; its most violent, the killing of Polonius; its most devious, the sending of Rosencrantz and Guildenstern to death in England; its most sinful, the contemplation of killing Claudius not when he is praying but when his heels will be kicking at heaven; its most cruel, the rejection of Ophelia which, coupled with her father's death, leads to her death-sex mad songs and to her suicide; its most philosophical, the thoughts on the death of politicians, courtiers, lawyers, and contemplation of suicide. Wherever one turns in the play, death lurks, the skull grins, the dead body rots—and the live body too, for the gravedigger's qualification in answering Hamlet's overly curious question, "How long will a man lie i' th' earth ere he rot?" pinpoints the condition of man in Denmark: "if 'a be not rotten before 'a die. . . ."

Therefore, by the time Hamlet physically and emotionally confronts Yorick's skull in the graveyard scene (5.1), death has become the most important condition of Hamlet's felt experience and of the audience's experience of the play. The picture of Hamlet contemplating the skull of Yorick, reacting to the death of someone in his past, must remind us of all the reactions to death in the play up to this point: his mother's haste in remarriage and speed in rushing to bed again; Claudius' commonplace sentiments on sons losing fathers and fathers losing fathers *and* his genuine pangs of conscience at his foul deed of murder, for he *has* a "conscience" that can be caught in the Mousetrap; Ophelia's madness caused by her father's death and her lover's departure; Laertes's impulsive actions as the avenger of his dead father; Fortinbras's calculating actions as the regainer of his dead father's lost land; Hamlet's melancholy because of his father's death; his callousness as he "lugs the guts" of Polonius and as he thinks of hoisting those engineers, Rosencrantz and Guildenstern, with their own petard; his self-chastisement for not speeding to the killing of Claudius in order to end the agony of his dead father's ghost; the gravediggers singing at their work of digging graves and throwing up skulls, for 'tis their vocation. In the center of all these actions and thoughts is the skull—covered by a leprous crust, as with the father; covered by a flesh plastered with cosmetics, as with the mother and all women; bare and mocking, as with Yorick. *Hamlet* offers us the dance of death, with the piper invisible, the source of the music secret.

Immediately after Hamlet's words on Yorick and to Yorick, the dead Ophelia will be brought on stage. Hamlet's reaction to her death will be flamboyant. He will jump into the grave, shout bombastic words, grapple with Laertes in the grave, and symbolically propel us forward to the final duel to the death in the play's last scene. Here, in the graveyard, Claudius the observer looks down into the grave, another kind of abyss, to witness Hamlet and Laertes at one another's throats; soon he will witness a duel that will end with his own death as well as their deaths, and the revenge play will end with revenge. The observed of all observers, that melancholy prince too much in the sun, will give his most persistent observer the last of many drinks. Pouring the contents of the poisoned cup down Claudius's throat, after sticking him with the poisoned sword, Hamlet will complete the process of death that began before the play started when Claudius poured poison into the ear of Hamlet's father. With this completion, Hamlet can now die, and death will be "felicity." But this last rush of activity to completion comes after Hamlet's contemplation of Yorick's skull, what has become a sentimentalized emblem of the play, having captured the popular imagination; but popularity notwithstanding, it is the most potent image of Hamlet's condition.

As he looks at Yorick's skull, Hamlet recalls his past, with father alive and mother doting on him, with song and merriment in the air. But now, *now*, looking at the skull makes his gorge to rise. The nausea caused by the visible and touchable representation of death—how Hamlet dwells on the features, as if he wishes to force himself to puke—surely recalls the nausea he felt when he contemplated his mother's and all women's sexual appetite. Death and sexuality come together in Hamlet's words to Yorick's skull: "Now get you to my lady's chamber and tell her, let her paint an inch thick, to this favor she must come—make her laugh at that." Hamlet had already visited the lady's chamber, and there he told his mother all that was breaking his heart. There in the bedroom he disgorged his sexual nausea, answering her question "What have I done?" by making her see the sheer physicality of her sexual union with the satyr Claudius, what seems to be disturbing him most.

> Such an act
> That blurs the grace and blush of modesty,
> Calls virtue hypocrite, takes off the rose
> From the fair forehead of an innocent love,

And sets a blister there—makes marriage vows
As false as dicers' oaths.
(3.4. 40–45)

         Nay, but to live
In the rank sweat of an enseamed bed,
Stewed in corruption, honeying and making love
Over the nasty sty—
(3.4. 91–94)

There in the bedroom he made his mother see herself as belonging to the nunnery-brothel where he sent Ophelia, where he would send all women, the proper home for all the diseased in Hamlet's world, including Claudius, who first reveals his guilt by referring to "the harlot's cheek, beautied with plastering art."[5] There Hamlet killed Polonius, thinking he was Claudius, for who else would be in his mother's bedroom? And there, while Hamlet is ranting on Gertrude's bestial sexuality, death enters the bedroom in the form of his father's ghost. For the only time in the play, the mother, father, and son are together, but how different from their togetherness of the past, when the mother and father were loving, and the son, happily in the sun, still had illusions about life and love. Now, Father— the father who *belongs* in the mother's bedroom—comes to "whet" Hamlet's "almost blunted purpose," revenge, *and* to stop his condemnation of Gertrude, for whom he still cares, it seems, and who remains the puzzling center of affection for all her men. But now Mother cannot see Father, who may be a figment of Hamlet's imagination in this scene although his presence was very real in the first movement of the play. The lady's chamber is on Hamlet's mind as he talks to Yorick, for in that chamber death and sex come together powerfully and unequivocally, the scene itself a culmination of a series of scenes in which death and sexuality are connected. This connection is made not only in the play's first movement, already discussed, but also when Hamlet's "To be or not to be" soliloquy is immediately followed by the "nunnery" scene, itself a rehearsal for the bedroom scene, and in the "praying" scene, where Claudius reacts to the killing of his brother and stresses the importance of Gertrude, and where Hamlet, as he hovers over the praying Claudius, dwells on murderous thoughts, hoping to kill Claudius when he is "drunk asleep" or "in the incestuous pleasure of his bed." So vitally connected is death and sexuality in the fabric of the play and in Hamlet's diseased imagination that Hamlet's delay surely must be based in part on his inability to separate the two. That is, to avenge his father's murder he must of necessity confront his mother's sexuality; it seems that he can only do the former when he has purged himself of thoughts of the latter. Only when his mother is dead at his feet does Hamlet kill Claudius, not once but twice, by sword and cup.

Hamlet looking at Yorick's skull remembers a former time, the happy past, as he now contemplates the present, which is filled with death and sexuality, only to realize that the past was illusion, its gaiety hid treachery and adultery, cosmetics covered the ulcer. He looks at his past—illusion—compares it with the present—reality—and realizes that reality was there in the past too, but not seen by him, a reality so powerful that it controls his present and will control his future. With past controlling present and future, Hamlet is truly "born" to his condition in a world he did not make and in a world he did not understand. Now, by act 5, he has confronted death and sex, the pervasive conditions of the world he inhabits, and although puzzled by causes and still questioning—"Dost thou think Alexander looked o' this fashion i' the earth?"—he seems to understand that his life is controlled, that necessity forces one to play roles in life, and that if you are Prince Hamlet the role-playing ends only at the final curtain of death, itself the final necessity. "The rest is silence." The play's whole movement is toward death, and the genesis of that movement is the death of a father and the death of the illusion of pure love between man and woman. Death is so pervasive that it becomes the play's central mystery. *Hamlet* is the most discussed and popular play in the tragic tradition precisely because it confronts what puzzles us all, what fills us with doubt, what we must come to terms with in order to be free. It not only presents verbal questions and doubts, but dramatizes the primal experiences that touch the core of our darkest selves: the death of a loved one, the return of a dead father, the love for a sexual mother, the visit to her bedroom, the fight in a grave, the sea journey to death, the abyss into which we hauntedly look and which threatens madness, the watch on a dark fortification at the edge of the world shouting "Who's there?"

The play offers us many determinisms—man's nature, the past, fortune, fate, divinity, death—to be named but never fully understood. The Player-King's words in the Mousetrap succinctly point to a general view of man's relationship with destiny: "Our wills and fates do so contrary run / That our devices still are overthrown, / Our thoughts are ours, their ends none of our own" (3.2. 221–23). This Hamlet comes to realize toward the end of the play, before his fateful duel with Laertes. From the beginning of the play and his return from Wittenberg, Hamlet is filled with fundamental doubts about everything he thought he once knew. He is emotionally shocked, and, being an intellectual, he tries to answer some basic questions about life, to find reasons for his present condition. The famous "To be or not to be" soliloquy is only one among many utterances that prod this condition. The precise meaning of the soliloquy, which many see as the central speech of the play, has been deeply disputed, but whatever view we hold of its complex ideas, of this we are certain: the soliloquy brilliantly brings forth unresolvable questions, essential questions on life and death, questions so dark that the answers must remain secret. These questions, in the play's middle, are prompted by Hamlet's deepfelt emotion, his turbulent consciousness. Finally, however, in the play's end—after killing Polonius, after disgorging his sexual nausea, after sending Rosencrantz and Guildenstern to death, after his contemplation of Yorick, after his heightened speech in Ophelia's grave—Hamlet seems to give up looking for answers or reasons or causes, recognizing and acknowledging the dark determinism at work in his life and in all men's lives. Only at the play's end, after his life has accumulated evidence of this determinism, do his intellect and emotion come together at a point of balance or rest. Until then, intellectual though he is, his whole being seems to be possessed by emotion, especially disgust, nausea, contempt of others and self. Now, in the play's last scene, he is able to tell Horatio, "There's a divinity that shapes our ends, / Roughhew them how we will." And he is able to squelch the sick, foreboding feeling in his heart at the thought of the proposed duel with Laertes with these words: "We defy augury. There's special providence in the fall of a sparrow. If it be now, 'tis not to come; if it be not to come, it will be now; if it be not now, yet it will come. The readiness is all." Hamlet has discovered through his felt experience and his intellectual probing that men's "fates" are often controlled by forces outside their "wills." He realizes—and this is why Nietzsche believed that Hamlet resembles Dionysian man—that man's "action cannot change the eternal nature of things," and, in fact, that action demands illusion, so that the man who truly perceives that something is shaping our lives cannot really act. Hamlet, in short, has discovered the "terrible truth" of man's determined existence, the terror of the secret cause.[6] Those critics who believe that Hamlet's stoical words suggest a humble faith in the Christian God or a belief in the world's order or a realization of the rightness of things are drawing from the words more than the words offer.[7] A play filled with questions and doubts should make us wary of assertions that are too positive. ("There are more things in Heaven and earth, Horatio, / Than are dreamt of in your philosophy.") All that we can say with assurance is that Hamlet's words here and his experience throughout the play posit a determinism of some kind or determinisms of many kinds, but it is as impossible to articulate the particular kind of determinism as it is to go beyond the reaches of the soul. Hamlet seems calmer as he faces death, not because he has confidence that he is doing God's work and not because he has experienced a religious conversion, but rather because he is facing the fact of determinism, the fact of mystery, finally realizing that he, like each of us, is playing in someone else's play, that there is no escape from this condition, and that the best he can do is be ready for the right cues. Hamlet's catharsis, therefore, comes from accepting the mystery, which is a kind of mastery over mystery. He now knows that life's essential questions cannot be answered, that the mysterious core of life is nonrational. Revenge, then, although still a necessity for Hamlet, is no longer a pressing necessity. The readiness to avenge is important to him, but immediate revenge is not. It is interesting and paradoxical that once Hamlet accepts the nonimmediacy of his task, he is *immediately* swept to his revenge, surely the final manifestation of determinism, producing the play's satisfying closure.

If anything is clear in this complex play that must continue to puzzle the will, it is that the questions have no answers, the doubts remain doubts, and the causes remain secret. Let us give Shakespeare credit for wanting to have it that way. He is always careful to manipulate our responses. That we end with the question mark and silence is the effect he desires, which should come as no surprise since question and doubt and secrecy are part of the play's texture and therefore part of the play's meaning. *Hamlet* is a play about a young man's look into the abyss of the past (life and love turned to death and lust, ideal relationships turned rotten, certainties turned to doubts), of the present (challenges impossible to meet quickly because they are part of a world of questions), and of the future (death). The abyss is dark and deep and mysterious. As Hamlet and we look into it, hearing the roaring sea beneath, he and we realize the impossibility of sounding its depth or recognizing the hidden soul beneath.

How different a reaction when we hear the sea in Tom Stoppard's *Rosencrantz and Guildenstern Are Dead*. The third act opens in pitch darkness to "soft sea sounds." The voices of Rosencrantz and Guildenstern pierce the darkness with the kind of dialogue Stoppard offers throughout—"Is that you?" "Yes." "How do you know?" As they talk, the sound of the sea builds to the point where Rosencrantz and Guildenstern realize they are on a boat. Darkness and the sound of the sea lead not to mystery but to the clear recognition that the sea is a literal sea. The sea in *Rosencrantz and Guildenstern Are Dead* offers no sea change and suggests no hidden soul. A waterway rather than a haunting symbol, the sea takes Rosencrantz and Guildenstern to their deaths. The "Dead" of the title is the key word in the play. Not only are Rosencrantz and Guildenstern going to their deaths, but for Stoppard the two characters, representing modern man, *are* dead, although seemingly alive. They died their off-stage deaths in Shakespeare's *Hamlet* and therefore must die here, victims of a literary determinism. But they also are men, and men must die. The twin issues of death and determinism that inform Shakespeare's *Hamlet* also inform this play derived from *Hamlet*. However, to move from *Hamlet* to *Rosencrantz and Guildenstern Are Dead* is to move from tragedy to something else, because Stoppard's play, brilliant though it is, does not allow us to feel the secret cause; it touches the mind, not the heart. In it the mystery is not felt experience.

A derivative play, correctly characterized by Robert Brustein as a "theatrical parasite,"[8] *Rosencrantz and Guildenstern Are Dead* feeds not only on Shakespeare's *Hamlet* but on Pirandello's *Six Characters in Search of an Author* and on Beckett's *Waiting for Godot*. Stoppard goes to Shakespeare for his characters, for the background to his play's action, and for some direct quotations; to Pirandello for the idea of giving extra-dramatic life to established characters; to Beckett for the tone of some scenes, the philosophical thrust, and for some comic routines. The play takes Shakespeare's Rosencrantz and Guildenstern—time-servers, who appear rather cool and calculat-

ing in Shakespeare, and whose names indicate the courtly deca-
dence they may represent—and transforms them into garrulous,
sometimes simple, often rather likable chaps. Baffled, imprisoned in
a play they did not write, Rosencrantz and Guildenstern must act
out their prearranged dramatic destinies. Like Beckett's Vladimir
and Estragon, they carry on vaudeville routines, engage in verbal
battles and games, and discourse on the issues of life and death.
However, whereas Beckett's play, like Shakespeare's, defies easy
categories and explanations, and remains elusive in the best sense of
the word, suggesting the mystery of life, Stoppard's play welcomes
categories, prods for a clarity of explanation, and seems more interested in substance than shadow.

Stoppard's play is conspicuously intellectual; it "thinks" a great
deal about the issues dramatized in both *Hamlet* and *Waiting for
Godot*—appearance vs. reality, identity, life as play and men as players, is someone watching?—and these issues are pondered against
the backdrop of determinism and death. Displaying a refreshingly
clear understanding of Hamlet's condition, Stoppard pits the condition of Rosencrantz and Guildenstern against that of the melancholy
Dane. Shakespeare's Hamlet is a prince, absolutely connected with
a state, forced to play a burdensome part in someone else's play but
understanding that he is a prince and grudgingly acknowledging
the action he must perform. Rosencrantz and Guildenstern merely
"swell a progress," to use T. S. Eliot's phrase for the Prufrocks of
this world; they question their identity ("Who are we?" "Who do
you think we are?") and do not wish to perform the parts they too
must play ("Why us?"). They were not "born" to set things right.
They were born to die, and this kind of mortality—not connected
with a large action ("Incidents! All we get is incidents! Dear God, is it
too much to expect a little sustained action?!")[9]—reflects the absurdity of their condition. In *Hamlet* we hear that "the time is out of
joint"; in *Rosencrantz and Guildenstern Are Dead* we hear the cliché,
"times being what they are." "The time" vs. "times," action vs. incidents, I vs. us—these separate Shakespeare's hero from Stoppard's
nonheroes. Yet, the difference between the two conditions and the
two worlds of the play does not altogether account for the differences in genres, since our "times" can produce tragedy, since action
can acquire a wide enough interpretation to include "incidents,"
and since the questioning of self surely belongs in tragedy. And
death and determinism inform both the Elizabethan play and the

modern play. Smaller men though they are, Rosencrantz and Guildenstern, like Hamlet, are men forced to play a part, traveling on a journey to death. It is precisely because Stoppard's play touches Shakespeare's *Hamlet* in so many and different ways that it offers a valuable contrast, allowing us to realize more fully the importance to tragedy of the secret cause.

Hamlet holding Yorick's skull is the emblematic objectification of what has been happening inside Hamlet throughout the play. Living with death every minute of his life since his return from Wittenberg, his encounter with the material skull in the literal graveyard reveals on the outside what Hamlet has been feeling in the graveyard of his soul, that "within which passeth show." Stoppard's Rosencrantz and Guildenstern carry death with them too; in fact, as the play progresses, they become obsessed with death. But their obsession is merely mental, the soul never reached, the without never leading to within. Stoppard does not root the intellectual in felt experience, does not fuse the thinking with feeling. This must be considered a shortcoming in Stoppard's dramatic art, especially if that art aims for a tragic representation of man. One problem, of course, is Stoppard's idiom, which is not rich enough to sustain a direct confrontation with the large issues of life and death. Consider, for example, Guildenstern's question: "The only beginning is birth and the only end is death—if you can't count on that, what can you count on?" Put in this pedestrian way, the idea behind the question loses its force. Or take Guildenstern's remarks on death: "Dying is not romantic, and death is not a game which will soon be over. . . . Death is not anything . . . death is not. . . . It's the absence of presence, nothing more . . . the endless time of never coming back . . . a gap you can't see, and when the wind blows through it, it makes no sound. . . ." Examples of this kind of direct philosophical probing can be found throughout the play. We hear a man talking but do not feel the pressure of death behind the words. The passage seems false because the language does not possess the elusiveness and economy that are essential if a writer wishes to confront large issues directly.

Perhaps a more important consideration—one that reveals the essential deficiency of Stoppard as a tragic dramatist but also his distinctiveness as a brilliant modern playwright—is Stoppard's relationship to the play he is writing, his *stance* as a dramatist. According to Stoppard himself, his play was "not written as a response to anything about alienation in our times. . . . It would be fatal to set out to write primarily on an intellectual level. Instead, one writes about human beings under stress—whether it is about losing one's trousers or being nailed to the cross."[10] Stoppard's words run counter to our experience of the play and indicate once again that writers are not the best judges of their own writing. Like all writers of drama, Stoppard wishes to present human beings under stress, but he does so in the most intellectual way. In fact, there is only one level in the play, one kind of stance, and that level is intellectual. The audience witnesses no forceful sequence of narrative, since the story is known and therefore already solidified in the audience's mind. One could say that the audience is given not sequence but status quo, and status quo points to a "critical" stance—a way of looking at the events of the play as a critic would, that is, experiencing the play as structure, complete, unmoving, unsequential.

In the act of seeing a stage play, which moves in time, we are in a precritical state, fully and actively engaged in the play's events. When the play is over, then we become critics, seeing the play as a structural unity and, in fact, able to function as critics only because the play has stopped moving.[11] In the act of seeing *Rosencrantz and Guildenstern Are Dead*, however, our critical faculty is not subdued. We are always *observing* the characters and are not ourselves participating. Not witnessing a movement in time, we are forced to contemplate the frozen state, the status quo, of the characters who carry their Shakespearean fates with them. It is *during* Stoppard's play that we function as critics, just as Stoppard, through his characters, functions as critic within the play. It is precisely the critical stance of Stoppard and his characters and his audience that prevents *Rosencrantz and Guildenstern Are Dead* from being a tragedy, even though death and determinism, those tragic ingredients, are essential to the play.

Stoppard's critical posture depends heavily on the play idea, the mask, the game, the show. Not only is the entire *Rosencrantz and Guildenstern Are Dead* a play within a play that Shakespeare has written, but throughout Stoppard uses the idea of play. Rosencrantz and Guildenstern, and of course the Player, are conscious of themselves as players, acting out their lives, and baffled, even anguished, by the possibility that no one is watching the performance. All the world is a stage for Stoppard, as for Shakespeare, but Shakespeare's art fuses world and stage, causing the barriers between what is real and what is acted to break down, while Stoppard's art separates the two, makes us observers and critics of the stage, and allows us to see the world through the stage, ever conscious that we are doing just that. The last is my crucial point: Stoppard forces us to be conscious observers of a play frozen before us in order that it may be examined critically. Consequently, what the play offers us, despite its seeming complexity and the virtuosity of Stoppard's technique, is clarity, intellectual substance, rather than the shadows and mystery that we find in *Hamlet* or the pressure of life's absurdity that we find in *Waiting for Godot*. Of course, we miss these important aspects of great drama, and some critics and reviewers have correctly alluded to the play's deficiencies in these respects,[12] but we should not allow what is lacking to erase what is there—bright, witty, intellectual criticism and high theatricality.

However, the praiseworthy intellectual clarity eliminates the complexities and ambiguities we associate with the death and determinism of tragedy. The determinism in *Hamlet* is rooted in darkness, and death, itself an inscrutable thing, is part of the felt experience of the play. Stoppard's determinism is the concrete image of a ship plowing its way toward death: "Where we went wrong was getting on a boat. We can move, of course, change direction, rattle about, but our movement is contained within a larger one that carries us along as inexorably as the wind and current . . ." (p. 122). The truth of this statement need not be argued (for who would disagree?), but so concrete an image, so clean an idea, erases the terror we associate with that journey into night. Stoppard forces us to reflect on man's absurd condition, as man travels toward the grave. Shakespeare forces us to experience the grave within Hamlet. The trapped condition of Rosencrantz and Guildenstern is man's condition; the condition of Hamlet is his own as well as everyman's—the anguish and nausea are his first, and ours afterward. And death is attached to the inner man, Hamlet. In Stoppard's play, death is concept, the object of cool speculation.

> *Ros.* Do you ever think of yourself as actually *dead*, lying in a box with a lid on it?
> *Guil.* No.
> *Ros.* Nor do I, really. . . . It's silly to be depressed by it. I mean one thinks of it like being *alive* in a box, one keeps forgetting to take into account the fact that one is *dead* . . . which should

make all the difference . . . shouldn't it? I mean, you'd never *know* you were in a box, would you? It would be just like being *asleep* in a box. Not that I'd like to sleep in a box, mind you, not without any air—you'd wake up dead, for a start, and then where would you be? Apart from inside a box. That's the bit I don't like, frankly. That's why I don't think of it. . . .
(p. 70)

Later, Guildenstern says: "Death followed by eternity . . . the worst of both worlds. It *is* a terrible thought." *Saying* it is, however, does not make it so. To feel the terror, an audience must receive the thoughts on death from the lips of an anguished character who is sick at heart and perhaps sick of mind. Stoppard comes closest to giving Guildenstern a genuine tragic anguish when Guildenstern, who all along has shown contempt for the players and for their cheap melodrama in presenting scenes of death, becomes so filled with vengeance and scorn that he snatches the dagger from the Player's belt and threatens the Player:

I'm talking about death—and you've never experienced *that*. And you cannot *act* it. You die a thousand casual deaths—with none of that intensity which squeezes out life . . . and no blood runs cold anywhere. Because even as you die you know that you will come back in a different hat. But no one gets up after *death*—there is no applause—there is only silence and some second-hand clothes, and that's *death*. (p. 123)

He then stabs the Player, who "with huge, terrible eyes, clutches at the wound as the blade withdraws: he makes small weeping sounds and falls to his knees, and then right down." Hysterically, Guildenstern shouts: "If we have a destiny, then so had he—and if this is ours, then that was his—and if there are no explanations for us, then let there be none for him—." At which point the other players on stage applaud the Player, who stands up, modestly accepts the admiration of his fellow tragedians, and proceeds to show Guildenstern how the blade of the dagger pushed into the handle. Here we seem to witness, for the only time in the play, an act being performed, a choice being made, not dictated by the events of Shakespeare's play, *and* a character whose innerness has forced him into a genuine individual gesture, only to discover that we have witnessed playing, theater. Guildenstern and Rosencrantz are taken in by the performance of a false death, bearing out the Player's belief, stated earlier in the play, that audiences believe *only* false deaths, that when he once had an actor, condemned for stealing, really die on stage the death was botched and unbelievable. What we have in Guildenstern's "killing" of the Player, therefore, is a theatrical re-enforcement of the earlier observations on audiences by the Player as critic. As we spectators watch the event—Rosencrantz had remarked earlier that he feels "like a spectator"—we intellectually grasp the fact that we had no real action, that no choice was made, Stoppard thereby making his philosophical point indirectly and with fine effect. In Stoppard a condition of life is most clearly understood, it seems, only when reflected in a critical, theatrical mirror. His only attempt to give a character's inner scream a tragic action is cerebralized and muffled by the coolness of his critical stance, by the *point* he wishes to make. When Guildenstern makes his point about death, it seems to be Stoppard's too: "It's just a man failing to reappear, that's all—now you see him, now you don't. . . ." A quick clean exit, exactly the kind that Rosencrantz and Guildenstern make at the end of the play—"Now you see me, now you——"

In *Rosencrantz and Guildenstern Are Dead* we do not have the kind of theater characterized by such phrases as "direct involvement," "emotional," "precritical," "theater of the heart," but rather a theater of criticism, intellectual, distanced, of the mind. In a very real sense, Stoppard is an artist-critic writing drama for audience-critics, a dramatist least effective when he points his finger directly at the existential dilemma—"What does it all add up to?"—and most effective when he confronts the play *Hamlet* and Elizabethan drama and theatrical art, thereby going roundabout to get to the important issues. Stoppard's play, because it feeds on both an Elizabethan tragedy and a modern tragicomedy, gives us the opportunity to consider the larger context of modern drama, especially Joseph Wood Krutch's well-known and ominous observations on the death of tragedy and his prediction of the devolution of tragedy from Religion to Art to Document.[13] Krutch receives an interesting answer, I believe, in *Rosencrantz and Guildenstern Are Dead*. Using Krutch's words, but not in the way he uses them, we can say that *Rosencrantz and Guildenstern Are Dead* is art that studies art, and thereby serves as a document—dramatic criticism as play presenting ideas on *Hamlet*, on Elizabethan drama, on theatrical art—and by so doing commenting on the life that art reveals. That is, Stoppard's play is holding the mirror up to the art that holds the mirror up to nature.

This double image causes the modern audience to take the kind of stance often associated with satire. And yet, Stoppard's play cannot be called satirical, for it makes no attempt to encourage the audience into any kind of action, as do Brecht's plays, or to cause the audience to change the way things are. The play examines the way things are, or, more precisely stated, it intellectually confronts the condition of man as player and the world as theater. By the pressure of its *critical* energy, the play awakens in the audience a recognition of man's condition, not in order to change that condition, but to see it clearly. In short, by presenting a theatrical, artistic document, Stoppard makes us think—the words "document" and "think" pointing to the modernity and particular value of *Rosencrantz and Guildenstern Are Dead* as well as to its impoverishment as tragedy. The play presents not revelation but criticism, not passionate art—Hamlet in the graveyard—but cool, critical, intellectual art—Hamlet playing with the recorders. *Rosencrantz and Guildenstern Are Dead*, in its successful moments, brilliantly displays the virtues of theater of criticism,[4] and perhaps shows the direction in which some modern drama will be going—"times being what they are"—but it is a direction clearly nontragic because death and determinism have lost their haunting quality and the secrecy of the cause is never felt.

5 BOUNDARY SITUATION

King Lear & Waiting for Godot

"Re-enter Lear, with Cordelia dead in his arms" is the most terrifying moment in Shakespearean drama, and perhaps in all drama.
Like Hamlet holding the skull, King Lear holding the dead Cordelia
is an emblem, an image pressing against our imaginations with such
pain and urgency that for us, as for those on stage, this is "the
promised end" or "image of that horror." The difference between
Hamlet's posture and Lear's points to the considerable difference in
texture of the two tragedies. A young prince is holding his dead
past, and philosophizing. An old king is holding his dead present,
and howling. The excruciating image is like all of *King Lear*, which
grips us with such immediacy and power that critics have been
forced to state that Shakespeare was fully and inevitably committed
to its creation. As if Shakespeare himself had come, like Lear, to a
boundary situation; as if Shakespeare, like Gloucester, was peering
into an abyss from the edge of a cliff. The play is so painful that
Samuel Johnson could not read the last scene until he had to edit the
play, so brutal that from 1681 to 1838 Nahum Tate's romanticized
version—with King Lear alive at the end, and with Cordelia the new
queen and Edgar the king—held the stage and pleased the audiences. The intensity of response, the pain and the horror, derive, I
believe, from two basic sources—the play's immediacy and the nature of Lear's passionate experience. And both sources touch the secret cause.

   In no other Shakespearean tragedy is the sheer present, the *now-
ness*, felt so urgently. Hamlet looks back; Macbeth looks ahead;
Othello and Antony look back and ahead. King Lear lives only in the
present. He seems to have no past, and that he has no future makes
the last moments of the play so unbearable that many critics posit an

afterlife for Lear, his eyes looking upward as he gets ready to join his angelic Cordelia. The mind produces its own defenses to protect itself. But the end of *King Lear* is the end of King Lear, and that is a fact that must be faced.

We hear not one word about Lear's younger years or about his wife, the mother of the two pelican daughters and the one daughter who redeems nature. (Even Shylock had a Leah who gave him a ring when he was a bachelor.) We hear nothing of the courtships of Goneril and Regan; we see them at their husbands' sides as mature women, with no hint offered that they had childhoods. (The most childlike child in the play is King Lear, for "old fools are babes again"; Lear, according to the Fool, has become the child to his mother-daughters and must now pull down his breeches to be spanked. Cordelia is also a "child" to the purged Lear. And the riddling, playful Fool is often childlike. But all of these are in the play's present.) The courtship of Cordelia takes place in the present, before our eyes. In the Lear story, then, what we see is what we get. In the Gloucester story, however, there are references to the past, always a sexual past—Gloucester flippantly telling Kent in the play's opening lines that he had an adulterous affair which produced his bastard son Edmund, and Edmund in soliloquy pleased with the nature of his bastardizing, with the forbidden act "in the lusty stealth of nature" which gave him his fierce quality. The sexual past causes the terrible present of the Gloucester story: "The dark and vicious place where thee he got / Cost him his eyes." Painful as that story is, it does not possess the concrete immediacy of the Lear story, one of many important differences between the parallel overplot and underplot. We confront the Lear story head-on; everything in it is self-contained. And the "Nothing" of that story's beginning relentlessly leads to the "no more" and "Never" of its end. Between beginning and end we witness what is happening on this great stage of fools; we see a man stretched on the rack of this tough world. The crying since birth is happening now; the hand of mortality is smelling now; a precious daughter is as dead as earth now. We urgently "feel" the weight of "this sad time"; "our present business" is woe. The absence of past and future, the this-ness and now-ness, give the Lear story a compelling immediacy.

So too does its emphasis on essentials, on the *physical* nature of man's being and predicament. An autocratic king, robed and furred, gives away everything in the first scene. In the play's central situation he wanders on a heath in a storm, exposed to the elements, in need of sleep and shelter. He feels what "poor naked wretches" feel; he has taken "physic." His loyal follower, Kent, is sent into exile, but returns in disguise to wander with the king who banished him; he too is exposed and searches for a hovel for shelter. A blind Gloucester enters the Lear story on the heath; he must feel his way through life, guided by his son Edgar, who takes on the disguise of a Tom o' Bedlam, as low a creature as a man can be without becoming a beast. And the Fool, although realizing that one should let go of a big wheel that is rolling downhill, stays with that wheel and becomes exposed to the pitiless storm, always wishing to go inside but remaining outside, forever the physical embodiment of the play's dialectic. The central storm scenes dramatize the exposure of Lear, Kent, Gloucester, Edgar, and the Fool, an exposure that prods philosophical utterances and inner anguish, but which is, on the first level of significance, physical. This must be stressed because the critical tendency—taking a cue from Lear himself—is to discuss only the inner storm, thereby reducing, I believe, the complexity of Shakespeare's presentation. The pressure of the physical remains at the center of our consciousness throughout the play. Not only the need for protection from a storm, the search for a hovel, the necessity of sleep, food, and clothing in the heath scenes—all terribly physical—but those other scenes and moments which stress the physical: Kent in the stocks; the on-stage blinding of Gloucester; the fetching of whites of eggs to soothe bleeding eyes; an Old Man's mission to get a covering for a naked Bedlam; the mortal wounding of Cornwall and of Edmund; the killing of Oswald; the cramps of Regan; the bodies of the dead Goneril and Regan dragged on stage (a significant reversal of the usual Elizabethan stage procedure of dragging bodies *off* stage); Lear's carrying the dead Cordelia; even the need to undo a button. What we witness in the play's middle and end is raw experience, not covered by the veneer of symbolism or civilization (as is the play's beginning), experience that prods us to think, of course, of larger, higher things, like justice and the gods, but never allowing us to forget the primacy and immediacy of the physical. So persistent is Shakespeare's emphasis on the flesh,[1] on the body, on the body's needs, on "the thing itself," that it must be the informing focus of any large interpretation of the play. So great is the concentration on man and what he essentially is, so relentlessly is man ground down to his roots—"a poor, bare, forked animal"—that we become indifferent to the outside battle between England and France and to the political ramifications of the action. It matters little "who loses and who wins, who's in, who's out," and the reference to the "gored state" at the play's end seems a token gesture. As if "the mystery of things," as Lear puts it, can only be confronted when the cosmic becomes more and more micro.

Shakespeare is dramatizing human existence by having his main character confront the thing itself. Instead of a speculative young prince uttering "To be or not to be," an old active king is experiencing what it is to be, and in terms of the play, to *be* is such an agony that it is no small accomplishment to endure. However, to *merely* endure does not seem "high" enough an action for most commentators, who attach to endurance systems of belief—from Christianity to absurdism[2]—which go *beyond* the physical and the now. But in *King Lear* Shakespeare—and this is why the tragedy is his most painful and powerful—is confronting life on its own terms, with no covering, no mask, and no recourse to systems of belief that push essential life beyond itself. References to the gods are many, and, of course, we are dealing with a Christian dramatist writing for a Christian audience, so that allusions to Christianity are present, especially in connection with Cordelia—but these supernatural solicitings are presented only to be negated *in the play*. Paradoxically, *King Lear* is beyond the gods, even beyond Fate, precisely because its focus is so microcosmic. Shakespeare seems to be telling us: make no mistake, I am holding my mirror up to the thing itself, to this life and nothing beyond life. Can he make this any more clear than by having Lear carry on stage the dead Cordelia immediately after Albany says: "The gods defend her"? Again and again we are brought back to the physical as an answer to the metaphysical. We are forced to dwell on "the art of our necessities," here and now, confronting experience on its own brutal terms. How comforting it is to justify existence, to redeem its agony, by going beyond it. The play, however, allows for no such comfort. It offers another kind of comfort, deeper and truer, the comfort that comes when we face the fact of an existence that is self-contained, inclusive, and—without the framework of higher symbolic or philosophical systems—intrinsically mysterious. In *King Lear* we seem to be looking directly at Dionysus; Apollo is not there to protect us, just as he was not there to protect King Lear who called for him in the play's beginning. To face Dionysus and endure—as does our representative Lear, ever-ripening—is its own high justification. It is not nothing; it is all.

Gods are presented by Shakespeare in order to be denied. But not just the gods. Reversals abound in *King Lear,* and that is why the phrase "handy-dandy" can be extracted from the play in order to apply it to the play.[3] I shall not rehearse the many instances of handy-dandy in action and in phrase. It is enough to state that the image of life that the play presents rests on capriciousness and gratuitousness, on reversals of expectations which produce charged dramatic moments. Witness Cordelia as she says "Nothing," for which we are prepared but Lear is not. Witness the sudden banishment of Kent. Witness the easy duping of both Gloucester and Edgar by Edmund. Witness the sudden violence of Gloucester's blinding (containing the brutal gratuitousness of Regan's request to Cornwall to put out "the other too"). Witness the surprising "good" action, especially in the context of animal evil, of the servant who mortally wounds Cornwall. And equally surprising is the action of a repentant Edmund who, dying, wishes to do "some good." In short, the play repeatedly forces us to experience the surprising or shocking moment of action, more immediate and more mysterious because unprepared for. The most devastating moment, of course, is Lear's entrance with the dead Cordelia—after Edmund says he will do some good, and after Albany says "The gods defend her." Edmund's "good" comes too late and the gods are not there or not listening. So sudden, so capricious, so gratuitous are the actions—both good and evil—that no statement in the play can explain them. They can only prod such a question as Lear's "Is there any cause in nature that makes these hard hearts?" To which we can add: "Is there any cause in nature that makes these good hearts?" And these questions can only be answered by some such phrase as Cordelia's "no cause" or James Joyce's "secret cause."

In a world of unexpected action, the statement "As flies to wanton boys are we to the gods, / They kill us for their sport" seems like the perfect philosophical gem to explain what is happening in the play, a gem so attractive that the romantic Swinburne and the modern Jan Kott, Peter Brook, and Martin Esslin have grasped it as the key to the play. But this pithy statement must be rejected as the explanation, as must every aphoristic utterance that seems like truth. "Ripeness is all." No. Not all, for we cannot believe that Cordelia is ripe for death unless we eliminate the connotation of physical maturity from the word "ripeness," which we cannot do in a play that stresses the physical. "Reason is madness." Not always, for in madness Lear denies the existence of human love, which he will discover anew in moments of sanity. Edgar, who utters most of the charged phrases, Edgar, the play's philosopher as well as Lear's "noble philosopher" and "learned Theban," himself denies or rejects his own philosophical utterances in the face of his agonizing experience as witness. At the bitter end of the play, this young man—whose aphorisms, like all aphorisms, seemed so loaded with truth—is more restrained, more modest:

The weight of this sad time we must obey,
Speak what we feel, not what we ought to say.
The oldest hath borne most. We that are young
Shall never see so much, nor live so long.

In short, we cannot cling to any one statement to explain life's experience, and we cannot be sure of anything, a condition that brings to mind Oedipus and Hamlet, and the Lear who *thought* he could travel to death unburdened, who *thought* he was ague-proof, who *thought* that he and Cordelia would never be parted. That suffering brings wisdom is a characteristic of tragedy; the largest wisdom *King Lear* offers is that no one statement about life can hold, that the question mark must persist and confound. The play has many imperatives, but the interrogative remains most potent, as always in tragedy.[4]

In fact, the play can be described as Lear's progress from imperative *to* interrogative, from the firm ground of a palace to an unlocalized chaotic heath, from a sure sense of self to a confrontation with mystery. That is, Lear's movement in the play is toward the most terrifying boundary situation possible, the abyss of himself. In this respect, as in so many others, Gloucester's movement and predicament literally echoes Lear's. Shakespeare brings Gloucester to his brink by physically stationing him at the edge of an imaginary cliff at Dover. His despair, the result of physical blinding and spiritual regret because of his treatment of Edgar, brings him to thoughts of suicide. Only the trickery of his good son—paralleling the trickery of his evil son, but here for the positive purpose of instilling hope—forces Gloucester to endure a little longer, to wait for a death less desperate. Technically troublesome, this scene at Dover often brings laughter to the audience, and has brought the influential Jan Kott to the conclusion that the scene presents Beckettian pantomime, pointing to Shakespeare's absurdist view of life. Kott seems not to notice that the imaginary leap changes a man's despair to hope, that the director of the scene is a purposeful Edgar. But the awkwardness of a man falling on the stage and thinking it is a great leap from the edge of a cliff does call attention to itself by its necessarily difficult staging, so difficult that we must believe Shakespeare recognized its difficulty and wanted it that way. (We need only look ahead to the more difficult lifting of a wounded Antony up to Cleopatra's monument to notice that Shakespeare wishes to call attention to the lifting itself, the movement upward, visually pointing to the nature of Cleopatra's "pull" throughout *Antony and Cleopatra*.) Shakespeare gives us a literal boundary situation for a literal, prosaic, outward, physical man. The moment may be terrible; the moment may be comical; the moment may be terrible becoming comical —in any case, it very literalness, its concreteness, is appropriate to the man *on* the edge. How different a boundary situation—with Shakespeare calculatingly designing the mirrors of reflection—for the larger, poetic, deeper Lear wandering on the heath.

The heath on which Lear roams, unlike Gloucester's imaginary cliff, has no edge. It is absolutely unlocalized, vague, bare, without landmarks, fully exposed to the storm, as "unaccommodated" as those wandering on it. A dark territory, this heath, so dark that it must be considered both a terranean reality and a subterranean reality, a landscape of the demonic, of Dionysus. In fact, this landscape is *all* boundary, where Lear is living at life's edge, forced to look at himself and at the world as he never did before, forced to ask the large questions about man's condition. Life at the edge is unequivocally terrible for Lear—as it is for Oedipus and Antigone and Phaedra and Hamlet—and it is richly complex. His experience on the boundary brings out the best and worst in this large man. His newly acquired selflessness—"In, boy, go first"—and his new awareness of man's physical needs—"Is man no more than this?"— and his deeper understanding of what love is: these are the positive wages of suffering, the discovery of a new humanity. But Lear's suffering also produces anger and rage, which Lear always possessed, but here tapped from a deeper source, and it gives rise to large utterances that deny justice and love, and it causes a sexual nausea more repellent than Hamlet's—is there a more gross representation of the womb than Lear's "There's Hell, there's darkness, there's the sulphurous pit, / Burning, scalding, stench, consumption, fie, fie,

fie! / Pah, pah! / Give me an ounce of civet, good apothecary, to sweeten my imagination"?—and it denies humanity in the ominous, revengeful repetition: "kill, kill, kill, kill, kill, kill!" In short, the experience of Lear on the heath, the abyss without and within, is passionate and inclusive—positive and negative, mad and sane, full. So full that we must be moved by his sheer capacity to endure both the physical hardships and the emotional extremes. His heart, containing pity and hatred, is bursting; his mind, possessed by dark madness (itself a boundary situation) and bright clarity, is also bursting. This pressure of heart and mind finds its most powerful expression in act 4, scene 6, when the mad Lear meets the blind Gloucester. Here the cruelty ("I remember thine eyes well enough. Dost thou squiny at me?") and the poignancy ("Oh, let me kiss that hand") are hardly bearable. Here too some of Lear's most important statements are given their clearest expression:

> They told me I was everything. 'Tis a lie, I am not ague-proof.
>
> A dog's obeyed in office.
>
> Robes and furred gowns hide all.
>
> Thou must be patient, we came crying hither.
> Thou knowest the first time that we smell the air,
> We wawl and cry.
>
> When we are born, we cry that we are come
> To this great stage of fools.

Edgar, the courtier-turned-beggar who is himself on the boundary between man and beast, gives voice to our thoughts as we witness the meeting of Lear and Gloucester: "I would not take this from report. It is, / And my heart breaks at it."

The central experience in Lear's burdensome journey toward death takes place on the heath, dark in itself and the place where dark and perturbing questions are prodded into expression. The autocratic king who demanded his dinner, the loud proclaimer of imperatives, has become everyman, not ague-proof, who asks elemental questions in a language stripped of embellishment. Even language can no longer wear robes.

> How dost, my boy? Art cold?
>
> Filial ingratitude!
> Is it not as this mouth should tear this hand

For lifting food to 't?

Is man no more than this?

What is the cause of thunder?

Is there any cause in nature that makes these hard hearts?

What was thy cause?
Adultery?

. . . handy-dandy, which is the Justice, which is the thief?

No rescue? What, a prisoner?

No seconds? All myself?

The play's darkest question, however, is asked by Lear after he has passed through his heath experience, when he is on another boundary, between life and death. After the respite that comes with sleep, after he has awakened to music and seen Cordelia, the "soul of bliss," after the kneeling and blessings and forgiveness, after love has provided a contentment that even prison cannot destroy, Lear's inhuman "Howl, howl, howl, howl!"—as he carries the dead Cordelia on stage—joltingly brings us back to the heath, the terrible heath of the soul, where an unanswered question exerts excruciating pressure: "Why should a dog, a horse, a rat, have life / And thou no breath at all? Thou'lt come no more, / Never, never, never, never, never!" The "nevers," those relentless trochees, force us to face the dark unequivocal finality of death, which offers—like the human experience of the play—nothing beyond itself. Whether Lear dies thinking Cordelia is alive—"Look on her, look, her lips, / Look there, look there!"—or knowing she is dead, whether he dies in comforting illusion or cruel reality (the focus of much critical debate) seems relatively unimportant, seems secondary to the primacy and finality of death. Death—which comes to both the evil and the good, which comes to the high and the low, which comes by way of violence or grief or joy or mere exhaustion, which must come, and once come, will come no more. The wonder is, as Kent asserts, that Lear has endured so long. Wonder and woe come together at the end of Shakespeare's most powerful tragedy, in which the inexplicable exerts its greatest pressure, in which the fact of mystery is painfully immediate (the culmination of all the sudden actions, the capricious and gratuitous and shocking moments, the reversals in action and language, the unanswered questions), in which the boundary is dizzying and dreadful. Lear carrying the dead Cordelia, kneeling (as he did once before, when she lived) in order to put his ears to her lips, hoping that she will say something, this lady-child who said "Nothing," focusing *all* his attention on the daughter who will "come no more" (that sexual word "come" allowing tragedy to touch once again the dark mystery of incest, as it did in *Oedipus Rex* and *Phaedra* and *Desire Under the Elms* and *Hamlet*), finally expiring with words that contain their own mystery—surely no other tragedy trembles so dangerously at the edge of the abyss. Shakespeare's potent art lays bare our deep ignorance and our pitiful vulnerability. His *King Lear* forces us to acknowledge the secrecy of the cause.

It would not surprise us if King Lear and the Fool met Samuel Beckett's Didi and Gogo on the heath. They do meet Edgar, disguised as the mad Tom o' Bedlam, a confrontation that has given seemingly strong support to Jan Kott's contention that Beckett can be found in Shakespeare. Edgar—an exile in a cruel world, disguised as the lowest of men in the order of nature, naked as the air that surrounds him, dirty as the road he tramps—fits most easily into a picture of the absurd and grotesque, so easily that Kott seems to misunderstand Edgar's larger purpose. For example, Kott denies Edgar the right to sustain "the gored state." "In *King Lear* there is no young and resolute Fortinbras to ascend the throne of Denmark."[5] There is no Fortinbras but there *is* Edgar who, as Shakespeare clearly indicates, will undertake the job of restoring the state. He, because of his symbolic disguise and his elemental life as Bedlam beggar, has suffered and witnessed the suffering of others. He is qualified to help restore harmony to a disordered world, if it can be restored at all; he has attained "ripeness."[6] Kott's ideas are provocative but he pushes so hard to find Beckett in Shakespeare that he sometimes forgets Shakespeare. Shakespeare, of course, contains potential Beckettism, just as Shakespeare contains a wide range of attitudes toward human existence. A more revealing, not to mention more logical, pursuit is to find Shakespeare in Beckett. And perhaps (Beckett's favorite word), *perhaps* the most revealing critical pursuit is to investigate the common ground on which both Shakespeare and Beckett meet. The atmosphere of tragedy hangs over that ground.

Certainly, Edgar (as Tom o' Bedlam) and Didi and Gogo belong on the heath, for all three represent the stripped quality of man, unaccommodated man, the thing itself. In *Waiting for Godot*, however, the heath is not the central scene, as it is in *King Lear;* it is the entire scene, the entire play. In fact, it is a scene presented in one act and then presented *again* in a second act. Beckett seems to be indicating there is nothing else. Another way of saying this is that in *Waiting for Godot* Beckett is dramatizing the condition of man, man frozen on the boundary, all heath, stasis. To recognize this point helps us to understand the basic difference in form between a Beckett play and a Shakespeare play—stasis vs. movement, condition vs. action— *and* it also makes more clear the similarity between *Waiting for Godot* and *King Lear* in evoking the feelings associated with tragedy. If we could imagine Lear and the Fool meeting Didi and Gogo in the beginning of *King Lear* and then meeting them *again* in the central heath scene, we would be close to the Pozzo-Lucky meetings with Didi and Gogo in the two acts of *Waiting for Godot.* The confident haughty Pozzo of act 1 becomes the helpless blind man of act 2; his last word "On"—the word of direction, the word for a journey— indicates his "progress" toward death, the tragic progression of Lear. But the frozen condition of Vladimir and Estragon is no less tragic. They are in a boundary situation, and they will remain there. They are exposed and vulnerable, and will remain so. The unanswered questions haunt them too. In short, moving or stationary, acting or waiting, king or tramp, Elizabethan or modern, tied to a macrocosm or merely tied to a friend, man facing mystery points to tragedy.

Admittedly, Beckett calls *Waiting for Godot* a "tragicomedy." Always a troublesome term, shifting its meaning through the ages, the word itself must be confronted. When Plautus first used the term in his prologue to *Amphitryon,* he was alluding to the mingling of gods (who belong to tragedy) and low characters like slaves (who belong in comedy). The Renaissance latched on to this "mingling" as the essence of tragicomedy, an irregular genre which blurred the neat classical distinctions between tragedy and comedy. When such a classicist as Sir Philip Sidney referred to the genre, he did so with contempt. For him, "mingling kings and clowns" produced "mongrel Tragi-comedy."[7] A formal definition was given to the term by John Fletcher in his letter "To the Reader" which prefaced *The Faithful Shepherdess:* "A tragi-comedy is not so called in respect of mirth and killing, but in respect it wants deaths, which is enough to make it no tragedy, yet brings some near it, which is enough to make it no comedy. . . ."[8] This definition points to the importance of endings.

Classically, a tragedy ends sadly, a comedy happily; a tragedy ends in death, a comedy in marriage. The tragicomedy that Beaumont and Fletcher wrote was "tragi" along the way but ended as "comedy." And with the years this kind of tragicomedy has been cultivated, with the greater emphasis placed on *how* exactly to manipulate a happy ending from seemingly tragic situations, an emphasis clearly recognizable in eighteenth-century sentimental comedy as well as in modern James Bond melodrama. But this is not the tragicomedy that modern dramatists are writing, nor do those modern writers who use the term take any cognizance of Plautus or Sidney or Fletcher. Ionesco, for example, says that in modern times "the comic is tragic, and . . . the tragedy of man is pure derision." He claims that for him there is no "difference" between "the comic and the tragic."[9] Friedrich Dürrenmatt, who labels his *The Visit* a tragicomedy, believes that in our time the tragic comes out of the comic, that comedy, in fact, brings forth the tragic "as a terrifying moment, as an abyss that opens suddenly."[10] His words "terrifying" and "abyss" traditionally belong to tragedy and indicate how difficult it is to state with any sense of exactness what modern tragicomedy is. Perhaps this is as it should be. "Times being what they are," a world without a center, essentially shapeless, must offer blurred terms for the dramatization of that world. Then again, perhaps the incomprehensibility of our modern world is the proper subject of tragedy. Yes, Beckett calls *Waiting for Godot* a "tragicomedy"; yes, the play contains much comedy—vaudeville turns, clever language, pratfalls, Laurel and Hardy routines; yes, laughter is evoked. But let us not forget that for Beckett, as Nell expresses it in *Endgame*, "Nothing is funnier than unhappiness. . . . It is the most comical thing in the world." Both laughter and weeping produce tears. And as we confront a specific term like "tragicomedy," let us acknowledge Beckett's own distrust of language, his belief that words "falsify whatever they approach." My point is simply this: in Beckett the "tragi" and the "comedy" are tied inextricably one to the other, but the "tragi" overwhelms the "comedy," producing the effect we have been describing as tragic. (Even if the dialectic between comedy and tragedy were so equally balanced that it led to uncertainty and doubt, we would still be closer to tragedy.) The effect of a reading of *Waiting for Godot*, the effect of a performance of the play, is tragic. The play prods the ultimate questions; it evokes the secret cause; it forces us to face the fact of mystery. Like *King Lear*, which

contains much comedy, often of the same kind as *Waiting for Godot,*
Beckett's play is a tragedy.

Like Edgar and Lear, Vladimir and Estragon are characters
stripped of those robes that hide all. Unlike Edgar and Lear, they
have no connection to society, no place in a historical scheme. For
this reason they seem purer representations of unaccommodated
man, man ground down to his essence, than Shakespeare's characters, who at least have been connected. Vladimir and Estragon possess none of the superfluities; their existence is comprised wholly of
man's basic physical and emotional needs. Beckett, like Shakespeare in *King Lear,* relentlessly emphasizes the physical. Estragon
struggles to take off his boot. Periodically, he is physically beaten.
Vladimir admires him for having found a good ditch to sleep in.
Both men discuss the advantages and disadvantages of eating a carrot. Estragon's feet stink; Vladimir's breath stinks. Vladimir has
trouble urinating; Estragon enjoys watching him urinate. And so
on. We can ask with Lear: "Is man no more than this?" Well, man *is*
this—a this we can never forget or neglect—but he is also more. He
needs a friend; he needs to pass the time; he has to look forward to
something. No matter how reduced man is, he wishes to believe life
has some meaning even though there's "nothing to be done," the
play's first words which reverberate throughout the play. He wishes
to believe there are answers to questions. And questions abound in
Waiting for Godot, making up one-quarter of the play. Half of these
questions remain unanswered, and among these are the questions
that touch the ultimate uncertainties. Add to this the many qualifi-
cations of statements that are not questions ("What is it?" "I don't
know. A willow.") and we have a play whose essence is uncertainty, whose mood is relentlessly interrogative.

In the play's beginning, after Gogo's "Nothing to be done"—
which specifically refers to his difficulty in pulling off his boot, but
becomes a refrain on man's predicament—Didi addresses himself to
Gogo: "So there you are again." To which Gogo replies: "Am I?"
This is the first question of the play, two little words that point to a
big uncertainty. He is there; no question about that since *we* see him.
But who *is* he? (A question which belongs in *Oedipus Rex* and *King
Lear.*) And is he there *again?* And is he the same "I" that was there
before? Or has he changed since then, whenever that was? Didi
learns, by means of a series of questions that are answered, that
Gogo slept in a ditch last night and was beaten as usual. When

Estragon, again referring to his difficulty with the boot, cries "Help me!", Didi asks: "It hurts?"

Est. (angrily). Hurts! He wants to know if it hurts!
Vlad. (angrily). No one ever suffers but you. I don't count. I'd like to hear what you'd say if you had what I have.
Est. It hurts?
Vlad. (angrily). Hurts! He wants to know if it hurts![11]

"It hurts?"—another refrain, verbally linking the two friends; another big question, this one indicating the pain of man's condition.

Shortly thereafter Vladimir, the more thoughtful of the two, brings up a biblical "fact" that troubles him and sheds an atmosphere of uncertainty over the entire play: "One of the thieves was saved. (Pause) It's a reasonable percentage." At this moment it is a reasonable percentage, but salvation becomes more uncertain, the 50/50 balance more precarious, when he goes on to wonder: "And yet . . . (pause) . . . how is it—this is not boring you I hope—how is it that of the four Evangelists only one speaks of a thief being saved. The four of them were there—or thereabouts—and only one speaks of a thief being saved." Estragon, obviously less troubled by such problems, more willing to accept mystery as mystery, says: "Well? They don't agree and that's all there is to it." Vladimir, unable to dismiss so easily a moment in the life—the death—of Jesus that has such large implications *for him* (will *he* be saved or will Estragon be saved?) repeats the problem: "But all four were there. And only one speaks of a thief being saved. Why believe him rather than the others?" This emphasis on the unreliability of witnesses informs the rest of the play and brilliantly brings into question the status of those witnesses of that very moment on stage—the audience.

Uncertainty hangs over everything that Didi and Gogo have experienced or thought they had experienced or are experiencing. "What did we do yesterday?" . . . "He said Saturday. (Pause.) I think." . . . "And is it Saturday? Is it not rather Sunday? (Pause.) Or Monday? (Pause.) Or Friday?" . . . "We met yesterday. (Silence.) Do you not remember?" Small wonder that Didi is filled with exasperation ("Nothing is certain when you're about") and with anguish ("I don't know what to think any more"). To be frozen at a precise moment in time, unable to *relate* with assurance to a time past, unable to predict with some degree of assurance a time future, is the worst kind of boundary situation. The self needs time as a frame of reference. Without such a frame, the self *must* say "Am I?" to so commonplace an utterance as "So there you are again." Without such a frame, man's experience has no continuity, and the sheer heaviness of the present moment—without a past or a future—could be unbearable. (That is why Vladimir can repeat with such relish Estragon's phrase "The last moment," perhaps thinking of the relief of an end.) To make the present endurable, the passing hours must be filled with divertive activities—verbal games, clowning, or the like—in order to allow man to forget that his life, surrounded by an uncertain past and future, is indefinable. In *Waiting for Godot* the condition of man is waiting, perhaps another way of saying "enduring," and the activity of man is to pass the time while waiting. Nietzsche was correct, of course, in asserting that the man who has a *why* to live will be able to endure any *how*. The most powerful evidence of this truth is found in our time. The survivors of Auschwitz and the other Nazi death camps endured the worst "how" in recorded history because they had a "why."[12] In Beckett's play, an artifact that has the pressure of our nightmarish history behind it, the how is waiting, the why is the arrival of Godot. Who or what is Godot is the play's most haunting and important question.

Becket's answer to Alan Schneider's question "Who or what does Godot mean?" has often been quoted: "If I knew, I would have said so in the play." Schneider should not have expected Beckett to answer the kind of question no writer will answer, and in this case a question that has no specific answer. But Beckett's honest indication that an element in his own creation can be as mysterious to him as it is to his audience should not deter that audience from speculating on the meaning of Godot. The play forces the question on us. And the answers have ranged wide and plunged deep. None should be dismissed—including such seemingly limited, because too precise, beliefs that Godot is De Gaulle or a character in a Balzac play—because the solution to the mystery will never be definitely solved. Beckett's word "perhaps" should inform all our speculations on Godot. Nevertheless, some speculations are more acceptable than others because the play itself allows them to exert considerable pressure. We can make the most general statement, as does William York Tindall, and say that Godot is "whatever man waits for,"[13] and we can say with Ruby Cohn that Godot is "the promise that is always awaited and not fulfilled."[14] Like Rolf Breuer, we can expand the idea that "Godot is that which gives meaning to Vladimir's and Estragon's waiting" by considering the waiting itself as both the problem and the solution.[15] These beliefs—like Hugh Kenner's that Godot is "the mysterious one for whom we wait"[16]—have the refreshing quality of stating clearly what we all can easily accept. But a play drenched in uncertainty causes such clear statements to serve as beginnings of larger, perhaps darker, interpretations. Of all the interpretations—and the play has received the attention of critics with every kind of interest, from sociological to existential, from Marxist to biographical[17]—those that touch religion hold the greatest interest. Not only because we as human beings seem to need the illusion of God, need to have explanations, need to know the causes of things, but because the play, with its important biblical allusions and echoes, prods us to consider the waiting for Godot as the waiting for God. Beckett may be playing games with us and our needs, but a view of the play that does not recognize the Christian *trap*pings (a word that is operable, perhaps) seems shortsighted.

Jesus' choice of one of the two thieves, as reported in one of the four gospels, has already been discussed as an important ingredient in the play's atmosphere of uncertainty, here the uncertainty of salvation. The tree on stage, the *only* piece of scenery, makes us think of the crosses on which Jesus and the thieves were crucified, as well as the tree of life and death (since the tree sprouts leaves in the second act and the two tramps discuss hanging themselves from the tree), and the tree of knowledge, and the Judas tree. Estragon says that he has always compared himself to Christ, and he claims that his name is Adam. Pozzo is mistaken for Godot, and he responds to the names of both Cain and Abel. The play is laced with references to the crucifixion, since "to every man his little cross." And the Godot who sends messengers has the characteristics of the Old Testament God; he beats one messenger but not the other, for reasons unknown, just as he was pleased with Abel but not with Cain, for reasons unknown. Of course, the name Godot compels us to think of God. Lucky's speech cryptically but forcefully confronts God. The speech takes on great importance because of the character of Lucky—who says nothing else in the entire play, who is literally tied to Pozzo by a rope and by his status as slave to master, who taught Pozzo beauty and truth, who dances a dance called "The Net," a name which pinpoints his condition and man's condition (as we dance our dances within our harnesses), a name which alludes to the Christian trappings of the speech he will proclaim. Because the speech relentlessly goes on for five minutes, it allows us to *experience* the exhaustion of thought. The thought itself—as we unravel bits and pieces and try to string together clauses and *feel* the pressure of key words—makes us realize the truth of Didi's later statement that "what is terrible is to *have* thought." Lucky's thought is terrible. His speech, despite its grammatical incoherence and the confusion of its end caused by Lucky's physical struggle against Didi and Gogo and Pozzo who try to stop his "thinking," does contain disturbingly recognizable thoughts. Lucky places before us and the three listeners on stage "a personal God . . . with white beard," divinely apathetic, lacking the capacity for amazement, speechless, who "loves us dearly with some exceptions for reasons unknown," and these exceptions will go to Hell. Man, in Lucky's speech, despite strides in science and art and sports, "wastes and pines wastes and pines . . . for reasons unknown." And the earth, "abode of stones,"—"in the great cold the great dark"—is also dying "for reasons unknown." The speech spurtingly approaches its abrupt end with the refrains "on on" and "the skull the skull the skull the skull" and "abode of stones" and "unfinished," a word repeated again and again in the speech and appropriately the last word of the unfinished speech.

That Lucky's "personal God" could be Godot is learned in the play's last minutes when the Boy tells Didi that Godot has a white beard. Didi's "Christ have mercy on us!" reveals his fear that Godot may be the God that Lucky described. That Jesus himself may be Godot—the Jesus who saves one thief, allowing the other to plunge into hell—is a logical speculation in the light of the speech's progress toward death and the image of Golgotha that it hearkens (the great dark, abode of stones, skull). But Lucky's last word is "unfinished," the opposite of Jesus' "finished," the last word he uttered in the sentence "It is finished" as reported in one of the four gospels. Beckett is suggesting, perhaps, that Jesus was more fortunate than modern man; his agony came to an end, a closure, finished. They crucified quicker in those days, according to Estragon. Modern man's agony, his uncertain thoughts about life and especially about death, seem everlasting. Lucky's speech is intolerable to the three characters on stage because his words stress the fact of mortality and the fact of mystery. ("For reasons unknown" is the most repeated phrase in the speech.) Lucky's speech forces them to see themselves on the cross, with the crucifixion an ongoing condition, unfinished. Lucky must be silenced.

The arrival of Godot would change uncertainty to certainty, would provide answers to haunting questions, would finish unfinished thoughts. In this sense he will "save" man from the perennial condition of living a question mark, living at the boundary between question and answer. That it is painful to live there needs little more evidence than Gogo's simple utterance: "I can't go on like this." That man *must* live there, must wait and endure, is indicated in Didi's equally simple rejoinder: "That's what you think." They would like to "go," but they remain frozen to their condition—at the end of the first act and the second act and every act that will follow.

Godot is hearkened in *Waiting for Godot* as often as the gods are hearkened in *King Lear,* and in similar ways. And, as in *King Lear,* capriciousness is emphasized (why punish the sheep boy and not the goat boy?) and fortuitousness (Pozzo's "handy-dandy" statement that he could have been in Lucky's shoes and vice versa) and man's essential helplessness and vulnerability (Estragon's hunger and beatings; Didi's mental anguish; Pozzo's blindness—*that* Pozzo who never had a single doubt about his high status, his power, his direction "on"; Lucky's dance within the net, his unfinished speech and eventual dumbness). Also emphasized is death, an important ingredient of tragedy and, for some, what Godot represents. Didi and Gogo, situated between question and answer, between apparent meaninglessness and possible meaning, between present and future, are frozen as well on the boundary between life and death. Beckett presents no specific emblem of death—as Shakespeare does in his pictures of Hamlet holding the skull and Lear holding the dead Cordelia—but the play dwells on mortality. Lucky's speech, though unfinished, progressed "on" toward the skull and the stones. References to the death of Jesus dot the play. Didi and Gogo twice contemplate suicide. They talk about the "dead voices" that make noises "like leaves" . . . "like ashes" . . . "like leaves." Estragon wants to be told about worms. Vladimir, looking at the audience, wonders, "Where are all these corpses from?" He exclaims: "A charnel-house! A charnel-house!" And so on. The play's two most haunting passages dwell on death. Pozzo in act 2, now blind, bewildered, furiously shouts these words to Didi as he leaves the stage:

> Have you not done tormenting me with your accursed time!
> It's abominable! When! When! One day, is that not enough for
> you, one day he went dumb, one day I went blind, one day
> we'll go deaf, one day we were born, one day we shall die, the
> same day, the same second, is that not enough for you?
> (*Calmer.*) They give birth astride of a grave, the light gleams an
> instant, then it's night once more. . . . On!

The "On!" leads to one place only, the grave, for the night of the play has come to make even darker the night of Pozzo's blindness. Pozzo's words echo in Vladimir's mind when he comes to the clearest realization of his horribly mortal condition: "Astride of a grave and a difficult birth. Down in the hole lingeringly, the grave-digger puts on the forceps. We have time to grow old. The air is full of our cries." The cries belong to tormented man and to newborn babe, leaving grave-womb with the help of gravedigger-doctor, crying at the first moment air is sucked in, and forever after filling the air with cries. King Lear's "We came crying hither" hangs in Beckett's atmosphere. Birth and death are tied together (as is one day to the next, act 1 to act 2, past to present, present to future, Pozzo to Lucky, Didi to Gogo, Didi and Gogo to Godot) and time holds us dying from the moment of birth.

Despite Beckett's insistent use of repetition (which is both a dramatic device and a theme), time in the play is not standing still, although for Didi and Gogo it seems to. It is going "on" to "the last moment," the promised end. The changed condition of Pozzo and Lucky is evidence enough, but more stunning theatrically is the appearance in act 2 of a few leaves on the previously bare tree. Nature, with time, seems to have some possibility of flourishing; in a wasteland even a few leaves are welcome. Man, with time, grows old and dies, but in his condition he is frozen, for there's "nothing to be done." The image of blooming nature vs. petrified man makes death even more insistent and points to an essential difference between comedy and tragedy, the ongoing quality posited by the former, the certainty of an end in the latter. Because the audience is composed of men—"corpses," "not a soul in sight"—interested more in men than in the tree, the human perspective forces us to place this tragicomedy closer to tragedy. Especially interesting and significant in this connection is the "dog" song that Vladimir sings in the beginning of the second act.

A dog came in the kitchen
And stole a crust of bread.
Then cook up with a ladle
And beat him till he was dead.

Then all the dogs came running
And dug the dog a tomb—

He stops, broods, resumes:

Then all the dogs came running
And dug the dog a tomb
And wrote upon the tombstone
For the eyes of dogs to come:

A dog came in the kitchen
And stole a crust of bread.

He stops, broods, resumes:

Then all the dogs came running
And dug the dog a tomb—

He stops, broods. Softly.

And dug the dog a tomb . . .

The structure of the song, like that of many "round" songs, seems cyclical and has been considered cyclical by many commentators who believe the song typifies the structure of the play: two acts, one day like the next, waiting for Godot in both, Pozzo and Lucky appear in both, Boy messenger in both, trouble with boots and hats in both, similar games, night falling at the end of both acts, Didi and Gogo say "let's go" but do not move at the end of both acts. The repetitions put enough pressure on the play to make one day seem like the next. But a closer look forces us to realize that time does flow. (Pozzo and Lucky change, boots are switched, a tree acquires leaves.) Certainly, the activity of act 2 is more desperate, more frenzied than in act 1. And death seems more imminent. A closer look at the dog song reveals that the seemingly cyclical pattern progresses to a song-stopping word, "tomb," repeated more than any other word except "dog." Didi's pauses, his repetitions, put great stress on death, and what seemed a circle becomes a line, inevitably drawing toward the last moment, more precisely, the last resting place. Like Lucky's speech—which relentlessly approaches images of death, the finish, although it is unfinished—the dog song approaches an end, death, although it is circular. Unfinished and finished, circular and linear, these paradoxes, centering on death, receiving added force from the atmosphere of uncertainty, from the question mark hovering over the entire play, tilt the seemingly balanced genre, tragicomedy, toward tragedy. And it is only in the context of tragedy that the question "Who or what does Godot mean?" receives its most satisfying answer. With the two tramps in their frozen condition, waiting for that which will give meaning to their lives, which will change uncertainty to certainty, with the two tramps on the boundary between present and future, life and death, Godot is the ultimate mystery, the answer to the question, the cause that will forever remain secret. Clowns in a tragedy, Didi and Gogo represent bewildered modern man facing the fact of mystery. In the most memorable moment of Peter Brook's Beckettian stage production of *King Lear*, when the blind Gloucester sits cross-legged, alone on the bare stage, unblinkingly staring ahead at the audience while the sounds of chaos are heard off-stage, modern audiences were able to feel the horror of man's vulnerable condition and to feel pride in man's ability to go on in the face of darkness and uncertainty, even when to go on means to sit on the ground and wait. That is the common ground of tragedy shared by Beckett and Shakespeare.

6 WAITING

The Three Sisters & Riders to the Sea

Chekhov's *The Three Sisters* could be called *Waiting for Moscow*. The changed title has descriptive accuracy and it reveals the closeness of Chekhov's play to Beckett's. In some essential ways, the Irish Beckett is the Russian Chekhov's heir. For both dramatists the condition of man is waiting; their characters are poised on a boundary situation. In both *The Three Sisters* and *Waiting for Godot* the precarious balance of tragedy and comedy tips toward tragedy; in both plays the secret cause exerts dark pressure. Chekhov called *The Three Sisters* a "drama," a troublesome term, but one that indicates that Chekhov considered this a darker play than *The Sea Gull* and *The Cherry Orchard*, which he called comedies. His dispute with Stanislavsky, who exploited the play's seriousness, suggests that Chekhov did not consider it a tragedy. In fact, although his own reading of the playscript to the actors produced tears in their eyes, he insisted that he had written a happy comedy and that his play was misunderstood. The misunderstanding continues. We cannot ignore Chekhov's opinion of his own creation, but there are times when an artist knows less about his creation than those who experience its effects. The actors of the Moscow Art Theatre who wept over the play, and we who respond to its heartbreak, are reacting to the play's dominant tone—and that tone is tragic.

Consider the play's movement in space and time, a movement which paradoxically (tragically) results in stalemate, kinesis producing stasis. The first of its four acts begins in the living room of the house of the Prozorovs on a sunny bright noon in spring. It is Irina's birthday, a joyful time, and before the act ends all the characters will be gathered for the celebration. The act begins with the audience's view of the three sisters—Olga in the dark blue uniform of a teacher,

Masha in her characteristic black, Irina in white. Time is the play's central theme, immediately evoked in Olga's first speech, important enough to quote in full because it sets the play's tone and introduces the first of the play's many balances.

> Just a year ago, a year ago on this very day, Father died—on your birthday, Irina, on the fifth of May. It was very cold, the snow was falling. I thought I'd never live through it; you had fainted, and lay there as if you were dead. But now a year's gone by and we can remember it calmly; you're already wearing white, your face is radiant. . . .
>
> (The clock strikes twelve)
>
> And the clock struck just the same way then. (A pause) I remember that as they took Father there the band was playing, they fired a volley over his grave. He was a general, he was in command of a whole brigade, and yet there weren't many people. Of course, it was raining. Raining hard—rain and snow.[1]

Their father died in the spring, but the cold and snow erase whatever is positive about springtime. The band played at his grave, but few people were present, and it was raining and snowing. At a birthday, a deathday is remembered. The clock's striking twelve tells us of present time, but also hearkens the exact noon of the past. Present and past come together with the sound of the clock's striking; time has passed *and* time is frozen. Spring as winter, birthday as deathday, time present as time past—Chekhov offers this kind of precarious balance throughout the play. Act 2 opens on the same room, but now the room is bathed in the darkness of a cold winter's evening. The sound of an accordion outside is a faint reminder of the festivities of the first act. A solitary figure, Natasha, enters in her dressing gown, carrying a flickering candle. Declaring that the servants are "impossible" because it is carnival time, she complains to her husband Andrei that baby Bobik is cold, so cold that she'll ask Irina to give up her sunny room to Bobik. What we have, then, is winter replacing spring, darkness replacing light, the outsider Natasha now the insider in control, and the cold, always the cold. The carnival, and whatever joyousness it represents, will not be entering the house of the Prozorovs; Natasha will see to that. During this act the father's death is again recalled, and again a sound of the present—this time the howling in the chimney—causes Masha to remember the exact sound "just before Father died." As with the striking of the clock in act 1, the repetition of a sound indicates time passes and time stands still. With act 3 we move to Olga's room (now also Irina's room because Bobik has hers), crowded with beds and screens because it serves as a refuge for those affected by the fire that has been raging in the town. The sound of a firebell offstage suggests activity and urgency, but onstage Masha, still in black, is lying on a sofa, and those who enter do so exhaustedly. The *imagined* frenzied activity offstage, combined with the *seen* onstage inactivity, offers another of Chekhov's many balances. The sense of outside emergency, however, seems to prod climactic moments within this, the most emotionally tense, act: Masha tells her sisters she loves Vershinin; Irina tells Olga she will marry Tuzenbach; Chebutykin reveals that his ineptitude as a doctor caused the death of a woman, and he breaks the precious porcelain clock (causing time to freeze?); Irina realizes she will never get to Moscow, although she ends the act with "There's nothing in this world better than Moscow! Let's go, Olga! Let's go!" (Here the "Let's go" of Didi ending act 1 of *Waiting for Godot* and the "Let's go" of Gogo ending act 2 must come to mind, and rightly so, for in both plays we are witnessing a tragic frozen condition—"They do not move.") That the curtain of act 3 rises to reveal a smaller crowded room visually indicates the narrowing of the sisters' spatial world, the inevitable narrowing of tragedy. Interestingly, act 4 takes us *outside,* in the garden of the house, with a view of "a long avenue of fir trees" and a river and a forest on the other side of the river, with people passing through. Here we *seem* to have an opening up, a widening of the sisters' world, which is the movement of comedy. Chekhov is again displaying the remarkable paradoxicality of his art. We are outside, not because the world is opening up for the sisters, but because the sisters no longer live in the house; Natasha's possession is complete. The outside vista and the road are not awaiting the sisters, who are literally frozen to their conditions, if not to their house. The road will be tramped by the soldiers who say goodbye. The possessors are dispossessed; the outside is not freer for the sisters than the inside; they, like Didi and Gogo, are near the road but cannot travel on it. Others "go"; they do not move. As the closing curtain descends on the cold autumn day, we see the three sisters, dreams shattered, huddled together, tied to their condition. Although we have gone from inside to outside, from spring to autumn, that is, although we seem to have moved in space and time, the final tableau is the initial tableau—three sisters, center stage, trapped. A still-life picture or, more precisely, a photograph, the kind of photograph Fedotik is taking in his last goodbye when he says "Stand still."

The frozen quality of the sisters' lives—so horrible in its sameness, so frustrating to their dreams—is bound up with the large notion of determinism which Chekhov presses into the play's fabric. Chekhov's life as a doctor, his own losing battle with tuberculosis, the influence of Darwin and Zola on his thought and writing, seem to have pushed him to the dark belief that man, for the most part, is the tragic victim of fate. The birds—how often they fly through Chekhov's plays—are fated to be free and to move to other places in the proper season. Man, in all seasons, is fated to be that prisoner talked about by Vershinin in act 2, confined to his cell while he watches the birds fly overhead. Danchenko said this about the characters in *The Three Sisters:* "These people are like chessmen in the hands of unseen players."[2] The idea brings us very close to Einstein's dancers dancing to the mysterious tune of an invisible piper. The soldiers, by the nature of their profession, come and go on orders from above. Andrei seems to have no control over his descent from potential professor to gambler to pusher of prams. Given the condition of his provincial life, his gambling is as inevitable as Olga's headaches as schoolmistress, Masha's love affair with Vershinin, and Irina's loss of Tuzenbach. Natasha and Solyony are the only characters who seem to have control over their lives, and both serve as the evil instruments of fate. Natasha's evil, despite her banality, is as relentless as Edmund's in *King Lear,* but she, unlike Edmund, is the unqualified winner at play's end. Her strong self-interest, her vulgar possessiveness, push the members of the Prozorov family ever closer to the abyss. The pedestrian Natasha and the more mysterious Solyony—who kills Tuzenbach and who is constantly sprinkling perfume on his hands (because they smell of "mortality"?)—are the instruments of fate in a play that never allows us to forget that life is controlled by fate. Vershinin, agreeing with Masha that they will be forgotten in time to come, says: "That is our fate, there is nothing we can do about it." Masha, in act 3, tells Olga she loves Vershinin—". . . it's my fate." When Kulygin states that, despite all, he loves Masha "very much," he adds: "And I'm thankful for my fate." Fedotik, playing the fortuneteller with cards in act 2, suggests that Irina is not fated to go to Moscow, which Irina realizes in act 4, when she says: "if it's fated for me not to live in Moscow, then that's that. It means, it's fate. There's nothing to be done about it. . . . It's all in God's hands, that's the truth." Here fate is linked with God, a linkage which the play exploits. Old Ferapont never went to Moscow: "It wasn't God's will I should." Olga tells us in act 1 that ". . . it's all as God means it to be," a conventional belief which takes on more serious overtones when, talking about Tuzenbach in act 3, she says to Irina: "But if it were God's will he should marry you, I'd be happy." It is not God's will, it seems, because Tuzenbach will be killed by Solyony, Irina will not marry, and Olga will not be happy. Irina's hopeful "Somehow God will help me!" as she contemplates a "new life" with Tuzenbach is heavy with tragic irony, as is Chebutykin's wish for Irina to "fly on and God be with you." The birds will fly on; the sisters will remain. Whatever the force of determinism is called—fate or God—the sisters are tragic victims mysteriously chained to the frustrating stasis of their lives.

Of course, the most common manifestation of determinism and inevitability in Chekhov's play, as in all tragedy and in life, is death. Death and dying so pervade the play that the controversy over the play's genre seems merely academic. True, Chekhov is the master of equilibrium and counterpoint, and he does mix his modes, but a tragic sensibility informs the play. Death in *The Three Sisters* is a pervasive experience. Remembrance of the death of the father begins the play; the death of Tuzenbach ends the play. In between, death enters in various ways—sometimes matter-of-factly, as when Ferapont tells Andrei that a contractor in Moscow ate forty pancakes and died, or when Ferapont tells Andrei that "last winter" two thousand people were "frozen to death" in "Petersburg or Moscow, I don't remember" or when Solyony, seemingly joking, tells Chebutykin that he'll put a bullet through his head; sometimes ominously, as when Solyony tells Irina that he loves her and that he'll "kill" any rival; sometimes philosophically, as when Andrei laments the way life is in his provincial town: "They just eat, drink, sleep, and then die"; sometimes enigmatically, as when Solyony repeatedly utters this couplet: "Before he'd time to get his breath /The bear was hugging him to death"; always exerting considerable pressure on the living —the death of the father; the death of Tuzenbach; the death of that woman of Zasyp killed by Chebutykin's incompetence, haunting Chebutykin, causing everything inside him to feel "all twisted, all vile, all nauseating"; the death of the son of that lady to whom Irina was stupidly rude at the telegraph office. Still, death *remembered,* painful though it is, is not so horrible as slow dying *experienced.* A tiredness, an exhaustion, a wasting-away, a growing old penetrate the souls of the Prozorovs and those around them. Olga's head aches all the time, and she realizes from the play's beginning that she has, at age twenty-eight, an "old woman's thoughts already," that strength and youth are being "squeezed out" of her "day by day, drop by drop." Throughout the play she complains that she is "exhausted." Chebutykin considers himself "a lonely worthless old man." Kulygin complains that he's "tired," "exhausted." Masha tells Vershinin when she first sees him: "But how old you've got! *(Tearfully)* How old you've got!" In a later act, Vershinin complains: "My hair's getting gray, I'm an old man, almost, and yet I know so little, oh, so little!" Irina, on her very birthday, laments: "For us three sisters life hasn't been beautiful, it's—it's choked us out, the way weeds choke out grass." Later, she remarks "how lifeless and old" her brother Andrei has become. And as she contemplates herself at age twenty-four in act 3, she realizes "my brain is drying up, I'm getting thin, getting ugly, getting old." Andrei wonders about life: "Oh, where's it gone, what's become of it—my past, when I was young and gay and clever, when I had such beautiful dreams, such beautiful thoughts, when my present and future were bright with hope? Why is it that, almost before we've begun to live, we get boring, drab, uninteresting, lazy, indifferent, useless, unhappy?" These words apply to all the Prozorovs. As we hear the laments, as we witness the slow dying on stage, we must agree with Vershinin who, saying goodbye in act 4, utters: "Everything comes to an end." A truism for life and play, but felt—and this is the artistry of Chekhov—*felt* from beginning to end in the play. A kind of endgame from the beginning: a deathday remembered at a birthday; winter and snow in the month of May. Of course, saying goodbye is a kind of death, and Chekhov is the dramatist of farewells. Parting in *The Three Sisters* is sorrow not so sweet. The soldiers leave to the sound of music; although not dead, like Cordelia, they'll "come no more"; they are "gone forever and ever," says Masha. Their departure is a form of death for the three sisters, remaining stationary, together, near the road that others travel.

The dying sounds of the retreating band bring us back to Olga's words in the play's beginning—the band played when they took

Father to his grave. The band playing now is taking the sisters to their grave, although they are not dead. The final sounds of music allow us to recall the other sounds in the play, used by Chekhov to provide sadness and heartbreak: the faint sound of the lone accordion at the beginning of act 2, as we look at the dark living room, no longer gay, controlled by Natasha, and never again to echo the lively sounds of carnival week; the distant mournful playing of harp and violin in act 4 at the moment when Andrei is saying: "The town will be deserted. It will be as if they'd put all the lights out"; the more immediate playing of the harp and violin when the musicians enter the garden, receive money from old Anfisa with the words "Good-bye and God bless you!" before they depart; Protopopov's playing "The Maiden's Prayer" on the piano offstage, a song Irina detests, probably because she associates it with Protopopov, but perhaps because she is still a maiden; the howling in the chimney, like the howling "just before Father died"; Fedotik's little top that "makes the most wonderful sound," its spinning leading to Masha's enigmatic words, repeated throughout, "By the curved seastrand a green oak stands, / A chain of gold upon it. . . ," words she utters when "a muffled, far-off shot is heard" offstage in act 4, words of mystery following the sound of death. The humming top of act 1 is a suggestive focus of attention, spinning around a "still" center, like the three sisters fixed while life is turning around them, like the green oak standing still while the sea's waters come and go. It is clear that Chekhov, like Shakespeare's Orsino, is fond of sounds and music that have a "dying fall." The talk of death, the growing old, the exhaustion, the shattered hopes, the litany of goodbyes, the dying sounds—all provide a requiem as the Prozorovs move toward the abyss.

The abyss. On first consideration, perhaps too heavy a word for a play presenting surface reality and less-than-heroic characters. But the abyss is there, Chekhov allowing us to feel its presence *while* we observe the surface reality. That is, Chekhov the realist, the brilliant depicter of exterior life, is at the same time "the explorer of inner space," to use the words of George Steiner.[3] Chekhov probes the subterranean areas of the soul, the interior life; his insight into those areas seems all the more terrifying precisely because his pictured world, the world he exhibits onstage, is real and quiet and genteel. In Chekhov we have no suicidal walk up the cliff at Dover, no journey through a stormy wasteland, nor do we have a ghost visiting a son at midnight to assign him a large task of revenge which results in a bloody and poisonous duel to the death. In *The Three Sisters* there is no dramatic climb or journey, no large task, no blood. But the sisters, like most tragic characters, live their lives enveloped by doubt and uncertainty. Listen to Irina, "getting old" at twenty-four: ". . . there's nothing, nothing—there isn't the least satisfaction of any kind—and the years are going by, and every day, over and over, everything's getting farther away from any real life, beautiful life, everything's going farther and farther into some abyss. . . . I am in despair, I can't understand how I'm alive, how I haven't killed myself long ago." Irina's "abyss" may seem shallow but it is sufficient for tragedy. In despair because life seems "weary, stale, and unprofitable," Irina, like Hamlet before her, considers suicide. Hers is not Hamlet's sustained gaze into the abyss, nor is her abyss as dizzying and deep as his; they belong to different worlds. But Irina recognizes her relentless movement toward the boundary situation, a recognition which leads to tears, not action. And her movement —her "going farther and farther into some abyss"—is taking place under a cloud of doubt which hovers over all the sympathetic characters. *Why* is life the way it is? Why have the Prozorov dreams been shattered? Why has a stifling stasis settled over their lives? Is life obeying "laws of its own," laws that, according to Tuzenbach, "we'll never be able to discover," laws that govern all animated nature: "Migratory birds, cranes for instance, fly and fly, and no matter what thoughts, great or small, wander into their heads, they'll still keep on flying, they don't know where, they don't know why." The "why" will never be known, a fact that Masha does not wish to acknowledge: "But still, it means something?" The question mark indicates that doubt is tied to her desire for meaning. Tuzenbach's rejoinder, "Means something. . . . Look, it's snowing. What does it mean?" accentuates the doubt and hearkens the secret cause. The falling of snow, the flying of birds, the birth of a child, the changing of seasons, the laws that govern all of nature, the sadness and frustration and suffering of mankind—all are at bottom mysterious. Deeper than the things we see, darker than thought, touching those inner spaces, a baffling uncertainty informs Chekhov's play. More baffling than the words of Masha's fragmented poem: "By the curved seastrand a green oak stands, / A chain of gold upon it. . . ." She asks: "What does it mean, *by the curved seastrand?* Why do I keep saying that?" More baffling than the vulgar hard-heartedness of

Natasha or the destructive sullenness of Solyony. More baffling than the great bell (Andrei) which fell and broke—"all of a sudden, for no reason at all." More baffling than the love that Andrei felt for Natasha. More baffling than the mysterious foreboding that Irina felt when Tuzenbach said goodbye for the last time. More baffling than the speed by which the years slip by and dreams are thwarted. We must say with Olga at play's end: "If only we knew, if only we knew!" But as we say it, we realize, as does Olga, that we will never know. When Chekhov's wife, also called Olga, asked him that question of questions, "What is life?", Chekhov answered: "That is just the same as asking what is a carrot. A carrot is a carrot, and nothing more is known about it." As in all tragedy, a question mark hangs over *The Three Sisters* and a dark uncertainty lodges at its center.

We feel the turbulence below the clear surface, and we go down far enough to touch mystery. Chekhov seems so elusive that it is difficult to examine his dramatic art with the usual language of dramatic criticism. (How often his plays are described in terms connected with that more elusive art, music—"harmonious," "rhythmic," "polyphonic.") He is unique in his ability to cast subterranean shadows while presenting surface clarity. We witness genteel people engaged in ordinary pursuits in a living room or garden, and we hear—we feel—the music of despair. As we leave the theater, a departure which mirrors the leave-taking of the soldiers as the three sisters remain frozen onstage (with audience mobility and character immobility very close to Beckett's technique in *Waiting for Godot* and *Endgame*), the resonance of that despair lingers. Now, if this is comedy, as some critics insist,[4] then it is the kind of comedy that gives conclusive proof to the truth of Socrates' assertion that ultimately comedy and tragedy are one. However, if we, like Socrates' listeners, have fallen asleep before we have learned how exactly comedy and tragedy *can* be one, then in our waking ignorance we must label *The Three Sisters* a tragedy. Chekhov is usually not considered to be a "tragic dramatist" because of his own statements on the comic nature of his plays and because his surface realism—comic and tragic, mirthful and sad—is close to the experience we have in our daily lives, experience that seems too mixed for tragedy, especially when we think of tragedy as a pure, "classical" genre. But the surface realism covers dark areas; the music of Dionysus throbs beneath the images of Apollo. This mingling of surface and sub-surface, combined with the ironic perspective that Chekhov gives to his audience—the fact that we are meant at times to take a different view of things than his characters—has caused most critics to emphasize the duality and irony at the expense of the tragedy.[5] Chekhov does present much irony in *The Three Sisters*, and he is the master of duality and balances, but he offers a felt experience that is closer to tragedy. The presence of duality or irony does not negate tragedy; if it did, Sophocles and Shakespeare would not be tragic dramatists. In Chekhov, as in any dramatist, the case for or against tragedy would have to rest on the total impression, on the tilting of the balance in one direction or another. A balance so finely poised that it allows neither comedy nor tragedy to be dominant would lead to confusion, the kind of confusion experienced by many at the end of *A Streetcar Named Desire* because Tennessee Williams has so evenly balanced Stanley Kowalski against Blanche du Bois.[6] At the end of *The Three Sisters*, we do not feel confusion; Chekhov clearly tilts the balance toward tragedy. He so involves us with the three sisters that we are not critical of them; rather, we feel compassion for them, just as we are not *finally* critical of Oedipus or Antigone or Hamlet or Lear or Didi and Gogo. Chekhov dramatizes the frustration of their lives, and he allows us to feel life's quiet but deep misery. Not the intense despair that causes a Faustus to go screeching to Hell, that causes Lear to die when he looks at Cordelia's unopened lips, that forces Enobarbus to "think and die"; rather, the kind of despair that Thoreau is referring to when he says "the mass of men lead lives of quiet desperation." Quiet desperation. That Chekhov ends his play with the three sisters, like Didi and Gogo, frozen to their condition, the still center of the humming top, quietly lingering, puzzled by life's mystery, is perhaps more terrifying than the death that ends all questioning. To say with Olga, "If only we knew, if only we knew!" may be more tragical than the rest that is silence. In short, Chekhov, like all tragic dramatists, looks into the mystery of things. That his dramatic presentation is less "pure," more oblique, more impressionistic—should I say more "modern"?—than other dramatists does not make his vision less tragic.

To move from Chekhov's *The Three Sisters* to Synge's *Riders to the Sea* requires a longer journey than the move from Russia to Ireland, or from a comfortable provincial house to a poor island cottage. Yet, a surface comparison of the two dramatists and their two plays reveals striking similarities. Both dramatists gave life to their respective country's theaters, Chekhov to the Moscow Art Theatre, Synge to the Abbey Theater. Both wrote comparatively few plays, including one-act plays and full-length plays. Both fell in love with actresses, Chekhov with Olga Knipper, whom he married, Synge with Molly Allgood, to whom he was engaged. Both lived with illness, and both died young, Chekhov of tuberculosis at forty-four, Synge of Hodgkin's disease at thirty-eight. The years of their lives overlapped, Chekhov dying in 1904, the year *Riders* was first performed. *The Three Sisters* and *Riders to the Sea* both dramatize the plights of women frozen to their condition and frozen to their physical environment, and in both waiting is the play's activity. Death and determinism pervade both plays. Both brilliantly present surface reality, helping to support the often-repeated claim that Chekhov and Synge are masters of modern realism. Despite these similarities, Chekhov's play is a tragedy and Synge's is not, and this clearly indicates the importance of the secret cause to tragedy. Whereas a baffling uncertainty informs Chekhov's play, a dark certainty informs Synge's play.

Synge's *Riders* has no inner spaces. In this intense one-act play Synge has not given himself the luxury of probing the interior life. Instead, he presents the way of life of a particular group of people, the Aran Islanders, whose daily battle with poverty and death is their lives' occupation. The enemy is the sea, but the means of livelihood is also the sea—in which fishing nets are cast and on which boats transport the horses to be sold on the Irish mainland. On boats or horses, the men of the Aran Islands are riders to the sea, and their ride inevitably ends in watery death. Synge's dramatic artistry is so effective, his presentation of the plight of the islanders is so intense, that the particular becomes the general and their ride becomes the ride of all men to confront mortality. But Synge, like the Aran Islanders, never questions this confrontation with mortality or the forces of mortality. He creates the atmosphere of doom, he dramatizes the inevitable, but the somber music of his prose-poetry never allows us to look into the abyss, to face question and mystery. In the half-hour playing time, Synge masterfully dramatizes the condition of man, showing the way life is, but his bare presentation, and the one-act form in which it is chained, does not allow him to investigate character, let alone have character or the play itself question life's demands or significance, or man's losing battle with the elements or death. As with all artistic creations of the highest order, the effect of

Riders is absolutely bound up with technique, and Synge's technique precludes tragedy. Precisely because *Riders* is a play of somber beauty, precisely because it contains important ingredients of tragedy but is not a tragedy—although its dark power has prodded some critics to label it that[7]—does it provide an interesting focus in a discussion of tragedy.

Riders dwells on the inescapable fact of death. The deaths of Michael and Bartley are the centers of concentration, with the two brothers coming together in Maurya's vision by the sea, coming together, that is, in death. Michael we never see, but his presence is felt from the play's beginning, when Nora enters the cottage kitchen with a bundle containing "a shirt and a plain stocking were got off a drowned man in Donegal." Nora and Cathleen will soon identify the clothes as Michael's, but their present attempt to do so is interrupted by the entrance of Maurya, the mother, causing Cathleen to hide the bundle in the turf-loft. That bundle containing a dead man's clothes serves to keep death as a focus of attention, as do the new boards for a coffin, standing against the wall. These props —bundle of clothes and coffin boards—are the *physical* reminders of the fact of death. The inactive old Maurya is waiting to learn whether or not her son Michael has drowned at sea, while her daughters Cathleen and Nora, busy with chores, are waiting to open the bundle when Maurya is not observing them. The attention of mother and daughters quickly turns to the youngest son, Bartley, who rushes into the cottage in order to get ready to take a boat to the mainland to sell his horses. Death hovers over this segment of the play, because Maurya fears that the one son she has left will also die. First, she tells Bartley not to take the new rope that he needs for a halter, giving as her reason that the rope will be needed when Michael's coffin is lowered into the ground. Bartley takes the rope. Then Maurya tells him he will be needed to make a coffin from the new boards when Michael's body is washed up. When Bartley says that the body can't be washed up after nine days, Maurya finally offers the true reason she wants Bartley to stay home: "If it was a hundred horses, or a thousand horses you had itself, what is the price of a thousand horses against a son where there is one son only?"[8] Bartley ignores his mother, gives Cathleen instructions on how to carry on with the work while he is away, takes off his coat and puts on another, and goes out with these words: "I must go now quickly. I'll ride down on the red mare, and the gray pony'll run behind me. . . . The blessing of God on you." That Maurya knows Bartley will die is revealed by gesture—she puts her shawl over her head—and by her words at his parting: "He's gone now, God spare us, and we'll not see him again. He's gone now, and when the black night is falling I'll have no son left me in the world." A confrontation between mother and son, but no confrontation at all—for the mother is ineffectual and the son is not listening. He has a job that must be done. On the Aran Islands a man, even so young a man, must go to sea; he has no choice. Rope, boards, a shawl—props visible and tangible, each touching death, giving fateful immediacy to the plight of an old woman who fails to keep her young son from his last ride.

With Michael gone, Bartley is now the man of the house. That he inherits the status of all the dead men before him is ominous but natural. That Maurya inherits her dead son's stick, as she leaves the cottage to bring a "bit of bread" and perhaps a blessing to Bartley, is unnatural, and indicates the special agony of this mother's condition: "In the big world the old people do be leaving things after them for their sons and children, but in this place it is the young men do be leaving things behind for them that do be old." On the Aran Islands, and in *Riders to the Sea,* the dead relentlessly press against the living. Maurya's departure allows Cathleen and Nora to get the bundle from the turf-loft in order to identify the garments. Synge here, as throughout, emphasizes physical detail—the knife needed to cut the string, the black knot on the string, the bit of sleeve, the shirt, the bit of stocking ("the second one of the third pair" that Nora knitted, "and I put up three score stitches and I dropped four of them"). When the girls wish to compare the shirt in the bundle with Michael's on the hook, they discover that Michael's shirt is gone, which reminds them that "Bartley put it on him in the morning, for his own shirt was heavy with the salt in it." Again, the living inherit from the dead, and again the two brothers are joined in our awareness. Realizing that the clothes are indeed Michael's, Cathleen cries out: "Ah, Nora, isn't it a bitter thing to think of him floating that way to the far north, and no one to keen him but the black hags that do be flying on the sea?" To which Nora adds her question: "And isn't it a pitiful thing when there is nothing left of a man who was a great rower and fisher, but a bit of an old shirt and a plain stocking?" Questions these are—and questions are the punctuation marks of tragedy—but these are not questions that touch the secret cause. These questions merely require simple answers—yes, it is a bitter thing; yes, it is a pity. More precisely, these are the rhetorical questions of Synge's lyrical prose, and therefore not questions at all, gathering to themselves no uncertainty. The pity of it all does affect us, but the terror of mortality or the sea's mystery or death's mystery is not invoked. Nor, surprisingly, is terror or mystery invoked in the one passage that seems to demand a terrified look into the abyss, when Maurya returns to tell her daughters of the fearful vision she saw: "I seen Michael himself."

> I'm after seeing him this day, and he riding and galloping. Bartley came first on the red mare; and I tried to say "God speed you," but something choked the words in my throat. He went by quickly; and "the blessing of God on you," says he, and I could say nothing. I looked up then, and I crying, at the gray pony, and there was Michael upon it—with fine clothes on him, and new shoes on his feet.

Although Maurya says she saw "the fearfulest thing," it does not appear so to us—because we've been prepared for the joining of the two brothers in death, and because the emphasis on the physical throughout has pushed even this supernatural revelation into the realm of the real. The vision seems not a fearful product of imagination, or the haunting premonition of an old woman, but a real happening, a believable fact. We think, yes, Maurya did see her sons. Even the horses, traditional symbols of terror, are merely horses—a gray pony and a red mare—conveying no sense of mystery.[9] That is, the supernatural seems natural. As natural as the inevitable claims of the sea. Through the years, a procession of dead men, as Maurya tells us, has been carried into her cottage, drenched by the sea. A procession so inevitable and mechanical that the terror is muted. When Maurya tells us of all the men she lost, she relives a past that will be repeated on stage momentarily.

> There were Stephen, and Shawn, were lost in the great wind, and found after in the Bay of Gregory of the Golden Mouth, and carried up the two of them on one plank, and in by that door. . . . There was Sheamus and his father, and his own father again, were lost in a dark night, and not a stick or sign was seen of them when the sun went up. There was Patch after was drowned out of a curagh that turned over. I was sitting here with Bartley, and he a baby, lying on my two knees,

and I seen two women, and three women, and four women coming after them, and they holding a thing in the half of a red sail, and water dripping out of it—it was a dry day, Nora—and leaving a track to the door.

That same door now opens, with old women coming in, crossing themselves, kneeling with heads covered, and then men carry in the body of Bartley. The baby that was Bartley on his mother's knees is now the dead young man on a plank placed on the table, with everyone around him on bended knees. Most important here, at this climactic moment, is the pattern of repetition, not the sea's deep dark mystery or the mystery of fated mortality. Past has become present, relentlessly and mechanically. The future, however, will be different, because Maurya has no more men to give to the sea. "They're all gone now, and there isn't anything more the sea can do to me." When Maurya "drops Michael's clothes across Bartley's feet, and sprinkles the Holy Water over him" the two dead brothers are again joined. A calm comes over Maurya. Whether her last words, the last words of the play, come from a woman of great religious faith or stoicism or a woman totally exhausted by a sea of troubles, all passion spent, is not so important to a discussion of tragedy as the fact that she accepts her condition; she does not question it. "No man at all can be living forever, and we must be satisfied." Before this ending, Synge had already returned to the world of the living, when an old man, asked to make a coffin with the white boards still leaning against the wall, asks if there are nails with them. Here, as throughout, the activities of the living relate to the dead, and again Synge stresses the physical, *dinglichkeit*. The Aran Islanders live with the terrible sea, and therefore they live with death, but death is so naturally bound up with their lives that they never question its mystery. Just as "it's the life of a young man to be going on the sea," as Cathleen asserts, it's the death of a young man to do so, with no questions asked.

Riders to the Sea is a play of great power; it is austere and dramatic and classical, in the truest sense. Its small world of the cottage represents the larger world, and its conflict of man against the sea has large implications. It contains two important characteristics of tragedy, death and determinism. But death and determinism are accepted, never fought or questioned. And the characters who are involved with death and fate are not individuals; they are types.

Maurya is one of the many keening women who have lost sons at sea. Cathleen and Nora are the young women, old before their time, who must carry on the difficult business of living. Bartley is one of the many men who must ride to the sea and death. We never go inside because Synge has no desire to explore the inner spaces. We view everything straight-on, at its own level, hearing the surface music only. We observe the bitterness of the characters' lives and we are affected by their unrelieved sadness. But they lack the complexity that comes to characters who shout against or quietly question their condition. Maurya never comes close to saying, with Lear who also lost a child, "Why should a dog, a horse, a rat, have life / And thou no breath at all?" Unlike Olga, she never wonders why she must suffer—"If only we knew, if only we knew!" She never approaches an existential or an ontological question. She does try, in her ineffectual way, to prevent Bartley from going to sea, that is, to stop the inevitable. However, she fails; the inevitable is fulfilled; she accepts—and that is all there is to it. The sea takes; the sea will take no more. As in all tragedy, there is no escape from the inevitable, but here there is no thought about the cause. *Riders* is all effect; it offers no residue of mystery. What Synge has accomplished is remarkable; there is no more effective one-act play in our language.[10] Part of the miracle of Synge's accomplishment is that he was able to write a play of such intense dark beauty without connecting it to the secret cause.

7 DOOM-SESSION

The Master Builder, The Visit, Death of a Salesman

Few would argue with the belief that modern drama begins with Ibsen, specifically with the presentation of his *Pillars of Society* in 1877. Fewer would attach the term "tragedy" to this early play or, for that matter, to such important Ibsen problem plays as *An Enemy of the People* and *A Doll's House* and, yes, even *Ghosts*, although Francis Fergusson makes as good a case as possible for its "tragic rhythm."[1] In his last plays, however, Ibsen's refinement of the use of myth and symbolic action, which was present in such early plays as *Brand* and *Peer Gynt*, and is present from *The Wild Duck* on, allows him to offer a vision of life that is essentially tragic. These last plays —*The Master Builder* (1892), *Little Eyolf* (1894), *John Gabriel Borkman* (1896), and *When We Dead Awaken* (1899)—all belong to the realistic tradition (and continue to support the claim that Ibsen is the father of modern realism in drama) but their powerful insistence on the symbolic and mystical pushes them toward the mystery essential to tragedy. Of the four, *The Master Builder* stands most centrally in the tragic tradition because it dramatizes most effectively the secret cause.

A bare plot summary of *The Master Builder* makes the play seem not so much tragical as "lamentable comedy." A middle-aged man, a successful builder by profession, unhappy in his domestic and professional life, constantly in fear of the younger generation, welcomes to his home a mysterious young woman who, ten years earlier when she was twelve or thirteen, had seen him climb the tower of the church he built in her home town. She claims to have extracted a promise from him that in ten years he would carry her off to an exotic place and buy her a kingdom. The strange attraction between master builder and young woman is immediate, and under her influence he, although afraid of heights, climbs the tower of his newly built home, and having reached the top, falls to his death. One could say, therefore, that *The Master Builder* is a play about a middle-aged man who tries to recapture his youth through an affair with a vigorous young woman and in an act of bravado fails disastrously. The stuff of comedy—except for the fall to death. But such a summary, merely narrative, and such a bare statement of what the play is about omit the play's appeal to deeper, more instinctual levels that are the important domain of Ibsen's dramatic art. This appeal links Ibsen to that other modern realist, Chekhov. Both pioneers of modern drama explore the darkness within, both brilliantly present the realism of surface and subsurface; with both, the tragic rests on the hidden spiritual and psychological reality. E. M. Forster, viewing Ibsen as a "romantic," characterizes him as a "lover of narrow passages and darkness,"[2] a phrase equally applicable to Chekhov, as we have seen. The two subterranean explorers are different, however, in the nature of their symbolism, Ibsen's being more mystical, more enigmatic, and therefore more difficult. Maeterlinck considered *The Master Builder* the first great symbolic play, and one of his comments on Halvard Solness, the master builder, and Hilda Wangel, the young woman, is an appropriate starting point for a discussion of the play's dark suggestiveness. Maeterlinck considered Solness and Hilda to be "the first characters in drama who feel, for an instant, that they are living in an atmosphere of the soul; and the discovery of this essential life that exists in them, beyond the life of every day, comes fraught with terror."[3] The crucial words here are "atmosphere of the soul" and "terror."

Solness's soul is torn apart by inner conflict, by mysterious forces, and perhaps by madness. He has served God by building churches, which he thought was "the noblest thing I could do with my life."[4] But this service, he believes, has caused a possessive God, a God who demands total dedication, to burn down the home his wife loved, thereby leading to the death of his twin sons and to the living death of his wife Aline. Shouting defiance against this God ten years earlier on the top of the last church steeple he was to build—the incident that Hilda vividly recalls—Solness then began building homes for men. But these homes did not provide happiness for the families occupying them. "Human beings don't know how to use these homes of theirs. Not for being happy in" (p. 379). Service to God and service to man have come to "nothing" for Solness except material success, which is empty and which has helped to produce his intense fear of the younger generation, especially of Ragnar Brovik, who works for Solness and is a potential master builder. The torment within Solness's soul is considerably compounded by his belief that he himself had a part in destroying his home and wife and sons. As he explains to Hilda, he is one of those "special, chosen people who have a gift and power and capacity to *wish* something, *desire* something, *will* something—so insistently and so—inevitably —that at last it *has* to be theirs." He wanted the house to burn down, and it did; that fire led to his eventual success as a builder. He was aided by "helpers and servers" who did what he willed. (Other men call it "luck," says Solness.) But what calls for these helpers and servers is *inside* us—"It's that troll in us, don't you see—that's what calls on the powers out there. And then we *have* to give in—whether we want to or not" (p. 356). Solness, it seems clear, sees himself both in control and controlled. His troubled imagination is trying to grapple with the terror of irrational impulses within his own nature. Small wonder that he considers himself somewhat mad, for he is looking into the abyss of self, the most dangerous darkness, according to Ibsen, who believed that "to live was to fight with the devils that infest the head and heart and to hold a Last Judgment over the self."[5] The troll—that dwarf *or* giant out of Norse mythology—is here the supernatural and uncontrollable creature who represents whatever is demonic in Solness's human nature. It is the name that both Solness and Hilda give to their own energies that cannot be mastered by the rational mind. What further complicates this enigmatic concept and what helps to make *The Master Builder* so difficult in its symbolism is that Hilda herself serves the function of troll, for she externalizes Solness's deepest desires. (In part, therefore, she serves a function similar to Aphrodite in the Phaedra plays, and proves equally destructive.) Hilda is a realistic character, no doubt, and her breezy manner and unusual dress (including a sailor blouse and sailor hat and an alpenstock) are very much of this world, strange though she may seem. But she is also the objectification of Solness's hidden desires and fears, which means that, as a character, she cannot fully exist without Solness, and Solness cannot be understood without her. In fact, the *relationship* of the two is what drives the play toward its climax and its meaning. On a purely realistic level, this relationship cannot be fully understood. For example, we never can be sure, because Solness is not sure, that the incident at Lysanger ten years earlier really took place as Hilda describes it. Note the tentative quality of Solness's responses:

> Hilda. And then you said that when I grew up, I could be *your* princess.
> Solness *(with a short laugh)*. Really—I said that too?
> Hilda. Yes, you did. And when I asked how long I should wait, then you said you'd come back in ten years, like a troll, and carry me off—to Spain or someplace. And there you promised to buy me a kingdom.
> Solness *(as before)*. Well, after a good meal one's not in the mood to count pennies. But did I really *say* all that?
> Hilda *(laughing softly)*. Yes, and you also said what the kingdom would be called.
> Solness. Oh? What?
> Hilda. It was going to be the kingdom of Orangia, you said.
> Solness. Ah, that's a delectable name.
> Hilda. No, I didn't like it at all. It was as if you were out to make fun of me.
> Solness. But I hadn't the slightest intention to.
> Hilda. No, it wouldn't seem so—not after what you did next—
> Solness. What on earth did I do next?
> Hilda. Well, this is really the limit if you've even forgotten *that!* A thing like that I think anybody ought to remember.
> Solness. All right, just give me a tiny hint, then, maybe—hm?
> Hilda *(looking intently at him)*. You caught me up and kissed me, Mr. Solness.
> Solness *(open-mouthed, getting up)*. I *did!*
> (p. 330)

Solness, of course, *wants* it to be true—"This all must have been in my thoughts. I must have willed it. Wished it. Desired it"—and it is the kind of truth that prods Solness to make plans to change his life. It is a truth buried in psyche and past, brought out of the darkness by the realistic character Hilda and what she symbolizes. That she symbolizes so much, perhaps carrying more weight than one character can successfully bear, makes her both more and less than realistic, a mysterious, troll-like figure, despite the clarity of her vigorous presence on stage.

Hilda represents the fear of youth that has been troubling Solness and that informs his relationship with Ragnar and Kaja. She is the young person knocking at the door at the precise moment that Solness says to Dr. Herdal: "Yes, Doctor, you better look out. Someday youth will come here, knocking at the door—" (p. 324). An obvious theatrical trick, so obvious that we must believe Ibsen wanted to make absolutely clear Hilda's symbolic representation of youth. By embracing Hilda, Solness embraces the very fear he has been living with. He seems to be joining youth instead of fighting it, but paradoxically and tragically the embrace of youth is the embrace of death as well, for Hilda will cause his fateful fall. The knocking at the door will be "the end of Solness, the master builder," as Solness says to Herdal without realizing the full implications of his statement. His falling death will provide the stunning climax to a play filled with *death*—Solness "chained to the dead," as he puts it, because he is bound to a wife whose lifeblood has been sucked out of her by his troll; the dead sons who perished because Aline dutifully insisted on nursing them, even though her milk was bad; Aline's "dead" dolls, for whom she has a stronger affection than for her dead children; the dying Brovik, forever frustrated in his attempt to have his son recognized as a competent independent builder, and in a dying coma when the recognition finally does come. Hilda's knocking at the door, although a more vigorous manifestation of death and echoing in a far different world, takes on some of the ominous overtones that we associate with the knocking at the gate in *Macbeth*. Hilda, like Macduff, is an avenging force that will pursue the hero to his death. The past, as always, controls the present and future, and the future in tragedy is death. Solness's bold deed of the past—his shouting defiance against God on the church tower in Lysanger—brings forth a witness (a literal witness and the physical manifestation of Solness's own guilt) who comes knocking to make her private claim of the past but who, at the same time, is linked to God's vengeance and to a pattern of sin and retribution. An avenging angel, a devil (Solness called her "a little devil in white"), a troll—whatever the designation—Hilda is central to the determinism which controls Solness's life and death, a determinism set in motion by such deeds of the past as willing the fire, shouting defiance at God, and promising a kingdom to a young girl. That little girl of the past whom he embraced and kissed (or did he?) returns after ten years to lead Solness to death. She prods him to repeat his former bold deed of climbing a tower, at the top of which he challenged the God for whom he built churches. At that precise moment of the past Hilda heard "harps in the air"; at the end of the play she will hear the same heavenly music. The past will be repeated, but with a difference—this time Solness falls. Solness wills Hilda as his helper and server but he has no control over her dark function as the troll who causes his death. For Ibsen, it seems, man's will allows for choice, but eventually man is pulled down by a larger determinism, psychological *and* metaphysical, whose essence is mysterious.

Solness the master builder is the victim of his own latent guilt—"there's this sense of some enormous guilt hanging over me, crushing me down"—resulting from his willing the fire and from what he considers to be a wasted life because his artistic energies have produced no happiness for anyone. He is also the victim of his own "luck" which, he realizes, was the means by which the angry God he defied exacted revenge. Solness, like all tragic characters, is trapped in his condition; for him, as for Oedipus and Hamlet and Phaedra and the three sisters, there is no way out. His grand attempt to be free from the restrictions of self and God, his daring climb to the top of his house-tower, leads to the ultimate restriction, death. Instead of waiting for Godot, Solness climbs toward Godot. Fated to fall—fulfilling "a destiny controlled by an invisible power," as Hermann Weigand puts it,[6] as "retribution at the hand of God," according to Sverre Arestad[7]—Solness escapes the frozen condition of his dead life by smashing into a stone quarry, metaphorical death followed by literal death. The fall itself is the repetition of a previous fall, which occurred in the world of dreams. Hilda, between acts 1 and 2, had a good sleep—"like a child in a cradle . . . like a princess"—but she had, as she tells Solness, an "awful" dream: ". . . I dreamed I was falling over a terribly high, steep cliff. *You* ever dream such things?"

> *Solness.* Oh, yes—now and then—
> *Hilda.* It's wonderfully thrilling—just to fall and fall.
> *Solness.* It makes my blood run cold.
> *Hilda.* You pull your legs up under you while you fall?
> *Solness.* Of course, as high as possible.
> *Hilda.* Me too.
> (p. 343)

Solness and Hilda share the experience of dreaming a fall. For Hilda the dream is "awful," but "wonderfully thrilling"; it turns Solness's blood cold. This doubleness of response toward the dream fall clings to the real fall at play's end. "Terribly thrilling" for Hilda; "how horrible this is," says Ragnar; *"a cry of horror"* from the crowd below. Beneath the external realism, moving toward it, making it happen, is the more mysterious, but not less real, power of fantasy, the kind of fantasy attached to building "castles in the air" for a princess instead of churches or homes. "Castles in the air"—like the dream of a fall, a death wish. Believing that he may be mad, fearful of the demonic troll controlling him, Solness is lodged on a boundary situation at the edge of reality. Whether he is on the "high, steep cliff" of a dream world or on the tower of a home in the more tangible world, his fall—thrilling or horrible, perhaps both at the same time—is inevitable. Although the climb may be his choice, he is pushed off the top by the irrational within and the unexplainable without.

From two directions, then, Solness receives the slings and arrows that flesh is heir to, and Hilda—that troll within and that angel or devil who works God's revenge—is connected to both. At the moment that Hilda knocks and enters, Solness has begun his "movement toward death";[8] he has taken a step toward the abyss into which his body will fall. Before he falls, Solness must climb, despite his intense fear of heights. Hilda makes him rise, literally and spiritually—and sexually. Concerning the last, there is no need to belabor the obvious Freudian interpretation that forces itself upon us when we contemplate a middle-aged man, still strong, whose "dead" and dutiful wife makes him think he is faltering, who is attracted and attractive to a vigorous young woman who prods him to climb, allowing her to hear heavenly music. What must be emphasized here is that Hilda is associated with an eroticism that makes us aware of Solness's darker desires and energies. That is why she, wearing sailor cap and blouse and carrying an alpenstock, represents both the sea and the mountains, Ibsen's two favorite symbols. Sea and mountain hearken the primitive and uncontrollable, depths and heights, Dionysus, madness. Hilda to Solness is sea and mountain; she helps us to experience the atmosphere of his soul and the urges of his body.

Solness's climb makes him rise in our admiration of him, makes him, in fact, a traditional tragic hero. A flawed character because of his selfish manipulation of Kaja and Ragnar and Old Brovik, because of his artistic compromises, because of his physical fear of heights, he emerges very high indeed in his solitary climb, which places a man apart, above other men. His is the isolation and desire for freedom of the artist. Wishing to stand alone, even independent of God, but bound to a wife and successful profession, and bound to an irredeemable past, Solness must make an enormous effort to be free, to release himself from the guilt that is crushing him down, to "test" himself by doing the "impossible" once again, as he did ten years earlier at Lysanger—climb a tower and tell *the* Master Builder that he, Solness, will be "a free creator—free in my own realm, as you are in yours." With Hilda's help, he is able to acquire a "robust conscience," to become a Viking—amoral, capturing young women, defying danger, sailing uncharted waters, achieving "a joy in life." He becomes, as Robert Brustein labels hm, a "Promethean rebel,"[9] for Solness revolts against God, carries the fire of artistic creation, asserts self, and demands our respect. Like Prometheus, he too will be a victim of a god's vengeance, but before vengeance comes, he will display courage as he tries to confront the troll within and as he painfully raises himself above those people below who watch the climb of others, who merely observe the fall of princes. At play's end we learn from Hilda that Solness is "struggling" with someone at the top. At the moment of victory, waving his hat, he falls. Victory and defeat come together—the paradox of tragedy. The choric commentators below give us the two perspectives on Solness's fall from the heights.

> *Ragnar.* How horrible this is. And so, after all—he really couldn't do it.
> *Hilda (as if out of a hushed, dazed triumph).* But he went straight, straight to the top. And I heard harps in the air. *(Swings the shawl up overhead and cries with wild intensity.)* My—my master builder!
> (p. 384)

I believe that Ibsen wants us to hold simultaneously both of these views of Solness's end. Failure and success, success and failure— the kind of rich ambivalence attached to the victory-defeat of such tragic characters as Sophocles' Oedipus and Antigone and Shakespeare's Hamlet and Racine's Phaedra and O'Neill's Abbie and Eben. That Solness reaches his peak and reasserts his "Non serviam" attitude toward God surrounds his high isolation with a Luciferian grandness. Like Lucifer, he falls, hurled headlong into the quarry, but the law of gravity that pulls him into the abyss is not more powerful or relentless than those mysterious forces within and without that determine his tragic fate.

Ibsen the dramatist is usually pictured as a plump, satisfied, bespectacled burgher, seated on a plush chair in a heavily furnished Victorian drawing room. This comfortable surface impression hides a tormented soul, forever, like Solness, fighting the demonic troll, forever, to use Ibsen's charged phrase, holding "doom-session" on the self. Obviously, there is more within. As with Ibsen the man, so too with Ibsen's dramatic art. The realism of the decorous social surface covers a deep, subterranean darkness. There is more within— and that "more" touches the secret cause.

Although he is not a master builder who climbs steeples to challenge God, Alfred Ill, a simple shopkeeper in the small town of Guellen, also holds doom-session on the self in *The Visit*, the finest play of the important mid-century dramatist, Friedrich Dürrenmatt. In acknowledging the guilt lodged deep within him, Ill is prodded by Claire Zachanassian, the richest woman in the world, whom he wronged forty-five years before and who now returns to her home town of Guellen to exact vengeance. Belonging to a different world than Hilda Wangel, seemingly different from her in every way— old, unnatural, wearing dark clothes, accompanied by a macabre entourage of Husband VII, eighty-year-old butler, two gum-chewing ex-gangsters, and two blind eunuchs, with a caged black panther and an empty coffin as part of her luggage—nevertheless, Claire shares with the breezy, young, natural Hilda the dramatic function of bringing out the best in, and causing the death of, the play's tragic hero. From the moment the train carrying Claire Zachanassian makes its stop in Guellen and Claire steps on the train platform, Alfred Ill begins his journey to his self and to his death.

On one level, *The Visit* is a realistic revenge-play with Claire Zachanassian as the relentless revenger[10] avenging herself against those who abused her forty-five years before. That the abuse, considered from one perspective, resulted in good fortune for her must be acknowledged. She is now the richest woman in the world because she was forced to leave the town of Guellen. Leaving town led her to the brothel in Hamburg where she met "old Zachanassian . . . the old, gold lecher!"[11] who was the first and the richest of the many rich men she married. Traveling on the road to prosperity, while Ill

remained stationary in his shopkeeper-husband-father role (but
with the possibility of rising to mayor of the town), Claire's crowded
life, calculatingly lived to "turn the world into a brothel" because it
turned her into a whore, has made her a different creature from the
seventeen-year-old victimized girl who left town almost a half-
century earlier. Although lucky in her worldly fortunes, Claire has
become an inhuman, grotesque figure, so strange and mysterious
that we are forced to go beyond the realistic in attempting to gauge
her full significance. Like Pozzo and Lucky (the latter's name clearly
applicable here, especially in its ironic dimension) Claire travels a
worldly road, but like Godot she takes on abstract significance. The
Didi-Gogo of this play, Alfred Ill—frozen, locked in his small-town
condition, "a broken-down shopkeeper in a broken-down town"—
need wait no longer for his Godot, who "from the heights" (Claire
literally waits on the balcony for the town to accept eventually her
proposal of killing Ill for a million) will cause him to be "plunged in
torment" although she "loves" him "dearly." (The quoted words
are from Lucky's speech.) Once she returns to Guellen, Claire
Zachanassian becomes the fixed power who forces Ill to move
toward an understanding of self and the world around him. That is,
Ill is now metaphorically on the road while Claire is fixed, perched
on high, "cast in a mold of stone," as Dürrenmatt describes her in
his postscript to the play. An avenging force, with her vengeance
aimed at the town as well as Ill, Claire Zachanassian's largeness and
dark potency compel us to approach the play—realistic at its base,
but at times expressionistic in its technique—by way of myth and
ritual. Dürrenmatt points us in that direction by having the Schoolmaster, the play's most articulate character, call Claire a Medea in
her "evil thoughts of revenge," and by the dramatist's own
statement in the postscript that she is "something like Medea."
Interesting and apt as this comparison is—for Claire is as absolute
and terrible in her demand for vengeance as that sorceress from
antiquity—it does not suggest the full power of Claire's other-
worldly stage presence, her Sphinx-like aura, her half-woman/half-
stone quality, and her function, not as central tragic heroine like
Medea, but as the nemesis of the play's central character, Alfred Ill.
Claire Zachanassian who, according to Dürrenmatt, is "purely and
simply what she is, namely the richest woman in the world" (postscript, p. 106), is certainly more than what she is. Like Ibsen's Hilda,
she is a realistic woman coming on stage to make sure a debt from

the past is paid; but also like Hilda, she is a mysterious force, beyond realism, whose presence controls the action of the play and the progress of its tragic hero. She is the play's Sphinx or gods to the play's Oedipus. The Ill-Oedipus connection is too tight to be accidental.[12] *The Visit* begins with a chorus of townspeople lamenting the sick condition of their community. They see as their deliverer Alfred Ill, the future mayor, who will know how to talk to the visitor and thereby change the town's condition. Like Oedipus at Thebes, Ill is the cause of the community's misery without knowing it, and like Oedipus, he, with heavy irony at work, is asked to be the deliverer. In an unmistakably classic sense, Ill in his past has committed an act that is now weaving around him the net of necessity, leading him to death. That act has at its core a sexual sin. Although the young Alfred loved the young Clarie Wascher—and some of that love can still be felt in the play's Village Wood scenes ("If only time hadn't put us asunder. . . . I do love you!")—he refused to claim the child born from their young union, he bribed two witnesses (the play's blind eunuchs) to swear falsely that they slept with Claire, and he allowed Claire to leave the town in disgrace. All of this in order to acquire material comfort (by marrying Matilda Blumhard "with her little general store"), the kind of comfort the townspeople will acquire when they murder Ill. Like Oedipus, Ill tries to avoid his fate, but eventually he, again like Oedipus, acknowledges his guilt: "I made Clara what she is, and I made myself what I am, a failing shopkeeper with a bad name. What shall I do, Schoolmaster? Play innocent? It's all my own work, the Eunuchs, the Butler, the coffin, the million. I can't help myself and I can't help any of you, any more" (p. 76). And, like Oedipus, he saves his community (although the word "saves" as applied to Dürrenmatt's play needs further discussion), thereby allowing the play to end in a communal chorus. Ill's inner guilt, again in accordance with classical formula, combines with a strong sense of external fate, here represented by Claire Zachanassian. Sphinx-like, she hovers over the town's destruction, not only having bought all the industries in order to close them down and produce poverty, but now spiritually destroying the town by offering one million pounds for the murder of Ill. ("I'll wait," she says knowingly at the end of act 1, when the Mayor rejects her offer "in the name of humanity.") Claire's ability to use words in such a way that crass vengeance becomes pure justice suggests the riddling quality of the ancient Sphinx, and like that

Sphinx, she brings death. Although this mechanical listing of parallels between *The Visit* and *Oedipus Rex* indicates the strong allusive dimension of Dürrenmatt's play, it does not altogether reflect the play's enormously rich suggestiveness. For Claire Zachanassian not only represents the Sphinx, she carries with her the force of the gods. She controls the fates of Ill and the townspeople, and she is linked to unalterable necessity. The Schoolmaster specifically calls her "an avenging Greek goddess . . . like one of the Fates." He believes "her name should be Clotho," and he suspects her of "spinning destiny's web" (p. 26). And her demonic dimension gives Ill's tragic status a Christian shading as well. She is the devil tempting Everyman: ". . . I've grown into hell itself" (p. 29); "I'm unkillable" (p. 31); my first husband was "a real devil. I've copied him completely" (p. 42). When Ill is unable to escape Guellen at the end of act 2, we see a large poster in the train station which reads "Visit the Passion Plays in Oberammergau," reminding us of that other figure tempted by Satan, also the ritual sacrifice of his people. At play's end, Ill is able to expiate his sin by going to his death. He refuses to commit suicide, the Christian sin of despair, but his death-wished walk to his death at the hands of the Gymnast seems like a kind of suicide. (Here Solness's fall from the steeple, also a kind of suicide, comes to mind.) With strong Greek and Christian echoes, what we have in *The Visit* is the classic confrontation of man with an inscrutable determinism, terrible in the fixity of its dark purpose.

The development of Ill as the play's hero is described briefly in Dürrenmatt's postscript: ". . . he is a thoughtless figure of a man, a simple man in whose mind something slowly dawns, by the agency of fear and terror, something highly personal; a man who in recognizing his guilt lives out justice and who, in death, achieves greatness. (His death should not be without a certain monumental quality.)" This is an important statement because Dürrenmatt clearly recognizes what seem to be traditional qualities of the tragic hero at the same time that he discusses his play as a comedy and labels it "a tragicomedy." The crucial words are "fear and terror" and "guilt" and "achieving greatness in death." As Ill begins to realize that his fellow townspeople and his family are yielding to temptation with each new acquisition ("How did you all get new shoes?" . . . "How are you going to pay?"), he is overcome by fear for his own life ("It's me you're hunting down, me" . . . "I'm scared") and by the terror that comes from making a new discovery about people you thought you knew. At first, he tries to avoid his fate, scurrying around "like a cornered animal." Finally, however, he faces his guilt with a dignity that is reserved for the respected heroes of tragedy. Not shirking his responsibility in causing Claire's fall—and let us not forget that even though she "rises" in her fall to become the richest woman in the world, she has fallen from wronged human being to vengeful stone-goddess—and not condemning the townspeople whose moral weakness he clearly recognizes, Ill accepts his own death at the hands of those townspeople. He is able to see, for the first time in his long life, the dark selfish core in all people, including himself. And what he sees makes him understand the justice of his punishment and makes him the instrument of whatever justice will come to the townspeople when they have murdered him. In the paradoxical nature of tragedy, Claire Zachanassian, the goddess of bitter vengeance, is also the goddess of justice, and Ill, the victim of justice, in the very act of being murdered, becomes the instrument of justice against the murderers. What kind of "justice" the townspeople receive is one of the play's many problems, but no ambiguity surrounds Ill's dignified walk to death. Death, of course, has been on stage since Claire's arrival. The black coffin that she brings with her is both a visual prop and the focus of discussion; empty when she arrives, it will contain Ill at play's end. The black panther (her pet name for Ill) arrives in a cage, but escapes and is hunted down and killed. Claire's blind eunuchs are two "sinister" fat men who seem to have arisen "from the infernal regions." Claire, herself half-dead with artificial limbs and Death itself in her symbolic suggestiveness, often talks about her previous dead husbands. To the Schoolmaster she's "a gruesome vision." Her first contact with the Priest brings forth her question, "Do you comfort the dying?" She asks the Doctor if he makes out death certificates. And so on. Death in all its aspects—from fleeting allusions to the Passion of Jesus to the "hunting down" of the main character—informs the play, and no escape from death is possible for Ill. His recognition and acceptance of his own guilt, combined with the fearful actions of the ordinary townspeople, push him along the ever-narrowing road to the boundary situation. That he travels on it with self-control and dignity gives his death the "monumental quality" that Dürrenmatt desired.[13] The dark power of the Sphinx-goddess-devil has doomed Alfred Ill into tragic significance.

The townspeople, on the other hand, have been doomed to murder and prosperity. The power that corrupts them is money, and the determinism that controls them is economic. The poverty caused by Claire's buying up and drying up the town's industry has produced hard hearts. Their descent from friends and neighbors properly shocked at Claire's demonic terms for obtaining the million pounds —". . . we are not savages"—to menacing hunters self-righteously doing the dark deed in the name of justice is a devastating comment on human nature. But their action should not be considered monstrous. What they did seems natural, given economic necessity. They, although nonheroic in succumbing to temptation and nontragic in their inability to recognize the horror of their deed, are also being pushed to a boundary situation. "Like the rest of us," according to Dürrenmatt, the Guelleners "must not, emphatically not, be portrayed as wicked" (postscript, p. 107). Precisely because they are like us, capable of horrible deeds when driven by economic necessity, the townspeople cause Dürrenmatt's play to enter the realm of satire, thereby complicating a discussion of genre. Dürrenmatt labels the play "a tragicomedy" ("eine tragische Komödie"), the difficult term that always demands careful examination. Dürrenmatt supports his label by asserting, in the last sentence of the postscript, that "nothing could harm this comedy with a tragic end more than heavy seriousness." The "tragic end," one must assume, is the death of Alfred Ill, but the very end of the play focuses on the chorus of townspeople: their satisfied reaction to Ill's death and to Claire's departure from Guellen (with Ill in the coffin), and their statements on their own rebirth as a thriving community. The tragic effect seems to blend into a comic effect, with our perspective shifting from Ill to the crowd, from the silence of one dignified human being to choric utterances, words expressing both dreadful truths (". . . the radiant mushroom grows / From the spoor of the atom bomb") and banal ideas ("Young guys with any future drive a Sports"), from the utter finality of one man's death to the ongoing life of a community. What we seem to have is not "comedy with a tragic end" but tragedy with a comic end, unless we are meant to think of the townspeople's final condition as tragic even though they joyfully and unitedly acclaim their "good fortune," the play's last two words. The townspeople in their last choruses display no sense of guilt that they have acquired their fortune by murdering a man. Once the moral slaves of their poverty, they are now the immoral slaves of their prosperity. Unaware victims of Claire Zachanassian, they are alive and prosperous, but they will never achieve the paradoxical death-freedom of that aware victim, Alfred Ill. In short, "our glorious town / Grown out of the ashes anew" is now more corrupt and morally plague-ridden than it was in the play's beginning; the town is materially born anew, but spiritually dead. It is for this reason that Dürrenmatt says in his postscript that Ill's death is "both meaningful and meaningless." Ill has redeemed himself, thereby earning tragic status, but he has not redeemed his town, unlike Oedipus who accomplished both tasks. The end of *The Visit* gives us the ironical triumph of a fallen town, with Dürrenmatt the satirist prodding us to judge the townspeople's behavior and to realize that they are "like the rest of us."

Our difficulty in absorbing both tragedy and satire in the same play is compounded by Dürrenmatt's fondness for the grotesque, that distortion of the natural that combines the horrible with the comical or, more appropriate to Dürrenmatt, hides the horrible behind the comical. The grotesque is an important aspect of Dürrenmatt's dramatic art and it is a clear indicator of his general attitude toward life. Murray Peppard, paraphrasing Wolfgang Kayser in his *The Grotesque in Painting and Poetry*, crisply describes the essence of the grotesque as a viewpoint that sees "a world in which the irrational and demonic may, at any moment, break through the veneer of convention and complacency to reveal fundamental and frightening truths. The grotesque has a mixed effect, turning laughter into horror, provoking a smile and then causing it to freeze on the face of the spectator."[14] The question that such a description raises—and it is a description that clearly fits Dürrenmatt's significant use of the grotesque—is whether the grotesque belongs more to tragedy or to comedy. If not more to either, then "tragicomedy" *is* the best word for Dürrenmatt's play. But this is not the case. As with Chekhov and Beckett, the balancing act of Dürrenmatt reveals a strong undercurrent of the tragic. Whatever laughter Dürrenmatt provokes is tragic laughter; behind the smile of the comic mask is the shriek of the tragic mask. In *The Visit* Claire Zachanassian is the most obvious manifestation of the grotesque. Stated simply, she is a grotesque human being; in fact, her grotesqueness, comical on the surface, invests her with those ominous symbolic overtones already observed. Take, for example, the exchange between Claire and Ill in the woodland bower of their youth. They reminisce about the "young days," that precious time when "we kissed each other on this spot." A soft scene, touching some tender memories, quickly destroyed not only by Claire's revelation about what happened to her when she left Guellen, but by her physical grotesqueness. Ill, in his excitement, slaps her on the shoulder, withdrawing his hand in pain because he hit one of the straps of her artificial leg. He kisses her hand, her "cool, white hand," having said to her "I do love you!", but releases it "horrified" because Claire tells him "it's artificial too. Ivory." That she is practically all artificial—and therefore "unkillable"—allows her, on the symbolic level, to be the stone idol, the Sphinx, the fixed goddess, inflexible fate. In this brief woodland scene of act 1, the grotesque causes a smile to freeze as the demonic truth about Claire is revealed.

A more complex example of Dürrenmatt's use of the grotesque—more complex because it involves the satiric mode, itself a problem, as we have noticed—occurs at play's end, when Dürrenmatt boldly places the tragic moment of Ill's murder within the context of a grotesque mockery of justice. Having said goodbye to Claire in the woodland setting, Ill, knowing he will soon die to become merely "a dead love" in Claire's memory, remains seated on the bench while the setting changes around him. A Radio Commentator announces that we are now in the auditorium of the Golden Apostle, where the Guelleners, dressed in new evening gowns and dress-suits, are assembling to hear formally about Claire Zachanassian's donation to the town of one million pounds. Photographers, reporters, and cameramen are present to make this a remarkable media event. The Schoolmaster, once a character who possessed a conscience, now articulates the town's position with what the Radio Commentator calls "moral grandeur": the townspeople will accept Claire Zachanassian's gift not because of their love of money but because of their love of justice; once they connived at injustice, now they promise to take their ideals seriously. The Mayor asks "those pure in heart who want justice done" to raise their hands in acceptance of the Claire Zachanassian Endowment. With only Ill remaining motionless, all other hands are raised "as if making one, mighty pledge for a better, juster world," according to the Radio Commentator. The Mayor then leads the townspeople in a choric litany, the blatant repetition reminding us of the characteristic mode of expression of the blind eunuchs, also the victims of Claire's machinations.

Mayor. The Claire Zachanassian Endowment is accepted.
Unanimously. Not for the sake of the money,
Citizens. Not for the sake of the money,
Mayor. But for justice
Citizens. But for justice
Mayor. And for conscience's sake.
Citizens. And for conscience's sake.
Mayor. For we cannot connive at crime:
Citizens. For we cannot connive at crime:
Mayor. Let us then root out the wrongdoer,
Citizens. Let us then root out the wrongdoer,
Mayor. And deliver our souls from evil
Citizens. And deliver our souls from evil
Mayor. And all our most sacred possessions.
Citizens. And all our most sacred possessions.
Ill (screams). My God!
(p. 94)

Ill's scream brings us back from communal self-righteous platitudes
mocking the ideal of justice to the single agony of a tragic figure who
recognizes the horror behind the mechanical repetitions captured
for posterity by the movie camera. With that scream of terror,
Dürrenmatt restores the tragic, only to subdue it again in the ensu-
ing stage business. The newsreel camera jams, and the Mayor is
asked to "do that last vote again" for the camera. The Mayor com-
plies, and we are given the exact repetition of the litany previously
quoted. Repetitions on repetitions, for the sake of the media, a gross
trivialization of what has already been trivialized. This time, however, Ill does not scream. His silence, like Cordelia's, is the most elo-
quent response possible in a world of hypocrisy. Moments later Ill
will walk into the lane formed by the Guelleners, reach the Gymnast, sink to his knees as the lane closes on him (the physical manifestation of the fate that has pushed him to this moment), and Ill will
be strangled. The media will report that he had a heart attack, that
he "died of joy"; one reporter informs us that "life writes the most
beautiful stories." The grotesque perversion of justice, punctuated
by hum of camera and flash of bulb, forces a satiric glance at modern
civilized society, but hidden behind the veneer of civilization lies the
horror. Dürrenmatt's use of the grotesque throughout *The Visit* reveals frightening truths that point to a tragic view of the world.

In his much-quoted critical essay, *Problems of the Theatre*, Dürrenmatt asserts that tragedy is not possible in our time. Because ours is a fragmented "unformed" world, a world about to end (because of the atom bomb, the "world butchers," and the "slaughtering machines"), a world containing no "responsible" men and therefore no "guilty" men in the personal sense, comedy "alone is suitable for us." Not wishing to discount the tragic entirely, Dürrenmatt allows the genre to enter modern drama in this way: "But the tragic is still possible even if pure tragedy is not. We can achieve the tragic out of comedy. We can bring it forth as a frightening moment, as an abyss that opens suddenly."[15] Here he seems to be describing what we have just discussed, the grotesque. That his words tilt the grotesque toward comedy conforms to his belief that comedy is the only possible genre in our time and (typical of many dramatists who write criticism) conforms to what he sees himself as doing. The problem here—in addition to the fact that a writer could be his own worst critic, as Dürrenmatt himself acknowledged[16]—is close to the problem we observed in Chekhov: a dramatist cannot always accurately judge the emotional response produced by his own play. When, as in *The Visit*, comedy gives us a glimpse of the "abyss," when the moment is "frightening," when irrational and demonic forces arise suddenly, when death and determinism reveal themselves as terrible truths, when the cause of man's helplessness and the cause of man's hard-heartedness remains secret, then what seemed to be a humorous view of the world—the distanced view that we associate with comedy—becomes the immediately felt tragic view, the open mouth of laughter freezing to a silent scream.

Perhaps the most intense discussion of whether a particular play is or is not a tragedy focuses not on a play labeled "tragicomedy," like *The Visit* or *Waiting for Godot*, or on a play whose writer considered it to be other than a tragedy, like *The Three Sisters*, but on one carefully conceived and meant to be received as a tragedy, Arthur Miller's *Death of a Salesman*. From its first performance on February 10, 1949, to the discussion I am about to enter, more than thirty years later, Miller's play has been the center of controversial debate on its genre, a debate prodded by Miller himself, whose critical essay "Tragedy and the Common Man," appearing in the *New York Times* seventeen days after the play opened, attempted to shoot down previous definitions of tragedy in order to uphold his firm belief that "the com-

MILLER SAY IT'S OK TO HAVE TRAGEDY OF A COMMON MAN .

mon man is as apt a subject for tragedy in its highest sense as kings were."[17] In this essay, and in the perceptive introduction to his *Collected Plays,* Miller eagerly takes on Aristotle and company, fueling a debate whose fire continues to throw sparks. *Death of a Salesman* is an important touchstone in any discussion of tragedy. It was written as a tragedy by an important American dramatist who has defended its status in his critical writings, and it contains many aspects of traditional tragedy, but its generic designation does not satisfy many academicians. To examine precisely why the label "tragedy" does not adequately describe Miller's play is to understand more clearly the importance of the secret cause.

What characteristics of tragedy does *Death of a Salesman* possess that allow it to be compared with the best in the genre? Its basic story is that of a man whose failure in life leads him to suicide; it dramatizes an agony and a death. In classical fashion, the man, Willy Loman, is picked up near the end of his life; not in classical fashion, the important moments of his past are shown to us on stage, instead of being presented in expository speech or dialogue. Miller's is the modern method of realism combined with expressionism, the latter made possible by advances in modern psychology and modern stage techniques. As in most tragedies—and as in the plays of Ibsen, the dramatist who had the profoundest influence on Miller—the past influences the thoughts and actions of the present. So immediate is the past in Willy's troubled mind that the past and present become one, and so powerful is the pressure of the past that it seems to determine the play's action. That is, the sense of fate is produced by the intensity of the past's impingement on the present, with Miller's expressionistic devices allowing us to see and hear Willy Loman thinking about a past that becomes now. Willy's false values, linked inextricably to the values of his society, shape his life and cause his death. What happens to Willy, his present frustration, is the direct result of his firm belief in the American dream of success.

Choosing the life of a salesman, Willy has as his ideal Dave Singleman who, at the age of eighty-four, was able to go into a hotel, "put on his green velvet slippers,"[18] pick up the phone, and make his many calls to buyers. But Willy cannot live up to the model of old Dave Singleman, whose "personality" made him a successful salesman. Willy is laughed at; "people don't seem to take to" him; he is not "noticed"; he can not squeeze out a living by selling. The violent death of the salesman Loman, which is followed by a funeral attracting four people (his wife, two sons, and one friend), is a sad contrast to the death of the salesman Singleman—still wearing his green velvet slippers on the train to Boston—whose funeral is attended by hundreds. Willy's other model, his older brother Ben, is equally difficult to imitate. Ben is "success incarnate"; he went into the jungle with only the clothes on his back and came out with diamonds, a rich man at the age of twenty-one. Ben's rugged individualism was inherited from his father, "a very great and a very wild-hearted man," who made and sold flutes as he traveled west. The closest that Willy can come to his father, whom he never really knew, is the fragile flute music that tells of "grass and trees and the horizon," an horizon that Willy never moves toward. His father traveled to the frontier and his brother went into the jungle. Willy's setting is the hotel room, the predictable locus for the salesman of the traveling-salesman jokes, and, for Willy, the taunting center of his most unsettling remembrance of the past, when his son Biff discovers him with the laughing undressed woman. As with Ill and Oedipus, a sexual sin is part of the root experience of a protagonist's feeling of guilt.

Unable to make a living, soon to lose his job, as obsolete as his Hastings refrigerator and Studebaker, Willy Loman rightly considers himself a failure as a salesman. This sense of failure extends to his relationship with his sons. Having instilled in Biff and Happy a set of false values (often conflicting values, although Willy does not recognize the contradictions) meant to make them successful—to be "well liked" and to walk alone into the jungle; to be a lively talker, always throwing in a few jokes, and to be a man of few words; to be decent and to steal if you know you will not be caught; to get an education and to feel contempt for bookishness—one son is a thirty-four-year-old drifter, and the other is a shallow, happy-go-lucky weakling. Limited and misguided though Willy is, damaging as he is to his sons whom he has filled with false values, the intensity of his fatherhood raises him in the audience's estimation. And his realization, toward play's end, that his son Biff loves him is his only important discovery in the play.

Willy Loman's financial and familial troubles, combined with his boxed-in physical situation (surrounded by apartment buildings, unable to see the sun, unable to plant a seed), place him in a trapped tragic condition and lead him to his death. The man of the play's beginning who enters in exhaustion with two large valises, who says

"I'm tired to the death," is very close to the death that will end his exhaustion. The intervening visions and monologues and dialogues help us understand what brought him to that death. Our last minutes with Willy—after he returns from the restaurant where he replayed in his mind the Boston hotel experience, punctuated with the sounds of knocking at the door and laughing of the woman—vividly reveal the conflicts within the man and clearly display his passionate grasp of the false values that have shaped his life. Appearing on the apron stage, carrying flashlight and hoe and seed packets, Willy, flirting with madness, is preparing to plant seeds in darkness in unreceptive soil. Madness in tragedy brings out truth, and the essential Willy—the Willy who desires to plant seeds, who laments the death of trees, who enjoys working with his hands, who instinctively possesses his father's need for horizon and who has transmitted to his son Biff the love of the outdoors—confronts the values, here symbolized by Ben, that have subdued and distorted his natural instincts. Knowing that "a man has got to add up to something," but never realizing that the "something" cannot be measured by money, Willy tells Ben about his $20,000 insurance policy. For Willy, the money is "like a diamond, shining in the dark," an image that allows him to see himself at one with Ben, that "genius" who went into the dark and brought out diamonds. At this moment, in physical and spiritual darkness, Willy chooses the values of Ben, diamonds over seeds. After Biff finally and emotionally tells him the painful truth—"We never told the truth for ten minutes in this house!" "Pop! I'm a dime a dozen, and so are you!" "Pop, I'm nothing! I'm nothing, Pop. Can't you understand that? There's no spite in it any more. I'm just what I am, that's all"—and then breaks down, sobbing and holding on to Willy, Willy recognizes the genuineness of his son's love, but pays no attention to Biff's words. He reverts to his sure belief in the values he has expounded all along—"Can you imagine that magnificence with twenty-thousand dollars in his pocket?"—and rushes to his suicide, making his final sale instead of "ringing up a zero."

The death of a passionate protagonist, his feeling of guilt, his heightened status as father, the sense of determinism produced by the pressure of both a personal past and the American dream—these are the elements in *Death of a Salesman* that allow it to be considered a tragedy. Yet, the designation, as it stands, without further discussion or qualification, seems misleading. The play contains tragic characteristics and it offers a moving dramatic experience, but the play's effect is not the effect of tragedy.

Two main reasons have been stressed by the critics who do not consider *Death of a Salesman* to be a tragedy: the character of Willy Loman and the play's heavy social criticism.[19] Concerning the former, it should be emphasized at the outset that Willy's "low" status, although mentioned at times by critics and although it is the issue that Miller confronts in his criticism, is not the crucial factor in rejecting Willy Loman as a tragic hero. Rather, it is Willy's distorted values, his limited mentality, his lack of awareness, his vulgarity that prevent his receiving the kind of admiration a tragic hero seems to demand. A prince—Willy himself is called a "prince" by, of all people, Biff—a prince with Willy's qualities would be equally disrespected. A tragic hero's dignity rests on his values and behavior, not on his hierarchical or economic status. Ill, Dürrenmatt's shopkeeper, acquires the dignity of a tragic hero. Willy, Miller's salesman, even though he is intense, and he suffers, and he dies, does not acquire such dignity because of the sheer mundaneness of his values and his acceptance and parrotlike repetition of phrases and ideas that typify the worst aspects of the American dream of success: his belief in "personal attractiveness" or "personality" or being "well liked" as the key to success; his easy acceptance of the claims of advertisers; his idolizing of Ben, whose advice to Biff reveals his cut-throat individuality: "Never fight fair with a stranger, boy"; his playing to the crowd, with a crude joke, a smile, a pat on the back. It would take little effort for a comic playwright to make Willy Loman the satirical object of ridicule and contempt. Miller invests him with pathos, and successfully forces us to pay attention to the man who cannot shed the values that have ruined him. However, paying attention to him and feeling the pain of his disappointments does not necessarily ennoble him. Biff's condemnation of Willy's values as "hot air" and his evaluation of Willy as a man who "never knew who he was" pinpoint Willy's severe limitations. The shallow, uncomprehending Willy Loman cannot be "well liked," let alone respected, because he never changes his mind about his values. Even though he feels guilt and knows he is a failure and recognizes his obsolescence, he persists in seeing the world as an arena where well-liked personalities find diamonds and make something of themselves. Willy's act of self-destruction is his last attempt to be well liked by his son. Because he does not accept what Biff is telling him, because the $20,000 will mean nothing to the man who has rejected his father's values, Willy's suicide becomes an arbitrary and essentially meaningless act. His death becomes one more wrong dream for the man who, according to Biff in the Requiem, "had the wrong dreams. All, all, wrong." Charley's answer to this, that Willy, a salesman "riding on a smile and a shoeshine," should not be blamed because "a salesman is got to dream, boy" does not satisfy; it runs counter to everything Charley has said up to this point. Either Charley is so affected by Willy's death that he has suddenly changed his beliefs, or Arthur Miller is nodding. Perhaps Miller wishes to give us something positive to hold on to when we leave the theater. In any case, Charley's gesture does not work. This salesman went to his death with wrong dreams and false values.

Willy's "personality" and values are conditioned by the society that fed him the business ethic and the myth of success. There is little doubt that Miller wants us to condemn the society that pushed Willy Loman to his lamentable obsolescence. This desire by Miller is the source of the second major obstacle to the play's acceptance as tragedy. Too much social criticism works against tragedy. Because Miller, with deep and genuine compassion for the low man, believes that in drama there resides "the ultimate possibility of raising the truth-consciousness of mankind to a level of intensity as to transform those who observe it,"[20] his plays tend to have a reformatory dimension that diminishes or subdues the tragic. *Death of a Salesman* has been accused of being a propagandistic play, which it is not. But there is enough social criticism in it, or "social causation," as John Gassner puts it,[21] to produce confusion of response. Eric Bentley's questions indicate the problem: "Is his [Willy's] littleness the product of the capitalistic system? Or is it Human Nature? What attitudes are we to have to it? Pity? Anger? Or just a lovely mishmash?"[22] Bentley's exasperation stems from his belief that Miller did not know whether he wanted to write a social drama or a tragedy. Each has a different purpose: social drama criticizes a social condition, making its hero a victim of society; tragedy goes beyond society to touch the human condition, making its hero a victim of a larger and more elemental force than society, making him, in fact, an actor in a more terrible, because more dark and cosmic, drama. The force that works against Willy is clearly discernible: a society based on ruthless competition, hollow success, the cult of personality, mechanization, and built-in obsolescence of machine and man. A short scene that brings this force into sharp dramatic focus could be called the wire-recorder scene, in which Willy goes to the office of Howard Wagner, his boss, to ask that he be taken off the road. When Willy enters, Howard is busy plugging in the wire-recorder, a machine Willy has never seen before. Willy cannot break Howard away from the newly acquired gadget; whenever he wishes to ask his "little favor" he is interrupted by the sounds from the machine—Howard's seven-year-old daughter whistling "Roll out the Barrel," then Howard whistling, then his five-year-old son's recitation of the capitals of the states, then Howard urging his wife to say something. When Willy finally manages to speak to him, Howard pays no attention to Willy's plight, and refuses his request for a desk job. Willy tries to appeal to Howard's human side: "Your father came to me the day you were born and asked me what I thought of the name of Howard, may he rest in peace." But for Howard "business is business." Willy, getting more desperate, tells a bored and inattentive Howard about his early decision to be a salesman, about old Dave Singleman who "dies the death of a salesman," about the importance of "personality" in the good old days. When he asks for merely forty dollars a week, Howard answers: "Kid, I can't take blood from a stone, . . ." A clichéd phrase, but touching the truth of this excruciating moment —Willy is shedding his heart's blood, but receives no response from the stone Howard. Interrupted by Howard when he is about to explain his relationship with Howard's father, Willy, himself very much a father, passionately exclaims: "I'm talking about your father! There were promises made across this desk! You mustn't tell me you've got people to see—I put thirty-four years into this firm, Howard, and now I can't pay my insurance! You can't eat the orange and throw the peel away—a man is not a piece of fruit!" The words reveal the agony and frustration of the obsolete man. When Howard leaves to see people, Willy hallucinates; he talks to Frank, Howard's father, and accidentally switches on the recorder. Howard's son continues his mechanical recitation of capital cities, as Willy leaps away in fright, shouting to Howard to shut off the machine. A charged scene, in which Miller makes clear that the machine has replaced man, who is now discarded like an orange peel. Because "business is business," an employer must fire an employee, despite the bonds of the past. Human relationships are replaced by mechanical voices, droning on and on. The wire-recorder, like the movie camera of *The Visit,* is a machine that trivializes life, diminishes it, turns blood to stone. Willy cannot control the machine, just as he cannot control his own mind. Immediately, Ben appears, and Willy asks: "Oh, Ben, how did you do it? What is the answer?" If Willy were the kind of man who could learn from his experience, he would know that Ben's answer—the answer of "success incarnate," the answer of the tooth-and-claw jungle mentality, the answer of get-rich-quick and never mind how you do it—must be rejected. But Willy is both the victim of society and its representative, which gives the wire-recorder scene an added dimension. For Willy himself would say "business is business"; Willy, like Howard, dotes on his son; Willy is even impressed with the names of the cities in which he sells. In short, a scene which represents a sharp criticism of American society and what that society does to its people (Howard as well as Willy) does not thereby lessen the faults of the individual or erase his intrinsic frailties. There is no question that Miller is criticizing a society that can so discard and transform its members, but he does not allow such criticism to eliminate individual responsibility. That is why he gives us Charley, who is Willy's contemporary, who is a businessman, who is not corrupted by society, who has retained his integrity, although he lacks Willy's intensity and has not been tested by failure. We return to Bentley's questions: "Is his littleness the product of the capitalistic system? Or is it Human Nature?" The answer is "Both," and both almost equally. Although both can be part of a powerful human drama, which *Death of a Salesman* is, the balance produces a blurring effect, which somewhat helps to explain the difficulty some critics have in calling the play a tragedy.

Well, then, is it a tragedy or not? It contains some important characteristics of tragedy, and Miller is calculatingly presenting it as a tragedy. That the play offers social criticism or that Willy Loman is a protagonist who lacks self-awareness may be compelling enough reasons to deny it tragic status, although tragedies have absorbed social criticism (e.g., *The Visit*) and not all tragic figures are fully self-aware (e.g., Antigone). What prevents *Death of a Salesman* from being a tragedy is the absence of the one dimension that seems indispensable to tragedy: the question mark, the mystery, the secret cause. The play disappoints critics precisely because more is expected from a play that touches tragedy in so many ways. The play catches its audience up in a moving emotional experience, terribly sad, approaching gloom. Miller gives us a Requiem in order to relieve some of that gloom. He is trying, I suspect, to give us the kind

of restoration or gesture toward normalcy that tragedy often contains. However, instead of experiencing such relief, the audience is
presented with upsetting contradictions. Charley's comment on
Willy the salesman is one such contradiction, previously discussed.
More damaging—and clear evidence that Miller realizes tragedy
rests on a question mark—is Linda's puzzlement over Willy's suicide, her statements gathering the force of a questioning refrain as
the Requiem progresses toward darkness: "I can't understand it." "I
can't understand it." "I don't understand it." "I search and search
and I search, and I can't understand it." Why, one must ask, can
Linda not understand it? From the play's beginning, she knew that
Willy was contemplating suicide, and she understood Willy's deep
frustration as a father and a breadwinner. Linda Loman, in fact, has
been paying the most attention to Willy. Her puzzlement at play's
end is not true to her character, and it has none of the resonance, for
example, of Olga's "If only we knew, if only we knew!" or Didi's
"Well? Shall we go?" It is there because Miller believes that tragedy
should "question absolutely everything," and that from this questioning "we learn."[23] However, in the Requiem the questioning
seems arbitrary. And the questions Miller asks throughout the play
are social questions, the kind of questions from which we can
"learn." Social questions *can* be answered; society *can* be improved.
For that reason, Willy's plight and death are not inevitable. The
questions of tragedy, in contrast, bring us closer to mystery; the only
thing we can learn from them is that they have no answers. Miller's
questions deal with man's place in society; tragedy's questions confront more primal, more vast mysteries. The experience that Miller
offers in *Death of a Salesman* is a closed experience, and his fine dramatic skill invests the play with the real and considerable power of
such an experience. But a closed experience, by its very nature, cannot be an expanding one. It is self-contained; it lacks resonance or
suggestiveness. When a dramatist allows his tragedy to ask compelling social questions that challenge society, then he is forcing his
question mark to become a period, thereby eliminating the terror of
the unknown. No large forces are felt in *Death of a Salesman;* no
primal urges are given dramatic weight. (Willy Loman's sexual sin,
for example, depends more on his loneliness and his desire to make
the best business contacts than on the dark needs of the body.) The
play contains no hint of the supernatural or religious, no sense of
macrocosm. When Miller expands his realism to get "behind the vis-

ible facades of life" (a pregnant phrase he uses in the introduction to his *Collected Plays*), he effectively dramatizes the passion of Willy Loman, but does not allow that passion to confront or be confronted by anything wider or deeper than Willy's society or a past determined by that society. Nothing mysterious intrudes, either from deep within or from vengeful or dark gods without. (Even Ben, who has an ostensibly symbolic function, lacks suggestiveness. He stands for something, and we know what that something is. Period. Think of Hilda Wangel and Claire Zachanassian, and the hermetic quality of Ben's symbolism becomes apparent.) Despite Miller's considerable use of music, nothing vibrates beneath or beyond the closed world of the play. In short, in *Death of a Salesman* Arthur Miller dramatizes the agony and death of his hero, but he omits the largeness that only mystery can invest in tragedy. This is a serious omission in light of Miller's obvious desire to write a tragedy for our time that will stand with the best in the tragic tradition. *Death of a Salesman* is able to move audiences to tears, but it does not touch the dark heart of tragedy where the secret cause resides.

8 ON THE ROAD AND ON THE ROCK

Easy Rider & Prometheus Bound

The previous chapters have stressed what I believe to be the essential ingredient of tragedy, the secret cause. The discussions have dealt with plays from different ages and countries, and have examined both heroes and conditions, those traveling a high road to success-failure, like Oedipus and Lear and Solness, and those frozen on the road, like Didi and Gogo and the three sisters of Chekhov. It is appropriate, therefore, that this last chapter of analysis should treat that very road—an archetypal idea, of course—and should deal with beginnings and endings, that is, with our first tragic dramatist and with a popular film that has had great impact on filmmaking in the 1970s. In the paradoxical fashion of tragedy, I begin with the modern film.

Despite the many reviews that have gathered around *Easy Rider*,[1] despite the heated discussion it has provoked both pro and con, despite the emphasis placed upon it as a cultural phenomenon— talking to and about the *youth* of our society—there is one aspect of the film that has escaped attention: its genre. This is understandable, because "genre" is a concept with literary overtones, and *Easy Rider* is a movie, to use the word Pauline Kael prefers, and thereby essentially nonliterary. Yet, if we pause to consider the generic tendencies of *Easy Rider*, we are surprised to find that so youthful and rebellious a movie, in fact, so popular a movie precisely because it reflects youth's break from society, contains most of the traditional trappings of tragedy. That is, its "message" contains a condemnation of a hateful, tight, tradition-bound society, but its "genre" displays what has been traditionally accepted as tragic. Not that Dennis Hopper, Peter Fonda, and Terry Southern necessarily had in mind Aristotle and company—the thought ravishes, but no matter!—but what they offer us can be called modern tragedy. It seems fitting that the question, raised again and again, about the possibility of modern tragedy has been answered not only in the theater, the center of almost all previous discussions of the question, but also in a movie, which is *our* popular form of entertainment, just as a play was the popular entertainment for the Elizabethans and the ancient Greeks, who produced the two great periods of tragedy in the Western world.

Tragedy, as we have seen, has a vital relationship with myth, infusing the original patterns with human passion and conflict. *Easy Rider* is related to a distinctly American myth, most powerfully and clearly presented in Mark Twain's *Adventures of Huckleberry Finn,* from which, as Hemingway asserted and allowed his own novels to partially prove, all American writing comes. Most critics, when confronting Hemingway's claim, go immediately to the new unliterary prose style that Twain had made literary for the first time. However, the statement refers not only to style but to Mark Twain's evocation in its purest form of the American myth connected with a journey of escape, of going away from the restrictions of society, from the evil and brutality in the world, only to meet it and be wounded by it. (This is a variation, a significantly American variation, of the kind of archetypal journey we find in Homer, but Odysseus is on a journey *to* his home, whereas Huck Finn is on a journey *away from* home.) This journey of escape takes on a mythic quality because we recognize a vital part of ourselves in the experience. On a deep psychological level we participate in the journey, for it is our vicarious chance to play hooky from school, to be Falstaff to the responsible Hal who is within us to confine us, to be Zorba to the plodding scholar, to be Dionysus to the clear, cool Apollo who restricts and channels our wilder energies. It is on this deep level that Huck Finn and the easy riders affect us. The similarities between the boy on the raft and the boys on the cycles seem compelling and give testimony to the vitality of the traditional pattern and its truth to experience. In both Mark Twain's novel and *Easy Rider* we have rides that usually lead to violence, but sometimes to peaceful interludes. In both we experience the beauty and mystery of natural surroundings, the river in the book, the land in the movie. Huck Finn and Captain America and Billy the Kid are young, masculine, alone; they belong to the open air. Each young man delights in the pleasures of the senses. Each has a natural distrust of people, each is an essentially "serious" young man. Most important, they all want to get away from society, from respectability, from restrictions. Feeling trapped, they have to keep moving. Huck's words could have been spoken by the boys on the motorcycles: ". . . when I couldn't stand it no longer I lit out." But all, in the very act of trying to avoid what society offers, meet brutality and pain. The novel's Huck Finn with Jim on a raft on the river becomes the film's Captain America with Billy the Kid on motorcycles on the road. Structurally, just as the river holds the novel together, the road holds *Easy Rider* together.

Mark Twain, however, allows Huck—a wiser, wounded, more experienced Huck—to come back at the end of the novel to the everyday, empty, comic world of Tom Sawyer. Hopper, Fonda, and Southern kill their easy riders. This important difference points the film toward tragedy. But it is not the only difference. Huck is an innocent when the novel begins, a kind of "innocent aboard." (The play on words is intended to suggest that the American myth I have been discussing belongs as well to those novels that feature "innocents abroad," naive Americans who become wounded and wiser because of an escape to Europe.) Captain America and Billy are soiled, tainted. The opening sequence in *Easy Rider* shows them peddling dope, experienced in handling the dust, sniffing it with cultivated nostrils, jittery with nervousness for fear of being caught. They, unlike Huck, have seen much of the world before we meet them. That is why they are lighting out, with the money they receive selling the dope. Huck's ride is on a raft; the easy riders use motorcycles—the difference between the two modes of transportation itself indicates the respective difficulties of the rides and of the escapes. Huck climbs aboard the raft and floats away, the river at these moments a shelter, a darkness that soothes mysteriously and silently. The machines grind their gears, the wheels rub against the ground, the noise deafens. The escape seems more difficult because less soothing, less mysterious. And a road—any road or highway— inevitably *leads* somewhere; its very essence suggests direction, shades of civilization, and therefore, of society and restriction. The road on land, the highway between states, offers no escape, merely connection. It loads the film with a sense of inevitability, always an important aspect of tragedy. The river is less restrictive, less connective, more elemental and dark and lazy.

Supported, vitalized by a mythic journey ending in brutal death, *Easy Rider* possesses other qualities of the tragic. A tragic atmosphere hangs over the film, a sense that wherever the riders go, whatever they do, they are rushing—literally, as we see and hear their speed—toward a calamity that will destroy them. This sense of foreboding is present even at those moments when we, and the riders, relax. The nude dip in the lake with the easy girls, the moments of levity in the hippie colony, the meal with the farmer and his large family—these are points of rest, but not altogether restful, because we know that the girls will be left behind, that the hippies are struggling to survive, that the farmer, rooted in the land (a natural, so to speak, whose wife is a multiplying earth-mother, and who even takes out his *false* teeth when eating his victuals), stands for a way of life in solid contrast to the moving, shiftless riders. A crude and obvious visual juxtaposition is achieved when we see in a single frame the farmer shoeing his horse while Captain America is fixing his cycle's flat tire.

The film's easy riders support Arthur Miller's contention that a modern hero's stature is not dependent on rank, but on the intensity of his commitment to go beyond the given bounds. In the case of *Easy Rider* the commitment is based on the desire to *avoid* confrontation, but the intensity is felt, projected in various ways: in the sense of live determination on the part of the motorcycles in negotiating the roads, in the cyclists' silent insistence on their way of life, in the camera's concentration on brooding eyes and sad faces. In a world in which heroism is reduced to an avoidance of confrontation, an escape from society, the hero is confined to a conflict that seems to be, at first glance, no conflict at all—and without conflict there can be no tragedy. A closer look, however, indicates that in terms of the movie the very state of being a nonconformist, of being on a motorcycle, of wearing long hair, is an act of defiance in a straight, distrustful, smug society that is filled with hatred for outsiders. If escape were possible, then conflict could be avoided. But the whole movement of the film, with the form containing its own inevitable dynamism, propels the riders toward confrontation in the very act of avoidance. Paradoxically, they are escaping *to* a fateful meeting—thereby investing the film with the kind of tragic irony we find in Greek and Elizabethan tragedy.

And in *Easy Rider*, as in all tragedies, character wages a losing battle with necessity. Captain America—here I wish to separate the two protagonists, for Billy the Kid is a sidekick, traveling with Captain America, but clearly not his equal in intensity of feeling or intelligence—rides on the fateful road of tragedy, a journey through what Karl Jaspers describes as the dark night of the soul where man tries to find some meaning to life but is necessarily defeated. Captain America pursues his dream of freedom to the end. His pursuit, his ride—the action of the film—is itself the realization of his character, the mark of his character. Captain America possesses some qualities of character that we can admire, others that we must deplore, but his tragic status depends on his ill-fated ride of freedom, his attempted escape from a cramping, destructive society, his condition of being an outsider. Whatever moral condemnation we wish to attach to his peddling dope and to his not helping a struggling hippie colony, despite their kindness to him and his bagfull of money, we still have a sympathy for him, an interest in him, because of his obedience to his own deep values. The values are not articulated, because the eloquence he possesses is not verbal. (Modern tragedy will never be able to project the verbal articulateness of deep feelings that we find in Shakespeare, for example.) But eloquence it is, and here the camera's eye compensates for the script's paucity of words. For the movie projects the eloquence of the ride—the easy movement of the motorcycles on straight smooth highways, the powerful surging uphill, the sense of control possessed by the riders. Captain America's motorcycle contains its own eloquence—the colors, the shine, the preciousness of its parts as it is handled firmly yet gently by its proud rider, of whom it is an extension. The eloquence of Captain America's personal good looks and lean strength, in such obvious contrast to the scruffiness of his sidekick and the large-stomached grossness and hatefulness of the people of the South (the latter too crude a cliché in all our films that depict Southerners). On a level both visual and thematic we witness the eloquence of the friendship of the two riders and their sympathetic treatment of the alcoholic Hansen, who, being a lawyer, can use words and is, therefore, the film's only articulator, making pithy comments on the challenge that a "free" cyclist hurls at a "freedom-loving" society.

Wishing to avoid conflict and pain, the riders ride into it. Pursuing in open spaces a life of freedom, they ride a road that narrows to death. Along the way they meet the evil and corruption of society. Sitting in the restaurant, watched by distrustful eyes, mocked by chummy insiders, they avoid a fight that would maim or kill them— how we wish they *would* fight, our own hatred bristling, needing some release—only to find wounds and death in a woods at night.

The fatal bludgeoning of Hansen, sudden, brutal—physically punctuating the truth of his comments on society—shocks the viewer, as it shocks the easy riders. They go to the New Orleans Mardi Gras celebration, their proposed destination with Hansen, try to eat and drink in high style in his memory, try to immerse themselves in the forgetfulness of whiskey and the intoxication of sex, only to end up with their prostitutes in a graveyard, where drugs and sex and religion and death combine in a crudely obvious symbolic attempt to crowd everything, all of life and death, into one scene. The scene fails to move the viewer because at a moment of high emotion the camera is working in an academic, one could say intellectual, way. The graveyard sequence is too studied, too rich, too symbolic. It presents activity, but not action. (The motorcycles, it is interesting to note, are not seen in the entire sequence; the riders *walk* to and through the cemetery.) Yet, the scene's very ineffectiveness helps to support Captain America's assertion—after the frenzy, alone with Billy, again in a wooded area—that "We blew it!" This is as close as we come in the film to a tragic recognition, but it is enough. It contains the sense of futility and defeat in the riders' search for freedom, in their journey to find some meaning in life. They were never able to articulate what they were searching for, and had they found it—which was impossible, given the conditions of the film and modern life—they would not have been able to express it. But the phrase "We blew it!" succinctly suggests the defeat that must come in the battle with necessity, the deep sadness connected with defeat, and the emptiness of life once defeat is realized. It only remains for the riders to meet death physically, for the sense of life is already gone.

Although we expect Captain America and Billy the Kid to die—with the tragic recognition behind us and the sense of inevitability always with us—the film's last sequence manages to shock, nevertheless. In retrospect, it all seems so fitting: that a commercial truck should be riding along the road; that the truck drivers, again Southern and hateful, should try to provoke the riders; that Billy should make his gesture, finger extended in the air, with the words "Up yours!" or "Screw you!" coming from the gesture itself, not from his lips; that the Southerners should kill Billy and then Captain America; and that they should ride away, safe, secure, on a road that is and always has been theirs. Yet the speed of the sequence and its visual effects—the large truck, the flash of gunshot, the motorcycles overturned, wheels spinning in air, riderless—produce a stunning emotional impact, for a number of reasons. First, the ride ends so abruptly. When a rhythm is set up, when speed is attained, we expect—our aesthetic sense demands—that the rhythm stop gracefully. Sudden stops always jolt. Second, we have formed an attachment to the riders who were doing our vicarious riding for us. Third, we witness in a few crowded seconds the result of an evil that is inherent in society, sometimes merely mocking and derisive, but sometimes coming with a club at night, and here coming with a rifle in the bright light of a Southern day. Last, and most important, the sequence affects us strongly because it fills us with terror, not only because death seems so quick and easy, but because a ride of freedom, a ride to escape from restriction, has led to the ultimate restriction. There is no escape. This terror clings to the tragic view of the human condition, in which no reassuring justice or god or moral order is asserted, in which we witness only senseless destruction—pointing to our frightening inability to fully understand the *meaning* of events, the cause forever remaining secret.

Easy Rider, by displaying the violence and hypocrisy of a society that merely gives lip service to freedom, is presenting a criticism of that society. Tragedy, however, demands more, because the evils of society can never be the whole story. In tragedy a condition of life must be confronted. In the movie this condition is the tragic paradox of escape leading to no escape, of freedom leading to restriction and death. The modern hero of tragedy, like his predecessors, is at the mercy of the human condition, but—and here is the measure of the man—he asserts his individuality knowing, or learning, that his action will lead to "shipwreck," to use Jaspers's word, to death on wheels, when we think in terms of *Easy Rider*. The ride itself becomes the meaning of life; to ride is to affirm oneself, even in the face of an evil, destructive society. Integrity and defiance—even when "we blew it"—is all a man has. He rides, and when the rhythm of the cycle (of both machine and life) is broken, death comes, and the tragic is born.

Easy Rider, a popular movie produced for popular consumption, reassures us, in a period of transition and crises, that despite changes in the medium, the audience, and the "times," a traditional genre can endure because it expresses truths that are permanent and real.

Which brings me to beginnings: to Aeschylus, the father of tragedy, and to Prometheus, a tragic figure whose mythic story is wide-ranging and far-reaching. So powerfully is necessity operating in Aeschylus' *Prometheus Bound*, so unalterable is its course, taking in man and gods, that Aeschylus can be credited with being the first dramatist to make imaginative use of one of the central mysteries of tragedy, an idea that has propelled the tragic form through the centuries, allowing it to encompass rebels on motorcycles on a modern road and the earliest rebel on a rock at the very end of every road.

The Prometheus story touches the roots of man's condition. It was Prometheus who gave man the basis of his civilization, fire, and who bestowed on man the uncertainty connected with "blind hopes." Because he was man's saviour in his rebellion against Zeus, who wished to destroy mankind, Prometheus must now endure Zeus' punishment; he will be chained to a rock for thousands of years, with an eagle coming daily to eat his liver which will nightly re-form. The punishment could cease if Prometheus reveals to Zeus a secret he learned from his mother, Earth, who gave him the power of seeing into the future. Revealing the secret will allow Zeus to continue his dominion over gods and men; it concerns Zeus' sexual alliance with Thetis, the offspring of which union will overthrow his father, just as Zeus overthrew Cronos. Zeus the tyrant has the power to punish Prometheus; Prometheus the rebel knows the secret that can either save or destroy Zeus. To put it another way, Zeus has power and Prometheus has forethought, making each the victim of the other—but both are controlled by necessity.

The conflict between Zeus and Prometheus is the focus of the drama. Prometheus is literally chained to a rock in the play's beginning, the play's action consisting of a series of visits by those who come to him for various reasons, usually to break his stubborn resistance to Zeus. Unbroken, Prometheus, at the end of the play, is hurled into an abyss, there to await the eagle and his agonizing punishment. Because *Prometheus Bound* is the first play of a trilogy whose other plays are lost, it can be assumed that Prometheus' prediction that he will be freed in time will come true. He will eventually tell the secret, it seems, but the nature of this revelation and its cause are bathed in mystery. Scholars have presented various interpretations concerning the missing two plays, the most popular offering an evolutionary theory whereby the tyrant Zeus learns compassion and becomes converted morally.[2] Although this view conforms to the evolutionary movement from cold justice to warm mercy in Aeschylus' *Oresteia*, the theory has some built-in flaws, not the least of which is its need of a threat of future disaster to cause a supposedly converted Zeus to pardon Prometheus. What we do know is that Hercules eventually will kill the eagle feeding on Prometheus' liver. What we do not know is the role of Zeus in this act. But there is no question that the Zeus of this first part of the trilogy is an unequivocal tyrant and that he must yield, as Aeschylus makes very clear, to necessity.

The play's first scene gives us a silent Prometheus, and how effective this silence is. Might and Violence appear with Hephaestus to chain Prometheus to a rock somewhere at the edge of the world, "an untrodden desolation." Might, an insensitive loyal servant of Zeus, enjoys taunting Prometheus, exults in his commands to Hephaestus to drive a wedge through Prometheus' chest, "drive it hard," insists on Zeus' sovereignty and Prometheus' stupidity for having a "man-loving disposition." Hephaestus, although unwilling to punish Prometheus, is forced to become an instrument of Zeus' might, and predicts the agony of Prometheus' future torture on the rock, asserting that "the mind of Zeus is hard to soften with prayer." Might chastises Hephaestus for his softness, and ruthlessly prods him on, insisting that "there is nothing without discomfort involved except the overlordship of the Gods. For only Zeus is free." This last statement will be proven false, but at the moment the action involved in having Prometheus nailed to a rock gives the audience an unforgettable picture of Zeus' power—connected with the large figures of a taunting Might and a mute Violence, connected with an unwilling instrument of torture, Hephaestus, and connected with Prometheus' silent endurance of both pain and insult.

How necessary it is for Prometheus, when his torturers leave him alone, to shout his speech of painful suffering to the only possible listeners, the elements, which include his mother, Earth.

Bright light, swift-winged winds, springs of the rivers,
    numberless
laughter of the sea's waves, earth, mother of all, and the
    all-seeing
circle of the sun: I call upon you to see what I, a God, suffer
at the hands of gods,—

see with what kind of torture
worn down I shall wrestle ten thousand
years of time—
such is the bond of despite that the Prince
has devised against me, the new Prince
of the Blessed Ones. O woe is me!
I groan for the present sorrow,
I groan for the sorrow to come, I groan
questioning when there shall come a time
when He shall ordain a limit to my sufferings.[3]

A god is suffering at the hands of gods, just as man suffers at the hands of gods throughout the tragic tradition. And this god *questions* his suffering condition, as do most tragic protagonists. But Prometheus possesses foreknowledge; unlike man, he sees into the future of things. Yet, his questioning, the result of his pain and suffering—which produces all questioning—seems a *human* response, itself immediately questioned.

What am I saying? I have known all before,
all that shall be, and clearly known; to me
nothing that hurts shall come with a new face.
So must I bear, as lightly as I can
the destiny that fate has given me;
for I know well against necessity,
against its strength no one can fight and win.
(p. 315)

Immediately, therefore, Prometheus links his undeserved suffering with necessity, an idea that informs the play, binding *Prometheus Bound* to all the tragedies that will be written by the heirs of Aeschylus. Himself a victim of necessity, Prometheus knows that all, including the god Zeus, are victims—a catharsis for him, perhaps the kind of catharsis that all men experience when they know that their true condition is controlled by a mysterious necessity.

The entrance of the chorus of sea-nymphs, daughters of Oceanos, seems to answer Prometheus' loneliness. Expressing sorrow for Prometheus' plight, wondering about Zeus' hardness of heart, the chorus extracts from Prometheus his story of the past and prediction of the future. He tells of his service to Zeus, the tyrant who now repays his service with pains, and he reveals Zeus' plans "to blot out" mankind: "Against these plans none stood save I: I dared." A high hero who dares disturb the universe, Prometheus gave men fire and blind hopes, for which Zeus tortures him "on this rock, / a bitterness to suffer, and a pain / to pitiful eyes." He knew, he says, he knew that he transgressed "nor will deny it." "In helping man I brought my troubles on me," he realizes, but he did not expect such a fearful torture, a strange assertion from one who has foreknowledge. About to tell the chorus "what is to come" in the future, Prometheus is interrupted by the arrival of Oceanos on a four-footed sea monster, a mildly comical interlude, displaying a well-meaning, essentially empty trimmer who advises Prometheus to "give up this angry mood" and look for ways to get "free of trouble"; he wants Prometheus to reform his ways, especially to curb his haughty tongue and accommodate himself to Zeus. Oceanos wishes to act as a mediary and offers to go to Zeus to plead for Prometheus. Prometheus treats him with sarcasm and contempt, scorns his mission as a "useless effort" by "a silly good nature," and dismisses Oceanos, who is happy to leave because his projected mission would perhaps vex Zeus. The shallowness of Oceanos and his compromising nature highlight the strength and pride of Prometheus the rebel, mankind's saviour, for whose plight the chorus, at their father Oceanos' departure, utters a lament.

> The wave cries out as it breaks into surf;
> the depth cries out, lamenting you; the dark
> Hades, the hollow underneath the world,
> sullenly groans below; the springs
> of sacred flowing rivers all lament
> the pain and pity of your suffering.
> (p. 327)

The continuation of Prometheus' story to the chorus reveals his specific gifts to mankind, a remarkable revelation of man's essentially brute nature transformed by the civilizing gift of fire. In Prometheus' disclosure Aeschylus presents us with nothing less than the process of time, a large picture of frail limited man struggling toward a higher existence with the help of Promethean intelligence. Fire is itself a mystery, the secret knowledge of the gods stolen from them by a rebel-god and given to mankind for its progress, a progress that testifies to Aeschylus' belief in the power of human intelligence, and therefore a progress that places the Greek audience's sympathy unequivocally with the rebel, who benefitted man and suffers for man, against the potential destroyer of man, Zeus. Fire, the highest of the elements, represents intelligence and the soul, that fire within, and is associated with every art and craft. Paradoxically, fire is the very passion of Prometheus, which causes him to save mankind and suffer Zeus' punishment, itself associated with fire. "I am burning in my own fire," says Prometheus in Robert Lowell's adaptation of the play.[4] The forbidden element, like the forbidden fruit of the Genesis myth, has made primitive, bewildered, puny man into a lesser god, a master of his mind.

> For men at first had eyes, but saw to no purpose; they
> had ears but did not hear. Like the shapes of dreams
> they dragged through their long lives and handled
> all things in bewilderment and confusion. They did not know
> of building houses with bricks to face the sun, they did not
> know how to work in wood. They lived like swarming ants in
> holes in the ground, in the sunless caves of the earth.
> For them there was no secure token by which to tell winter
> nor the flowering spring nor the summer with its crops;
> all their doings were indeed without intelligent calculation
> until I showed them the rising of the stars, and the
> settings, hard to observe.
> (p. 327)

Prometheus taught men numbers and writing and medicine and astronomy and divination and skill in handling animals and making boats and finding metals in the earth. "One brief word will tell the whole story: all arts that mortals have come from Prometheus."

In addition, as Prometheus had previously told the chorus *before* mentioning his gift of fire, Prometheus' philanthropy has "caused mortals to cease foreseeing doom." "I placed in them blind hopes." This seems an interesting gift in the light of Prometheus' own ability to foresee his fate, an ability that at times seems to heighten his despair because he *knows* he cannot die even though his punishment and anguish are great. For man to foresee his doom, to have specific knowledge of his own death, is worse than the uncertainty of death. Man's hope—what Robert Lowell has his chorus call "consoling blindness"—allows man to build and plan and at least endure, even when he is at the end of the road. Witness the importance of this gift to Beckett's Didi and Gogo and to Chekhov's three sisters. Witness the suffering of Prometheus who can foresee his punishment for thousands of years, even though he knows he will eventually be set free.

Helpless men, "swarming ants," have been transformed into creatures of craft and intelligence and hope. However, man, like his benefactor Prometheus and like his potential destroyer Zeus, remains inferior to the dark power of necessity, for no mind, not even a god's, can penetrate the darkness of necessity or overcome its power. Immediately following the revelation of man's glorious control over the elements, we hear about necessity. When asked directly by the chorus whether Zeus is weaker than the Fates, Prometheus answers, "Yes, for he, too, cannot escape what is fated." What is fated for Zeus is Prometheus' secret, which will in the course of time free him from his bondage. Whereas in the other Greek tragedies the mystery of the gods was connected with the mystery of necessity, here the gods themselves are not in clear control; they too cannot escape what is fated—making the mystery even deeper. Small wonder, then, that at least one critic allies *Prometheus Bound* with *King Lear* and *The Brothers Karamazov* as works that have the quality of "touching final doubts."[5] What we have in *Prometheus Bound*, therefore, is a rebel against Zeus who is in servitude to destiny, and Zeus the tyrant who is controlled by necessity, and intelligent, hopeful mankind in bondage to "the ordered law of Zeus" and to necessity. This is the tragic condition, here encompassing god and man, macrocosm and microcosm, and brilliantly displaying the contradictory perspective of tragedy, whereby a victorious tyrant is the victim of destiny and his defeated, suffering victim is victorious in possessing knowledge of that destiny—while intelligent mankind, victoriously piercing through layer after layer of ignorance and chaos, progressing in the course of time to mastery of his world, remains helpless beneath the arbitrary and dark control of both Zeus and destiny. Man, thanks to Promethean fire, is no longer an unreasoning ant, but his reason has led him where it always leads him in tragedy—to unanswered questions about the working of destiny, the injustice of gods, the secrecy of causes.

The play's most effective embodiment of mortal man's bewilderment in the face of dark necessity and torment at the hands of an unjust god is Io, the only mortal in the play, the horned maiden, once loved by Zeus, now driven across the world by flies that goad her tortured body and soul. The confrontation between the wandering

Io, on the road and attempting to escape like the easy riders, and the stationary Prometheus, on the rock, vividly accentuates the unjust workings of Zeus, who has victimized both. In addition, the past of Io, as revealed by her, and her future, as revealed by Prometheus, span the ages, while her wanderings which seem to take in the known world of the time, widen the canvas—so that Aeschylus' *Prometheus Bound*, having already presented the progress of human consciousness through the years, seems to gather all time and all space to itself, thereby making the mood of fatalism pervasive and extensive.

The entrance of Io immediately stresses the agony of her restlessness, not only by displaying the sheer nervous physicality of her movements as compared with the chained Prometheus' fixedness, but by having her utter tormented O's in the midst of her report on her condition. I quote her entrance speech in full because its effect is cumulative.

> What land is this? What race of men? Who is it
> I see here tortured in this rocky bondage?
> What is the sin he's paying for? O tell me
> to what part of the world my wanderings have brought me.
>
> O, O, O,
> there it is again, there again—it stings me,
> the gadfly: the ghost of earth-born Argos:
> keep it away, keep it away, earth!
> I'm frightened when I see the shape of Argos.
> Argos the herdsman with ten thousand eyes.
> He stalks me with his crafty eyes: he died
> but the earth didn't hide him, still he comes
> even from the depths of the Underworld to hunt me:
> he drives me starving by the sands of the sea.
> The reed-woven pipe drones on in a hum
> and drones and drones its sleep-giving strain:
> O, O, O,
> Where are you bringing me, my far-wandering wanderings?
> Son of Kronos, what fault, what fault
> did you find in me that you should yoke me
> to a harness of misery like this,
> that you should torture me so to madness
> driven in fear of the gadfly?

Burn me with fire: hide me in earth: cast me away
to monsters of the deep for food: but do not
grudge me the granting of this prayer, King.
Enough have my much wandering wanderings
exercised me: I cannot find
a way to escape my troubles.
Do you hear the voice of the cow-horned maid?
(p. 331)

Terrified by gadfly and image of Argos, her exhausted body always on the move, driven to distraction, wondering what her fault was, wishing for death to end her suffering, harnessed to misery and finding no escape, Io is a powerful representation of bewildered humanity tormented by an inhuman destiny it does not understand. The mind of Prometheus, once used by Zeus, brought Zeus' wrath down on him; the body of Io, her sexuality, which is desired by Zeus, results in her persecution. Aeschylus gives us a Zeus who is brutal and ruthless in his dealings with god and man, with mind and body, with male and female; he gives us victims whose suffering is unjustified. Io's plight is particularly poignant because the curse on her comes not from an act of defiance, as is the case with Prometheus, but from her being what she was, a defenseless woman who happened to be attractive to an amorous god. She tells how Zeus entered her dreams, haunting her in her "maiden chamber," exhorting her with words of lust. His nightly visitations —touching the mystery of desire that Freud tried to penetrate— terrified her. Her own sexual desire for a god, as Robert Lowell would have it, overcomes her resistance, and she rushes into the fields, where Zeus enters her. In Aeschylus, Io does not have a literal union with Zeus. Instead, she rushes to her father to tell him of her "nightly terror." Consulting the oracles, her father is told to drive her from the house. She must "wander to the limits of the world." When her father shut his doors on her, Io's form changed; she became a horned maiden, a cowlike woman chased by a gadfly, "that god-sent scourge," from land to land. A maiden's nighttime haunting visions of the Bull, Zeus, turns her to a cow; desire, a condition of man and god, remains mysterious and destructive. Aeschylus in *Prometheus Bound* has given us a literal "moocow" on the road, briefly pausing in her restless wandering to learn of her fate from a chained Prometheus.

The foreseeing Prometheus tells Io of her agonizing itinerary through continents and seas, through various and dangerous places. The painful details cause Io to wish for death now, but fate has determined that her wanderings must continue until she gets to the land of the Nile where she will found a colony. Before that, however, she will bear her first son, and in the thirteenth generation of her descendants another son, Hercules, will come to this edge of the world to free Prometheus. The fates of Io and Prometheus are intertwined, therefore, and their revenge on the persecutor Zeus is part of their joint future. Like all mortals, Io now has blind hope, but her agony will continue for a long time. She leaves the stage as she entered—in a frenzy of movement and in "mind destroying madness"; she will continue to endure the senseless persecution of a relentless god.

The meeting of Io and Prometheus is the central episode of the play. It tells us of the future; it reminds us of the past; it covers the geography of the known world; it re-enforces our image of a cruel, arbitrary Zeus; it makes us recognize the force of inevitable destiny, the necessity that controls victim and victimizer, mortals and gods, those moving and those chained. Prometheus' recognition of this necessity gives him the strength to resist Zeus; Io's recognition of this necessity allows her to continue her frenzied wandering in blind hope. It is the nonrecognition of necessity by Zeus, who does not as yet understand that he "cannot escape what is fated," that prompts him to send Hermes to Prometheus to extract the secret that will keep him on his throne.

Hermes is the last visitor to the fixed Prometheus, the last challenge to Prometheus' rebelliousness, the last instrument of Zeus' harsh tyranny, and the prod to Prometheus' most passionate outbursts of defiance. Prometheus displays utter contempt for this pompous "lackey of the gods" who has come to learn the secret of the marriage that will drive Zeus from power. Prometheus says that he would not change his own "misfortune" for the "slavery" of this footman of Zeus. He scorns the insolent Hermes who proudly carries Zeus' threats, and who seems to exult in his condemnation of Prometheus: "Your words declare you mad." "Bring your proud heart to know a true discretion—O foolish spirit—in the face of ruin." "These are madman's words, a madman's plans." But his insults and savageness do not bend an obstinate Prometheus. "Do you think I will crouch before your Gods, / —so new—and tremble?

I am far from that." "There is not / a torture or an engine where-
withal / Zeus can induce me to declare these things, / till he has
loosed me from these cruel shackles." "Me he shall not / bend . . . to
tell him who is fated / to drive him from his tyranny." Hermes' mission is not accomplished; Prometheus will not reveal the secret. And
the threats of a destructive Zeus become reality, as Prometheus' last
words—the last words of the play—indicate.

> Now it is words no longer: now in very truth
> the earth is staggered: in its depths the thunder
> bellows resoundingly, the fiery tendrils
> of the lightning flash light up, and whirling clouds
> carry the dust along: all the winds' blasts
> dance in a fury one against the other
> in violent confusion: earth and sea
> are one, confused together: such is the storm
> that comes against me manifestly from Zeus
> to work its terrors. Holy mother mine;
> O Sky that circling brings the light to all,
> you see me, how I suffer, how unjustly.
> (p. 351)

The words are accompanied by earthquake, thunder and lightning,
as Prometheus, still nailed to the rock, falls into the abyss, disap-
pearing into a dark future of punishment for thousands of years.

Prometheus' anguished cry of suffering to his mother Earth at the
play's end recalls his first cry to his mother after his silence while he
was being nailed to the rock in the play's beginning. The play is
framed by cries of suffering and shouts against injustice, and the
play itself dramatizes both the injustice of Zeus and the justified rebelliousness of Prometheus. From our first image of a haughty
Might and a mute Violence, to our last view of the destruction
wrought by Zeus, we are exposed to a building crescendo of Zeus'
tyrannical power and arbitrary dealings with god and man.[6]
Prometheus denounces him as a tyrant; his agents of tyranny—
Might, Violence, Hermes—are proud of his destructive power;
Oceanos acknowledges and accepts his tyranny; the chorus recognizes and deplores it; Io is brutally victimized by it. Zeus' despotism
is heartless, as stony as the rock on which he nails Prometheus; his
violence is wanton. So exaggerated is his tyranny that we are forced
to see him as symbolic of all the forces in nature that help to destroy

man—from wanton lust to uncontrolled storms, from the darkness of desire to the terror of thunder. Yet, he is not a law unto himself, for we can never forget that Zeus is controlled by necessity, which is greater and darker and more primal than even this unequivocally powerful tyrant. The chainer himself is chained by an iron necessity; the terrors connected with Zeus' godhead are bounded by a darker deeper secret than either god or man can fathom.

The suffering Prometheus, therefore, plunged into the abyss, shouting against injustice, represents man's weakness against a larger, arbitrary power; he shouts out man's defiance of destiny. The shout itself and his sheer endurance give him height and win our sympathy. We, like the chorus, refuse to desert him—first, because this thief of fire is man's benefactor; second, because he is a victim of those dark and destructive forces we all face; third, and perhaps most interesting, because Prometheus, though a god of intellect and forethought, is like us in being a creature of feeling, which is an aspect of his character too often ignored by those commenting on the play. Hermes' charge that he is "mad" strikes the chord of truth, for upholding a cause that overwhelms one is a form of madness, a fine madness, but madness nonetheless. Witness Antigone and Hamlet and that other thief who gave man knowledge, Satan. Prometheus' loyalty to man, his obsessive defiance of Zeus, his emotional outpourings of feeling for Io and his emotional outpourings of scorn for Hermes, display him as a slave of passion. That Aeschylus wants us to view him in this way is clearly brought out in Prometheus' confrontation with Hermes, for here Prometheus' emotions have led him to *hope* for the fall of Zeus. Now we know, as Prometheus knows, that Zeus will not fall, that some kind of accommodation will be made in the future, that, in short, the downfall of this tyrant is not what necessity has in store for him. Here Prometheus' hope—the blind hope he gave mankind but which he, as god and foreseer, should not possess—is fed by his feelings and not by his intelligence. This puts him very close to us, allowing him to represent a Greek humanism that has always confronted the terror of necessity with passion as well as intellect.

In every respect, then, this very early tragedy in our Western tradition encompasses those elements that I have been discussing throughout this book. Prometheus is the prototype of the tragic protagonist, and *Prometheus Bound* is the purest dramatization of the tragic condition. At the end of the road at the end of the world, where Prometheus is nailed to his rock, we have the clearest view of what happened *on* that road. Alone, at his boundary situation (literally at the end of both road and world), chained to his condition (literally nailed to his rock), controlled by iron necessity, ready to be plunged into the abyss, suffering both physical punishment and the gods' mockery, he shouts against injustice. He is a rebel, a saviour of mankind and a representative of mankind, a winner and a loser, defiantly expressing the will to endure whatever the outside forces of darkness and destruction offer. At the same time that he cries out to his mother in his helplessness, Prometheus, a god-man of intelligence and feeling, gathers to himself the mystery of things, especially the mystery of undeserved suffering. Unlike other tragic protagonists, he cannot die, but death, as he tells Io, would be preferred; not dying means that he has no relief from pain. His suffering, although it will end one day, seems everlasting, like the suffering of Sisyphus. Sisyphus, thanks to Camus, has given us our image of the absurd hero. Prometheus, thanks to Aeschylus, has given us our image of the tragic hero.

And as we contemplate the archetypal Prometheus nailed to his rock, how can we avoid seeing two other large figures of our tradition, also victims of undeserved suffering, also facing the mystery: Hebraic Job on the ashheap, Christian Jesus on the cross. Some scholars speculate that the author of the book of Job may have read Aeschylus' *Prometheus Bound,* but such a notion, though interesting, is not necessary—because man has always been bewildered by the buffets of the world outside him, man has always been crying out against his precarious state in a world he did not make, man has always questioned the gods and injustice and the causes of his suffering. That he has dared to question, whether in a shout or a painful cry, is tragic man's dignity. The Voice from the Whirlwind never directly answers Job's questions, never confronts the injustice of his suffering, in fact, deepens the mystery—and Job seems to understand that the mystery must remain. He questions and he receives no answer; there is no direct answer for mankind. The questions remain; the ambiguities remain; life's contradictions and injustices remain. But for Job, even though his suffering is undeserved, the despair does not remain, because *facing the fact of mystery* is itself a catharsis. We can ignore the tacked-on ending to the book of Job which restores possessions to Job and gives him other children, which turns this rich tragedy into a shallow comedy. What we remain with, what we *feel* as we witness Job on his ashheap, is the terror of man's precarious state and the mystery of its cause. And Job's questioning, his defiance, his refusal to believe those easy comforters, his endurance in the face of terror, give significance to his manhood and to the mystery.

So too does manhood and mystery inform the suffering of Jesus, only here the tragic figure is attached to a vision of life that accepts the mystery and thereby threatens his tragic status. We have only one biblical account of Job by a masterful writer whose Hebraic tradition allows him to stress the darkness of man's hard and questioning condition. We have four accounts of the Jesus story, written by men whose new religion miraculously transforms the darkness to light, making the suffering a prelude to eternal joy. But two of these writers, Matthew and Mark (a reasonable percentage, as Didi would say), indicate that Jesus' agony on the cross, both physical and spiritual, causes him to question God: "My God, my God, why has thou forsaken me?" In these words we feel the pressure of undeserved punishment, we witness, as we did with Prometheus, the loneliness and pain of a saviour of mankind, and we experience man's fragile status in the face of mystery. Here Jesus is tragic man bewildered by the secret cause. When Jesus is given his halo of salvation, is resurrected, is intrinsic to the doctrine of atonement and grace, then the terror is erased, replaced by joyous hope; the questions become solutions. Since the resurrected Jesus is the Christ of the Christian tradition, he becomes the most important player in a divine comedy. Any discussion of the possibility of Christian tragedy must, in the last analysis, be based on one's perspective of the image of Jesus on the cross. If we see the bleeding man, body stretched, a victim forsaken by man and god, bewildered and questioning, then we have a tragic Jesus. If we see a serene face framed by a halo, forgiving, at one with the cause no longer secret, then we have the very opposite of the tragic view.[7]

Prometheus, Job, Jesus—all suffering, all questioning because they are unable to fathom the mystery—are the most potent and universal representatives of tragic man in the Western tradition. In *Prometheus Bound* Aeschylus the humanist, like most writers of tragedy, applauds the sheer power of human consciousness and human endurance, but he acknowledges forcefully and truthfully the mystery at the heart of man's existence. On the rock with Prometheus or on the road with the easy riders, the question mark pervades.

9 THE MYSTERIOUS TUNE

Tragic Pleasure

Witnessing or reading tragic drama arouses many and different emotions. Of course, what a particular member of the audience or a particular reader feels must depend, in part, on where he is coming from. One person's deep compassion may be another person's easy pity; one person's grudging respect may be another's high admiration; one person's fear may result in a palpitating heart, another's in numbness or awkward laughter. Pity and fear, thanks to Aristotle, are the most discussed of the emotions connected with tragedy (and probably the most potent), but these do not, nor should they be expected to, exhaust the possibilities. Because tragedy can take so many forms, because tragedy is derived from different myths and stories, because the tragic figure can be a brooding, intellectual Hamlet or a physical, carrot-eating Gogo, a defiant Antigone or a frustrated Olga, a climbing Solness or a kneeling Ill, because tragedies are always reinterpreted at the time of performance, it is reasonable to expect the emotions aroused by tragedy to be many. Aristotle's notion that catharsis in tragedy comes from the purging of pity and fear has gathered to itself not only much discussion as to what exactly he meant, but also an academic encrustedness that must be chipped away. To say what we feel, not what we ought to say, would push us to declare that our emotional response to tragedy, the effect it has on us, is itself bathed in mystery. In tragedy we witness suffering and pain and death and man's losing battle with necessity, yet we do not feel utter despair, and we come back for more. Whatever the explanation for this phenomenon, it is rooted deeply in our psyches, just as it was rooted in the psyches of those early audiences watching Prometheus cry out his anguish in the chilly dawn of an Athenian day. And there may be many explanations. Those writing on tragedy, from Plato and Aristotle through

Hegel and Nietzsche to such modern critics and theorists as Jaspers and Unamuno and Frye and Langer, cannot avoid offering some explanation of what is particularly cathartic about tragedy. To review their explanations—a challenge I gladly avoid—would result in a textbook on the psychology of emotions, a rather full textbook in which every emotion is either closely examined or fleetingly mentioned. My explanation—which unsurprisingly both rubs against and rubs with the explanations of previous commentators—is offered as the logical result of my discussions of the specific plays and my emphasis throughout on the secret cause. The only originality I claim for it is the kind that arises naturally when a critic sifts ideas through his individual perspective and through his particular thesis. I present it in this short concluding chapter without the support of discussion of particular plays and therefore at the expense of some subtlety.

In tragedy we confront the secret cause, which is within the play or behind the play, which is part of the play's felt knowledge, and, perhaps most important in discussing tragic effect, which is verified by our own experience of life. This knowledge is *felt*—here, as throughout, I am stressing the immediacy and physicality of tragic drama—in worlds (of both plays and audiences) that possessed gods and aristocratic heroes and in worlds that lost their gods and heroes. It is the kind of knowledge, beyond good and evil, that leads to neither pessimism nor optimism because the question mark neither denies nor affirms. If drama in general holds the mirror up to our lives, then tragic drama reflects life's mystery. For how does life appear to man? As precarious, filled with unanswered questions, uncertain progressions, unaccountable evil, secret motives, dark passions, at time madness. In short, life as we experience it seems not to have a clear and intelligible direction or purpose. It is not surprising, therefore, that our response to tragedy is related to our response to our darkest fears and questions. Art does our dreaming for us. When the dream is a nightmare touching our emotional fears, then we have tragedy. In the profoundest sense, we, as human beings, are what we question, and we usually question the secret cause. This questioning is part of the basic pattern of human experience, dramatized from age to age, from country to country, precisely because it is there. "In the beginning was the Word," we read. After the Word came the Question Mark. Tragedy, as we have seen throughout my discussion, is lodged on the curve of that question mark. It forces us to wonder about the roots of our anguished experience of life; it draws us toward the largest mysteries. It does so because the tragic protagonists themselves are drawn to the secret cause. We must remember that "Who's there?" applies as much to the condition of Didi as to the condition of Hamlet. When we view the tragic character's confrontation with, or relationship to, the secret cause, the character is seen and heard, is concretely felt by the audience. However, the secret cause, by whatever name or means it manifests itself, is felt without being seen or heard—impersonal, awful, dark, unfathomable. In tragedy, and tragedy alone, the secret cause is ever present, just beyond the boundary of consciousness and clear discussion, with the dramatic artifact forever reminding us that darkness occupies the core of life, that the sheer reality of suffering and death cannot be avoided. The tragic character faces this reality, if not with high nobility, then certainly with dignity; if not by shouting and dying, then by quietly questioning and enduring. In any case, the tragic character is placed by the dramatist on the brink of the unknown and incomprehensible—and that is exactly where we are situated. (That is why such terms as "abyss" and "boundary situation" are remarkably apt in a discussion of tragedy.) Of course, we—as we carry on our daily lives, getting and spending, half awake and more than half asleep—try not to think about the threatening questions that haunt our lives. But at certain moments we are forced to. The death of a loved one, a sickness, a change of fortune that changes one's life, or those perturbing thoughts that arise *for no apparent reason,* usually in the small hours of the night (Fitzgerald's three-o'clock in the morning?) causing those "tears, idle tears" that our psyches force from deep within. The tragic dramatists touch these dark feelings and thoughts, and their appeal to mystery vibrates responsive chords within us that are too deep for intellect to reach, let alone explain. That is why, it seems to me, the clear and reasonable arguments of many fine tragic theorists and critics somehow seem inadequate in attempting to describe the appeal of tragedy. That is why a subjective commentator like Nietzsche, allying tragedy with the spirit of music—the most mysterious of the arts and the one that acts upon us so powerfully without our knowing why—seems closer to whatever truth we can discover about tragic emotion and tragic pleasure. That is why no single theory or definition of tragedy seems complete, or can be complete, and why those commentators who are most successful are those who are least prescriptive, most openended and tentative.

Of course, the pleasure derived from tragedy has a close relationship to the pleasure that comes from most products of the artistic imagination. When a satisfying form is imposed on whatever is by nature formless or chaotic, pleasure is the result. The attractiveness of the Apollonian illusion need not be questioned. But the satisfaction derived from tragedy seems to tap deeper sources. What tragedy offers is peculiar to tragedy alone: the pleasure that comes when the truth is verified. The art that affirms what we know, affords pleasure, even if it affirms a dreadful fact. Seizing terror by the hand, facing the unknown *as* unknown, provides its own special satisfaction. What we know is that our lives are surrounded and informed by mystery—from our mysterious beginning when we "enter crying" (in some uncanny way predicting life's condition?) to our equally mysterious end when we "exit dying." What we know is that a dark mystery is connected with fundamental instincts (like love and hate and desire and fear), with the inexplicable guilt that seems to demand expiation, with the evil and injustice and hardness of heart that produce pain and suffering and frustration, with the net of determinism that catches all of us in its intricate webbing. What we know is that the cause, whatever we name it (and we are forever attempting to name the unnameable), will remain secret. Tragedy thus stirs within us *what is already there*, what we bring to it as thinking, feeling mortals. It allows us to come to terms with what we know, and it makes us realize that we *can* live with the question mark. There is pleasure in clearly facing a fact, any fact. Facing the fact of mystery is no exception. (Is this not comparable to dying patients who, facing the fact of death, come to accept calmly their ends once they are forced to confront the truth? Is this not the lightening before death?) This pleasure is bound up with the comfort we feel in sharing the mystery, both with the tragic characters during the play and with the audience at play's end. While experiencing the play, that is, while participating in the tragic character's condition as he faces mystery, we are intensely alone, in perfect sympathy with the character's aloneness. When the play is over, we transfer feelings from the character to those around us—ideally, the larger audience at the theater, but also the larger audience of readers—because we all share instinctively the common darkness and determinism, we all share the knowledge that we shall never know the answers, that the cause will always remain secret for all of us. In a sense, after the play we all become the chorus feeling the same uncertainties and thinking the same thoughts, precisely because we have shared the experience of the play and because we share this common dark experience of life. The wisdom to which tragedy brings us is the recognition, not of cosmic justice, as Hegel suggested, or of cosmic evil, as Schopenhauer affirmed, but rather of cosmic mystery, as Einstein believed. When we look at the tragic mask, the silent scream speaks of suffering. It is the mask of the sufferer. The cause of that suffering is so secret that no mask for it is conceivable. Its contours cannot be frozen; its intensity cannot be sculptured. It has been given names—God, gods, fate, necessity, passion, blood—but no epithet adequately captures the mystery. The secret cause remains secret—and this is the fact tragedy forces us to acknowledge.

"Nothing is here for tears." How often Milton's words have been quoted to indicate the kind of reaction tragedy elicits. Usually, however, no tears need be shed because the play, like Milton's *Samson Agonistes*, is informed by a religious faith, by the affirmation of a positive outcome to direful events. At times, too, nothing is *here* for tears because we are witnessing an artifact, always aware that we are not really involved. I believe, however, that we respond to tragedy on a more profound level than these explanations suggest. "Nothing is here for tears" because our realization that mystery is a basic element in our lives calls for neither tears nor laughter. It evokes resignation, the feeling that indeed our lives are precarious, that indeed we are often victims (or, as Thomas Gould brilliantly suggests, innocent sufferers, who derive pleasure from knowing we are not guilty, who derive comfort from knowing we are indeed innocent),[1] that indeed it is difficult to know where free will begins or ends, that indeed we, like that Renaissance prince, are often forced to play roles we would rather not play. Resignation is comforting because it allows us to see ourselves as able to face life without delusions, as able to live with the question, not because the question mark has become a period, but rather because we know a solution will never come. That is the paradoxical certainty of uncertainty. We know that we cannot know. Tragedy, by making us realize the cause will forever remain secret, pleases us because of its utter truthfulness. It is left for us to dance to the mysterious tune as best we can, knowing—and it is the highest kind of knowledge because it is *felt* knowledge—knowing that the piper will always remain invisible.

NOTES

1 The Invisible Piper

1 / In a letter from Albert Einstein to Max Born, dated December 12, 1926. This quotation comes from Ronald W. Clark, *Einstein: The Life and Times* (New York: World, 1971), p. 340.

2 / In an interview, cited in Clark, p. 346.

3 / Albert Einstein, *Ideas and Opinions* (New York: Crown, 1954), p. 11.

4 / Four books that contain fine discussions of *Oedipus Rex* are: G. M. Kirkwood, *A Study of Sophoclean Drama* (Ithaca: Cornell University Press, 1958); H. D. F. Kitto, *Greek Tragedy* (New York: Doubleday, 1954); B. M. W. Knox, *The Heroic Temper: Studies in Sophoclean Drama* (Berkeley: University of California Press, 1964); C. H. Whitman, *Sophocles: A Study of Heroic Humanism* (Cambridge, Mass.: Harvard University Press, 1951). Richmond Y. Hathorn, *Tragedy, Myth, and Mystery* (Bloomington: Indiana University Press, 1962) was helpful not only for this discussion of Oedipus, but throughout my book. He makes excellent use of the concept of mystery which he derives from Gabriel Marcel's *The Mystery of Being*.

5 / Sophocles, *Oedipus Rex*, p. 6, in Sophocles, *The Oedipus Cycle*, trans. Dudley Fitts and Robert Fitzgerald (New York: Harcourt, Brace, and World, 1949). This is the text used in all references to Sophocles.

6 / H. D. F. Kitto, *Form and Meaning in Drama* (London: Methuen, 1960), p. 243.

7 / For a fine discussion of Apollo's role in the play and for the most refreshing interpretation of *Oedipus Rex* to date, see Thomas Gould's introduction to his *Oedipus the King* (Englewood Cliffs: Prentice-Hall, 1970) and his article, entitled "The Innocence of Oedipus and The Nature of Tragedy," in the *Massachusetts Review* 10 (1969): 281–300.

2 Love

1 / William Arrowsmith, "The Criticism of Greek Tragedy," in *Tragedy: Vision and Form*, ed. Robert W. Corrigan (San Francisco: Chandler, 1965), pp. 320–21.

2 / Sophocles, *Antigone*, p. 186, in the Fitts-Fitzgerald text.

3 / Richmond Y. Hathorn discusses this principle in *Tragedy, Myth, and Mystery*, pp. 66–78.

4 / Friedrich Hegel, *The Philosophy of Fine Art*, quoted in Corrigan, p. 438.

5 / H. D. F. Kitto, (*Form and Meaning*, pp. 138–78), Richmond Hathorn, and William Arrowsmith argue effectively for the importance of love.

6 / To my knowledge, Arrowsmith is alone in mentioning Creon's belief that love can only exist in a stable society. In Corrigan, p. 328.

7 / Bernard M. W. Knox, *The Heroic Temper*, p. 106.

8 / See especially Kitto, *Form and Meaning*, pp. 171–73, and S. M. Adams, *Sophocles the Playwright* (Toronto: University of Toronto Press, 1957), p. 55.

9 / Jean Anouilh, *Antigone*, p. 3, in Anouilh, *Five Plays* (New York: Hill and Wang, 1958). Subsequent references are to this text.

10 / Leonard Pronko discusses Antigone's commitment to herself in *The World of Jean Anouilh* (Berkeley: University of California Press, 1968), pp. 24–28.

11 / Alba della Fazia probably is correct in asserting that "in historic perspective, Anouilh will take his place among the mid-century pessimistic writers" (*Jean Anouilh* [New York: Twayne, 1969], p. 138).

3   Passion

1 / Richmond Y. Hathorn, *Tragedy, Myth, and Mystery*, p. 99.

2 / The following contributions to the controversy were helpful to my discussion, even when the interpretations were ultimately rejected: D. J. Conacher, *Euripidean Drama* (Toronto: University of Toronto Press, 1967); E. R. Dodds, *The Greeks and the Irrational* (Berkeley: University of California Press, 1956); L. H. G. Greenwood, *Aspects of Euripidean Tragedy* (Cambridge: Cambridge University Press, 1953); G. M. A. Grube, *The Drama of Euripides* (London: Methuen, 1941); H. D. F. Kitto, *Greek Tragedy;* Gilbert Murray, *Euripides and His Age* (London: Oxford University Press, 1965); A. W. Verrall, *Euripides, The Rationalist* (Cambridge: Cambridge University Press, 1895).

3 / Euripides, *Hippolytus*, p. 163, in *The Complete Greek Tragedies: Euripides*, vol. 1, ed. David Grene and Richmond Lattimore (Chicago: University of Chicago Press, 1955). Subsequent references are to this text.

4 / George Steiner, *The Death of Tragedy* (New York: Hill and Wang, 1961), p. 84.

5 / Especially critical of Racine's tragic sense are Francis Fergusson, *The Idea of a Theatre* (New York: Doubleday, 1954) and N. Joseph Calarco, *Tragic Being* (Minneapolis: University of Minnesota Press, 1969). More balanced views on Racine's contribution to tragedy are the following: Geoffrey Brereton, *Principles of Tragedy* (London: Routledge & Kegan Paul, 1968); Lucien Goldmann, *Racine* (Cambridge: Rivers Press, 1972); John C. Lapp, *Aspects of Racinian Tragedy* (Toronto: University of Toronto Press, 1955); Eugene Vinaver, *Racine and Poetic Tragedy* (Manchester: Manchester University Press, 1955); Bernard Weinberg, *The Art of Jean Racine* (Chicago: University of Chicago Press, 1963).

6 / Jean Racine, *Phaedra*, p. 186, in Racine, *Five Plays*, trans. Kenneth Muir (New York: Hill and Wang, 1960). This is the text used throughout.

7 / Eugene O'Neill, quoted in Arthur Hobson Quinn, *A History of the American Drama* (New York: Crofts, 1945), 2:199.

8 / Travis Bogard, *Contour in Time: The Plays of Eugene O'Neill* (New York: Oxford University Press, 1972), p. 213. Other books, in addition to Bogard's, that were helpful to me in my discussion of O'Neill are: Doris V. Falk, *Eugene O'Neill and the Tragic Tension* (New Brunswick: Rutgers University Press, 1958); Arthur and Barbara Gelb,

O'Neill (New York: Harper, 1962); Clifford Leech, *Eugene O'Neill* (New York: Grove Press, 1963); Louis Sheaffer, *O'Neill, Son and Playwright* (Boston: Little, Brown, 1968); Richard Dana Skinner, *Eugene O'Neill: A Poet's Quest* (New York: Russell & Russell, 1964).

9 / No biographer or critic has mentioned O'Neill's acquaintance with Racine, and no external evidence exists to establish this acquaintance—which accounts for my "perhaps." However, it is difficult to believe that O'Neill, a voracious reader of plays, did not know *the* French tragic dramatist.

10 / Edgar F. Racey, Jr., pinpoints the parallels between *Desire Under the Elms* and Euripides' *Hippolytus* in "Myth as Tragic Structure in *Desire Under the Elms*," *Modern Drama* 5, no. 1 (May 1962): 42–46.

11 / Eugene O'Neill, *Desire Under the Elms*, p. 2, in Eugene O'Neill, *Three Plays* (New York: Random House, 1959). Subsequent references are to this edition.

12 / Bogard, p. 202.

13 / John Henry Raleigh, *The Plays of Eugene O'Neill* (Carbondale: Southern Illinois University Press, 1965), p. 53.

14 / From a letter to Barrett Clark. These words are quoted by Clark in *Eugene O'Neill, The Man and His Plays* (New York: Dover, 1947), p. 59.

4 Death

1 / Harry Levin's *The Question of Hamlet* (New York: Viking, 1961) is indispensable reading for every student of Shakespeare.

2 / Maynard Mack, "The World of Hamlet," *Yale Review* 41 (1952): 502–23.

3 / William Shakespeare, *Hamlet* 1.2.129–59, in *Shakespeare: The Complete Works*, ed. G. B. Harrison (New York: Harcourt, Brace & World, 1952). This is the text used in all references to Shakespeare.

4 / To cite all those who have contributed to the debate would result in hundreds of references. I merely pinpoint seven studies that have been helpful to me and to all students of Shakespeare: A. C. Bradley, *Shakespearean Tragedy* (1904); Francis Fergusson, *The Idea of a Theater* (1949); John Holloway, *The Story of the Night* (1961); Ernest Jones, *Hamlet and Oedipus* (1949); G. Wilson Knight, *The Imperial Theme* (1931); L. C. Knights, *An Approach to Hamlet* (1960); J. Dover Wilson, *What Happens in Hamlet* (1935).

5 / For a fuller discussion of the image and idea of the prostitute in *Hamlet*, see my *The Base String: The Underworld in Elizabethan Drama* (Rutherford: Fairleigh Dickinson University Press, 1968), pp. 192–96.

6 / Friedrich Nietzsche, *The Birth of Tragedy*, in *Philosophy of Nietzsche*, ed. Clifton Fadiman (New York: Random House, 1954), p. 984.

7 / Theodore Spencer, for example, asserts that by the end of the play Hamlet's "experience" has made him "aware of the world's order" (*Shakespeare and the Nature of Man* [New York: Collier, 1966], p. 109).

8 / Robert Brustein, "Waiting for Hamlet," *The New Republic*, November 1967, p. 25.

9 / Tom Stoppard, *Rosencrantz and Guildenstern Are Dead* (New York: Grove, 1967), p. 118. Subsequent references are to this text.

10 / Tom Prideaux, "Uncertainty Makes the Big Time," *Life*, February 9, 1968, p. 76.

11 / Here Northrop Frye's comments are especially illuminating. *A Natural Perspective* (New York: Harcourt, Brace & World, 1965), pp. 8–10.

12 / In addition to the Brustein article, cited above, the following provide useful commentary on the play: C. J. Gianakaris, "Absurdism Altered: *Rosencrantz and Guildenstern Are Dead*," *Drama Survey* 7 (1968–69): 52–58; Andrew K. Kennedy, "Old and New in London Now," *Modern Drama* 11 (February 1969): 437–46; Walter Kerr, *Thirty Plays Hath November* (New York: Simon & Schuster, 1969), pp. 50–53; Jack Kroll, "R & G," *Newsweek*, October 30, 1967, pp. 90–92.

13 / Joseph Wood Krutch, *The Modern Temper* (New York: Harcourt, Brace & World, 1957), p. 143.

14 / I call attention to the play's value as "theater of criticism" in "*Rosencrantz and Guildenstern Are Dead*: Theater of Criticism," *Modern Drama* 16 (December 1973): 269–77, which contains material found in this chapter.

5 Boundary Situation

1 / We find more references to the word "flesh" in *King Lear* than in any other Shakespeare play except *The Merchant of Venice*, in which a pound of flesh is an important element in the plot.

2 / A good example of a "Christian" reading of the play is Paul N. Siegel, *Shakespearean Tragedy and the Elizabethan Compromise* (New York: New York University Press, 1957). For a scholarly and sober study of the religious readings of the play, see William R. Elton, *King Lear and the Gods* (San Marino: Huntington Library, 1968). The most influential example of an "absurdist" reading is Jan Kott, *Shakespeare Our Contemporary* (New York: Doubleday, 1966).

3 / John F. Danby, *Shakespeare's Doctrine of Nature* (London: Faber & Faber, 1949), pp. 102–13.

4 / This is one of those rare times I disagree with Maynard Mack, who acknowledges the interrogative but insists on the imperative as the dominant mood of the play (*King Lear In Our Time* [Berkeley: University of California Press, 1965], p. 89).

5 / Kott, p. 109.

6 / For a fuller discussion of Edgar as Bedlam beggar, see my *The Base String*, pp. 201–6.

7 / Sir Philip Sidney, *An Apologie for Poetry* (1595), in *European Theories of the Drama*, ed. Barrett H. Clark (New York: Crown, 1918), p. 105.

8 / John Fletcher, *The Faithful Shepherdess* (1608), in *Elizabethan and Stuart Plays*, ed. C. R. Baskerville, V. B. Heltzel, and A. H. Nethercot (New York: Holt, Rinehart & Winston, 1965), p. 1147.

9 / Eugene Ionesco, *Notes and Counter-Notes* (New York: Grove, 1964), p. 27.

10 / Friedrich Dürrenmatt, *The Marriage of Mr. Mississippi* and *Problems of the Theatre* (New York: Grove, 1966), p. 32.

11 / Samuel Beckett, *Waiting for Godot* (New York: Grove, 1954), p. 7. Subsequent references are to this edition.

12 / Viktor E. Frankl confronts this essential idea in his brilliant book, *Man's Search for Meaning* (New York: Simon & Schuster, 1959).

13 / William York Tindall, *Samuel Beckett* (New York: Columbia University Press, 1964), p. 9.

14 / Ruby Cohn, *Back to Beckett* (Princeton: Princeton University Press, 1973), p. 131.

15 / Rolf Breuer, "The Solution as Problem: Beckett's *Waiting for Godot*," *Modern Drama* 19 (September 1976): 232.

16 / Hugh Kenner, *A Reader's Guide to Samuel Beckett* (London: Thames & Hudson, 1973), p. 29.

17 / Of the many books on Beckett, the following are especially interesting: David H. Hesla, *The Shape of Chaos* (Minneapolis: University of Minnesota Press, 1971); Michael Robinson, *The Long Sonata of the Dead* (New York: Grove, 1969); Eugene Webb, *The Plays of Samuel Beckett* (Seattle: University of Washington Press, 1972).

6 Waiting

1 / The translation is by Randall Jarrell (London: Macmillan, 1969), used in the Actors Studio production that opened in New York City on June 22, 1964. Chekhov has many translators, including Constance Garnett, Stark Young, Ronald Hingley, Ann Dunnigan, Tyrone Guthrie and Leonid Kipnis, and Elisaveta Fen. Jarrell's translation is modern, colloquial, and stageworthy.

2 / This Nemirovich-Danchenko quotation is taken from M. N. Stroeva's essay, "*The Three Sisters* in the Production of the Moscow Art Theater," in *Chekhov: A Collection of Critical Essays*, ed. Robert Louis Jackson (Englewood Cliffs: Prentice-Hall, 1967), p. 134.

3 / George Steiner, *The Death of Tragedy*, p. 303.

4 / Prominent among the critics who consider *The Three Sisters* a comedy are David Magarshack, *Chekhov the Dramatist* (New York: Hill & Wang, 1960) and J. L. Styan, *Chekhov in Performance* (Cambridge: Cambridge University Press, 1971). Tom Driver's fine discussion of Chekhov in *Romantic Quest and Modern Query* concludes that Chekhov writes "tragicomedy."

5 / Two excellent discussions of Chekhov's duality are offered by Maurice Valency, *The Breaking String* (New York: Oxford University Press, 1966) and John Gassner, "The Duality of Chekhov," in *Chekhov*, ed. Jackson, pp. 175–83.

6 / I discuss this balance in "Complementarity in *A Streetcar Named Desire*," in *Tennessee Williams: A Tribute*, ed. Jac Tharpe (Jackson: University Press of Mississippi, 1977), pp. 97–103.

7 / See especially the following: Robin Skelton, *J. M. Synge and His World* (New York: Viking, 1971), p. 72; Donna Gerstenberger, *John Millington Synge* (New York: Twayne, 1964), p. 52; T. R. Henn, *The Harvest of Tragedy* (London: Methuen, 1956), p. 201.

8 / The edition used throughout is *The Complete Plays of John M. Synge* (New York: Knopf, 1935).

9 / Some critics believe that the horse symbolism is indeed communicated. See, for example, Henn, p. 202.

10 / Some critics consider *Riders* less a play than a poem. James Joyce, in a program note for a production of the play in Zurich on June 17, 1918, asserts that *Riders* is the work of "a tragic poet" but not a tragedy (mentioned in Herbert Gorman, *James*

Joyce [New York: Farrar & Rinehart, 1939], p. 258). F. L. Lucas believes *Riders* "may seem less drama than dirge—yet in its simple sincerity it remains a deeply moving dirge" (*The Drama of Chekhov, Synge, Yeats, and Pirandello* [London: Cassell, 1963], p. 185).

7 Doom-session

1 / Francis Fergusson, *The Idea of a Theater*, pp. 161–74.

2 / E. M. Forster, "Ibsen the Romantic," in *Ibsen: A Collection of Critical Essays*, ed. Rolf Fjelde (Englewood Cliffs: Prentice-Hall, 1965), p. 176.

3 / Maurice Maeterlinck, *Le Tragique Quotidien* (1896), quoted in Maurice Valency, *The Flower and the Castle* (New York: Grosset & Dunlap, 1966), p. 380. Valency offers a fine discussion of Ibsen.

4 / *The Master Builder*, p. 377. The text of the play is found in *Ibsen: Four Major Plays*, trans. Rolf Fjelde (New York: Signet, 1965).

5 / The quote is Eric Bentley's paraphrase of an Ibsen poem, found in "Henrik Ibsen: A Personal Statement," *Columbia University Forum* 1 (Winter 1957): 11.

6 / Hermann J. Weigand, *The Modern Ibsen* (New York: Dutton, 1960), p. 275.

7 / Sverre Arestad, "Ibsen's Concept of Tragedy," *PMLA* 74 (1959): 295.

8 / Charles R. Lyons, *Henrik Ibsen: The Divided Consciousness* (Carbondale: Southern Illinois University Press, 1972), p. 120.

9 / Robert Brustein, *The Theatre of Revolt* (Boston: Little, Brown, 1964), p. 76.

10 / Robert B. Heilman calls Claire Zachanassian "a Renaissance revenger in avant-garde modern costume" (*Tragedy and Melodrama* [Seattle: University of Washington Press, 1968], p. 60).

11 / Dürrenmatt, *The Visit*, trans. Patrick Bowles (New York: Grove, 1956), p. 29. Subsequent references are to this text.

12 / Critics have observed the connection. See the following: Melvin W. Askew, "Duerrenmatt's *The Visit of the Old Lady*," *Tulane Drama Review* 5 (June 1961): 89–105; Adolf D. Klarmann, "Friedrich Duerrenmatt and the Tragic Sense of Comedy," in *Modern Drama: Essays in Criticism*, ed. Travis Bogard and William I. Oliver (New York: Oxford University Press, 1965), p. 128; Maurice Valency, "*The Visit*—A Modern Tragedy," *Theatre Arts*, May 1958, p. 91; Heilman, p. 45.

13 / Murray B. Peppard believes that accepting one's fate is "the greatest virtue extolled in Dürrenmatt" in all his works (*Friedrich Dürrenmatt* [New York: Twayne, 1969], p. 39).

14 / Ibid., p. 21.

15 / *The Marriage of Mr. Mississippi* and *Problems of the Theatre*, p. 32.

16 / See Vera Sheppard, "Friedrich Dürrenmatt as a Dramatic Theorist," *Drama Survey*, Winter 1965, p. 245.

17 / Arthur Miller, "Tragedy and the Common Man," *New York Times*, February 27, 1949; reprinted in *The Theater Essays of Arthur Miller*, ed. Robert A. Martin (New York: Viking, 1978), p. 3.

18 / Miller, *Death of a Salesman* (New York: Viking, 1949), p. 81. This edition is used throughout.

19 / See especially the following: M. W. Steinberg, "Arthur Miller and the Idea of Modern Tragedy," *Dalhousie Review* 40 (1960): 329–40; Eleanor Clark, "Old Glamour,

New Gloom," *Partisan Review* 16 (1949): 631–35; Joseph A. Hynes, "Attention Must Be Paid," *College English* 23 (1962), 574–78; Richard J. Foster, "Confusion and Tragedy: The Failure of Miller's *Salesman*," in *Two Modern American Tragedies*, ed. John D. Hurrell (New York: Scribner's, 1961), pp. 82–88.

20 / Arthur Miller, "The Family in Modern Drama," *Atlantic Monthly*, April 1956, pp. 35–41; reprinted in *Theater Essays*, p. 84.

21 / John Gassner, *The Theatre of Our Times* (New York: Crown, 1954), p. 347. Gassner, however, believes that the play deals more with "personal destiny" than "social causation." So too does Leonard Moss, *Arthur Miller* (New York: Twayne, 1967), p. 57.

22 / Eric Bentley, *In Search of Theater* (New York: Knopf, 1955), p. 83.

23 / "Tragedy and the Common Man," in *Theater Essays*, pp. 6, 4.

8 On the Road and On the Rock

1 / *Easy Rider* (New York: New American Library, 1969). Screenplay by Peter Fonda, Dennis Hopper, and Terry Southern; directed by Dennis Hopper. My article, "*Easy Rider*: Touching the Tragic," *Hartford Studies in Literature* 3 (1971): 12–18, contains material found in this chapter.

2 / The evolutionary theory of Zeus' development has won the support of many scholars. See, as examples, H. W. Smyth, *Aeschylean Tragedy* (Berkeley: University of California Press, 1924), pp. 120–22, and Gilbert Murray, *Aeschylus: The Creator of Tragedy* (Oxford: Oxford University Press, 1940), p. 110. Some have rejected this theory, the best arguments coming from H. Lloyd-Jones, "Zeus in Aeschylus," *Journal of Hellenic Studies* 76 (1956): 55–67.

3 / Aeschylus, *Prometheus Bound*, p. 314, in *The Complete Greek Tragedies: Aeschylus*, ed. David Grene and Richmond Lattimore (Chicago: University of Chicago Press, 1959). Subsequent references are to this text.

4 / Robert Lowell, *Prometheus Bound* (New York: Farrar, Straus & Giroux, 1967), p. 67.

5 / John H. Finley, Jr., *Pindar and Aeschylus* (Cambridge: Harvard University Press, 1955), p. 220.

6 / Zeus' tyranny is stressed by most commentators on the play. See especially the following: Anthony J. Podlecki, *The Political Background of Aeschylean Tragedy* (Ann Arbor: University of Michigan Press, 1966), pp. 103–6; George Thomson, *Aeschylus and Athens* (London: Lawrence and Wishart, 1950), pp. 320–23; E. A. Havelock, *Prometheus* (Seattle: University of Washington Press, 1968), pp. 57–58; Jan Kott, *The Eating of the Gods* (New York: Random House, 1973), pp. 23–26. They were all anticipated by Shelley's *Prometheus Unbound*, in which Shelley clearly contrasts Zeus' tyranny to Prometheus' justified rebelliousness.

7 / The possibility of Christian tragedy is an ever-present critical controversy, attracting some of the ablest critics. See D. D. Raphael, *The Paradox of Tragedy* (Bloomington: Indiana University Press, 1960) and Laurence Michel, "The Possibility of a Christian Tragedy," *Thought* 31 (1956): 403–28, for cogent arguments against such a possibility. See Nathan A. Scott, Jr. *The Tragic Vision and the Christian Faith* (New York: Association Press, 1957) for arguments in favor of such a possibility. And see

W. H. Auden's interesting distinction between Greek and Christian tragedy in "The Christian Tragic Hero," *New York Times Book Review,* December 16, 1945.

9   The Mysterious Tune

1 / Thomas Gould, "The Innocence of Oedipus and The Nature of Tragedy," *Massachusetts Review* 10 (1969): 281–300.

INDEX